HETEROACTIVISM

T0347721

About the Authors

Catherine Jean Nash is a Professor Emerita in the Department of Geography and Tourism Studies, Brock University, St Catharines Ontario. Her research interests include geographies of sexuality/queer/feminist and trans geographies, mobilities and digital sexualities. She is currently working with Kath Browne (and Andrew Gorman-Murray) tracing transnational oppositions to LGBTQ rights in Canada, the UK and Ireland, and with Andrew Gorman-Murray on new mobilities and digital life and the transformations in LGBT and queer neighbourhoods in Sydney, Australia and Toronto, Canada. She has published in a wide range of journals and is co-editor with Kath Browne of *Queer Methods and Methodologies: Queer Theories in Social Science Research* (2010), co-editor with Andrew Gorman-Murray of *The Geographies of Digital Sexuality* (2019) and co-author of the Canadian edition of *Human Geography: People, Place and Culture* (2015).

Address: Department of Geography and Tourism Studies, Brock University, 1812 Sir Isaac Brock Way, St. Catharines, Ontario, Canada. L2S 3A1

Email: cnash@brocku.ca

Website: www.catherinejeannash.ca/

Kath Browne is a professor of geography at University College Dublin. Her research interests lie in sexualities, genders and spatialities, where she seeks to use research to make a difference to people's lives. She has worked on LGBT equalities, lesbian geographies, gender transgressions and women's spaces. She has worked with Catherine Nash (and Andrew Gorman-Murray) on understanding transnational resistances to LGBT equalities. She has authored over 100 publications including journal articles and she co-wrote, with Leela Bakshi, *Ordinary in Brighton: LGBT, Activisms and the City* (2013) and, with Sally Munt and Andrew Yip, *Queer Spiritual Spaces* (2010), and co-edited *The Routledge Companion to Geographies of Sex and Sexualities* (2016) and *Lesbian Geographies* (2015).

Address: School of Geography Department, University College Dublin, Belfield, Ireland

Email: kath.browne@ucd.ie

HETEROACTIVISM

Resisting Lesbian, Gay, Bisexual and Trans Rights and Equalities

CATHERINE JEAN NASH
AND KATH BROWNE

ZED

Heteroactivism: Resisting Lesbian, Gay, Bisexual and Trans Rights and Equalities was first published in 2020 by Zed Books Ltd, The Foundry, 17 Oval Way, London SE11 5RR, UK.

www.zedbooks.net

Typeset in ITC Galliard by River Editorial Ltd, Devon, UK
Index by Julia Hamill

A catalogue record for this book is available from the British Library.

ISBN 978-1-78699-646-6 hb
ISBN 978-1-78699-645-9 pb
ISBN 978-1-78699-647-3 pdf
ISBN 978-1-78699-648-0 epub
ISBN 978-1-78699-649-7 mobi

Contents

Figures

Acknowledgements

We would like to thank everyone who has supported the writing of this book, particularly Heather Maguire, without whom this work would not have been so well researched and edited. Her support and outstanding work is unsurpassed and her keen eye for the dreaded referencing process has meant the book was delivered much more quickly than would otherwise have been possible. We would like to thank Andrew McCarten and Dean Mizzi for their research assistance, and Will Andrews and Julia Hamill for their help in the final stages.

Our thanks go to everyone who has listened to, read and commented on draft chapters and to the reviewers who pushed us to develop our ideas within and beyond our published papers. We would like to thank Laine Newman for her excellent and insightful readings that pushed us to deepen some of our analysis. Our thanks to Stefanie Boulila for her readings that gave us key insights into some final materials. The feedback from reviewers, editors and conference colleagues has also shown us what is and is not possible for this project.

Our earlier writings have provided an important springboard for this book and although we built on this work across all chapters, we developed from the following scholarship for specific chapters. For Chapter 1, on same-sex marriage, we drew on Browne and Nash, 2014; Nash and Browne, 2015; Browne and Nash, 2015; Browne and Nash, 2018. For Chapter 2, on schools, we drew on Nash, Gorman-Murray and Browne, 2019. And for Chapter 4, on freedom of speech, Nash and Browne, 2018.

We gratefully acknowledge two research grants from the Canadian Social Sciences and Humanities and Research Council (Grant numbers: 435-2014-0071; 403-2012-0032).

Introduction

Introduction

In August 2018, we attended a conference in Dublin, Ireland that advertised itself as a 'Conference of Catholic Families' (www.lumenfidei.ie/a-conference-of-catholic-families/).[1] At this conference, keynote speakers from Ireland, Canada, the UK (and elsewhere) worked hard to undermine LGBT (Lesbian, Gay, Bisexual and Trans)[2] equalities,[3] denigrate the acceptance of same-sex marriage in Ireland, and dismiss the need for protections for gender identity and expression.[4] As the speakers noted, these objections are now no longer accepted as the common-sense norm in places like Ireland, Canada and the UK. Speakers and attendees alike recognised that simply vilifying homosexuality and LGBT people (and/or wayward women) was no longer effective and speakers presented alternative forms of resistances to LGBT (and broader) sexual and gender rights throughout the conference. In doing so, the conference was not only about resisting LGBT equalities but finding ways to reassert the superiority and centrality of hetero- and gender- normative, individuals and families as the foundation for strong and healthy societies, what we term heteroactivism.

The central premise in this book follows from these experiences. In undertaking an exploration of heteroactivism from 2012 to 2019, we show that resistances to LGBT equalities have not disappeared in the equalities era of the 21st century in places like Canada, the UK and Ireland. Instead, we contend that there needs to be new analytical understandings of resistances to LGBT equalities. These analytical engagements include understanding both direct attacks around, for example, the dangers of 'gender ideology', or the LGBT agenda in terms of trans rights or LGBT people in classroom instruction, and also tangential claims about freedom of speech, parental rights and the protection of children and society. These resistances to LGBT equalities in Canada, the UK and Ireland move beyond focusing on 'anti-gay' rhetoric and, we would argue, are not fully conceptualised in scholarship on anti-gender, gender ideologies and associated social movements (see Kuhar and Paternotte, 2017a). In many cases, heteroactivists take an apocalyptic view of LGBT equalities as 'destroying' the foundations of what they see as Western civilisation through the loss of what is constructed as the 'traditional'. When they (and in turn we) use 'traditional', they are referencing a particular version of a white, colonialist, Christian past that seeks to reaffirm the hierarchical position of the (white and Christian) heteronormative family developed in particular Anglo-American contexts and bound up in understandings of the nation-state. We offer heteroactivism as a tool to theorise the ways in which the superiority of heterosexual and gender normativity is asserted as underpinning 'civilised' Western (predominantly white Christian) societies. Heteroactivism is thus a term we use to conceptualise oppositions to LGBT equalities, in ways that seek to assert a particular form of heteronormative sexual and gender order.

To set the stage, we begin with a brief discussion of current scholarship regarding sexual and gender equalities in the 21st century. Much of this is critical of the effects of LGBT equalities and its exclusions for those who do not fit specific normativities. While it is important to recognise that LGBT equalities seem to privilege certain segments of the LGBT population, it is crucial to also attend to how oppositions to LGBT equalities are being created in contexts where legal and social norms shift towards protections, and acceptances, of LGBT people and lives. In this introduction, we review what we mean by the term heteroactivism and how, as a conceptual framing, it provides insights into ongoing oppositions to LGBT equalities. We then discuss our transnational methodological approach to researching this issue, demonstrating the importance of understanding both historical and geographical context. Finally, we detail the structure of the book as it supports our argument, that is, that heteroactivist opponents to LGBT equalities are making myriad arguments in Canada, the UK and Ireland to undermine LGBT equalities by reasserting the superiority of heteronormative relationships and family forms.

Sexual and Gender Equalities in the 21st Century

Sexual and gender political and social transformation has been one of the hallmarks of the start of the 21st century in countries such as Canada, the UK and Ireland which have experienced significant shifts in sexual and gender equalities (see Healy et al., 2016; Kinsman, 2018; Neary, 2016; Smith, 2008; Weeks, 2007). Legislative initiatives including same-sex marriage, and anti-discrimination legislation for employment, goods and services have ensured LGBT people are included in the institutions of the state and can defend themselves against discriminatory actions. Concurrent and substantive social and cultural transformation have made LGBT people and families more visible in media representations, sports, politics and cultural events (see e.g. Barker and Monk, 2015; Formby, 2017; Richardson and Monro, 2012). As a result, LGBT people are increasingly integrated into the fabric of everyday life, which is particularly apparent in places such as Canada, the UK and Ireland. As Healy et al. (2016) contend, perhaps optimistically, this has created nations of 'equals'. These countries are often portrayed, both academically and in the popular imagination, as champions and protectors of

sexual and gendered difference and as places where sexual and gender rights have been 'won' (Browne and Nash,
2014; Weeks, 2007).

Despite these gains, academic scholarship on LGBT
equalities in the 21st century has interrogated the limits of
these 'successes'. Non-normative, queer and LGBT lives,
identities and communities have been extensively explored
through a diffuse scholarship particularly, but not exclusively, undertaken in the Global North (e.g. Brown, 2005;
Brown and Browne, 2016; Browne et al., 2007; Formby,
2017; Gorman-Murray and Nash, 2014; Knopp, 1995;
Nash, 2005, 2006, 2011; Nash and Gorman-Murray,
2014; Richardson and Monro, 2012). These literatures
highlight the ways that ongoing experiences of non-
normative sexual and gender identities position LGBT
people as 'out-of-place' in everyday spaces and are enforced
by heteronormative discrimination, stigmatisation and violence (e.g. Bell and Valentine, 1995a, 1995b; Browne,
2005, 2006; Nash, 2005, 2006, 2011; Smith, 2008; Taylor,
2007). Often these exclusions are complicated by racialised,
classed and other markers of identity and social positioning (e.g. Boulila, 2019; Braun, 2017; Bryant, 2008; Chin,
2019; Diaz, 2016; Hunt and Holmes, 2015 Kojima et al.,
2017; Langstaff, 2011; Nayak, 2016; Taylor et al., 2010).
Therefore, as scholarship demonstrates, LGBT people and
other sexual and gendered minorities' lives are negatively
affected by discrimination and marginalisation impacting

health, mental health, safety, housing, schooling and employment (Browne and Bakshi, 2013).

Contemporary scholarship in the Global North has also been highly critical of the 'progress' narrative associated with the nature of the success of sexual and gender equalities. The concept of homonormativity refers to the reconstitution of a neoliberal sexual politics that incorporates certain normatively gendered, monogamous and middle-class same-sex couples into the normative fold (Brown, G., 2012; Duggan, 2002; Puar, 2007; Richardson, 2005, 2017). Gays and lesbians in the Global North are then portrayed as being both co-opted and complicit in the nation-building project that allows countries to assert their human rights *bona fides* because of their so-called acceptance of gays and lesbians (e.g. Oswin, 2006; Puar, 2007, 2011). Puar (2007) coined the term homonationalism to describe how the relationship of LGBT people and nation-states has been transformed through LGBT activism and the resulting equalities. This has resulted in broader shifts in international relations between states where those nations espousing tolerance, even protection, of sexual diversity are portrayed as advanced or progressive in terms of 'gay rights, women's equality and sexual freedom' (Puar 2007: 354; see also Adam et al., 1992; Altman, 1997a, 1997b on the globalization of LGBT politics). Other nation-states can then be tested against this measure of 'progress' and, within potentially racist and/or neocolonial discourses, presented as 'backward' or uncivilised, thereby justifying intervention including military or otherwise (Browne and Bakshi, 2013; Kulpa and Mizielinska, 2011; Oswin, 2006; Puar, 2007, 2011).

While scholarship on homonormativity and homona-tionalism is critical to understanding the ideologies of and transformations in sexual and gender equalities in the 21st century, it is also essential to understand the activism and ideologies of those groups that remain opposed to LGBT equalities. The current sexualities and gender literatures do not fully consider how heteronormativities continue to be manifest in contests around LGBT equalities. While many have presumed that opposition to sexual and gender equal-ities will simply 'die out', the rise in organised resistances to LGBT rights across Europe and North America clearly calls this assumption into question (see e.g. Burack, 2014a, 2014b; Kuhar and Paternotte, 2017a; see also Browne and Nash, 2014; Nash and Browne, 2015). Given the contem-porary (and arguably escalating) polarisations in Canadian, Irish and UK societies around issues of gender and sex-uality, it is paramount that scholars and activists critically engage with these new forms of activism, which we have termed heteroactivism.

Heteroactivism: Beginnings

The term heteroactivism names, and conceptualises, the organised resistances to sexual and gender politics that defines the sexual and gender politics of the 21st century.

Heteroactivism is both an ideology and a form of activism that seeks to reassert heteronormative understandings of home, family and society, and is opposed to the perceived (or perhaps experienced, see Conclusion) impact of the unwanted gains in sexual and gender politics (Browne and Nash, 2017: 645; Nash and Browne, 2015). As this book will show, in contemporary contexts where LGBT rights are seen as 'won', organised groups advance novel and at times effective strategies designed to roll back or evade the impact of LGBT equalities. Heteroactivism is a 21st-century form of resistance, which we set alongside investigations of more long-standing 'homophobic', 'transphobic' and 'biphobic' namings of objections to sexual and gendered equalities[5] (Browne and Nash, 2017; Murray, 2009; Weiss and Bosia, 2013).

Beyond Christian Right: Not Necessarily Christian, Not Necessarily Right

A key area of scholarship in North America that does consider resistances to LGBT equalities focuses on the US Christian Right, paying particular attention to activities in the United States (Kuhar and Paternotte, 2017a, see e.g. Burack, 2014a, 2014b; Fetner, 2008; Griffith, 2017; Herman, 1997; Jordan, 2011; McDonald, 2010; Reimer, 2003; Stein, 2001; White, 2015). Much of this considers historical and contemporary objections ground in religious Judeo-Christian precepts and operating largely on the political right. Political science scholarship offers a long-standing and extensive engagement with the Christian Right and conservative oppositional activism in the United States (Andersen and Fetner, 2008a; Burack and Josephson, 2005; Burack and Wilson, 2012; Buss and Herman, 2003; Nicol and Smith, 2008; Rayside and Wilcox, 2012; Todd and Ong, 2012; White, 2015). Scholarship largely understands LGBT rights campaigns and Christian Right opposition as mutually constitutive, which has been a key contention of those engaging with social movement theories (Altman and Symonds, 2016; Langstaff, 2011; Tremblay et al., 2011). This predominantly US-focused literature relates specifically to 'anti-gay' rhetoric that vilifies homosexuality, trans people and others as 'deviants' and as outside of the moral order (Stein, 2001). Part of the work that the term heteroactivism does is that it allows analysis to move beyond a focus on 'anti-gay' discourses that can characterise the Christian Right in the USA. This enables explorations of the multiplicity of heteroactivist forms that can operate obliquely across race, religion and the right/left political divide.

These emerging ideologies opposing sexual and gender rights in places such as Canada, the UK and Ireland require a new term that moves beyond labelling such opposition as anti-gay, homophobic, biphobic and transphobic. As we discuss in Chapter 4, these terms are contested and do not capture the depth and specificity of the distinctive historical or geographical foundations of more contemporary activism against LGBT equalities (Boulila, 2015; Murray, 2009).

Heteroactivism names a foundational shift in how groups opposed to LGBT equalities conceive of their resistance. Opposition to LGBT equalities has always asserted that heterosexuality is superior but within specific religious or more broadly moral frameworks. These moralities see homosexuals vilified as 'perverted', 'immoral', 'criminal', 'mentally ill' and as preying on children. Objections to the decriminalisation of homosexuality in places like Canada and the UK revolved around the risks associated with the loosening of moral codes, worries about the impact on children and the loss of regulation or control over certain kinds of sexual conduct (Bell and Binnie, 2000; Kinsman, 2018; Nash, 2005; Warner, 2002). In the contemporary period, and where gender and sexual equalities are now in place, we demonstrate how heteroactivists in certain contexts strategically avoid overt vilification of LGBT people and develop alternative arguments although homophobic or transphobic commentary has not entirely disappeared. Heteroactivism, then, reflects both social and political forms of engagement that create a space for oppositional groups to openly oppose LGBT equalities while deflecting criticisms that those holding such views are discriminatory, bigoted or homophobic (see Chapters 1 and 4).

Heteroactivism also refocuses attention on the types of opposition to LGBT equalities that are not necessarily religious or conservative (although they may be). Research does demonstrate that religion has played a key role in oppositions at a legislative level as well as through national and local practices (Andersson et al., 2013; Johnson and Vanderbeck, 2014; Vanderbeck et al., 2010; Vanderbeck and Johnson, 2015). Further, scholars do regard 'conservative understandings of religion as a catalyst for opposition to gender and sexual equalities' (Kuhar and Paternotte, 2017b: 3). However, scholarship also demonstrates the plurality of positions within Christianity around acceptance of LGBT equalities in Anglo-American contexts, where sexual politics can divide the church (Andersson et al., 2013; Griffith, 2017; Vanderbeck et al., 2010). In contrast, Islam is often presented as a hindrance to more permissive policies, and as challenging the 'embrace of gender and sexuality equality' despite the complexities of acceptances and practices of LGBT Muslims (Kuhar and Paternotte, 2017b: 4; see also Browne et al., 2010; Yip, 2008, see also Chapter 2 and the Conclusion).

Contemporary explorations of resistances to LGBT equalities that focus on Europe point to the rise of anti-gender politics, 'gender ideology' and 'genderism' (Kováts, 2018; Kuhar and Paternotte, 2017a; Nicholas, 2019). Gender ideology is a term used extensively by the Catholic Church (and others) which signals a different religious outlook than that of the US. Catholic objections which focuses on the pope's critique of gender ideology as undermining the natural and immutable differences between biological men and women are based on Catholic teachings (Paternotte and Kuhar, 2018). Objections to 'gender ideology' have now spread globally and are now no longer seen as being rooted primarily in the teachings of Catholicism (see Corrêa et al., 2018; although they are often seen as rooted in the far right, Gunnarsson Payne, 2019). Our conceptualisation of heteroactivism recognises the importance of this work and seeks to augment it by articulating the major underpinning ideologies of anti-gender social movements and, critically, other related resistances to LGBT equalities.

There is a heterogeneity to heteroactivist organisations, campaigns and supporters that defies easy categorisation, rendering it impossible to easily predict their social or cultural make-up (e.g. class or religious) or their political stance (e.g. liberal or conservative, 'left' or 'right'). In the contemporary era, where the 'far right' and 'populism' are extending their reach, it is critically important not to simplistically conflate heteroactivism with these movements, given that even within Europe the populist right takes various positions on sexual and gender rights (Siegel, 2017; Browne and Nash, 2017). We have seen oppositions to sexual and gender equalities emerge from various points along the political spectrum that cleave or segment both the 'left' and the 'right'. This book will show how heteroactivism is complex and differentiated. We turn now to consider how heteroactivism is inherently geographical in ways that further problematise understandings of opposition to LGBT equalities as the activities of the Christian and/or conservative right based in the USA.

Geographies of Heteroactivism:
The Transnational

Critical geographical scholarship on homonationalism and heteronormativity emphasises the importance of 'place' in understanding how 'sexuality' and 'gender' are conceptualised, questioning the US orientation of queer theory (Brown, 2012; Brown and Browne, 2016; Mikdashi and Puar, 2016; Oswin, 2006). Similarly, heteroactivist resistances are always crafted somewhere. Our focus is on locations in which particular laws, policies, histories and cultural norms and values that support LGBT equalities are inscribed. This requires a geographically nuanced approach that recognises the multiple, interacting and variable scales though which heteroactivism emerges and is manifest. Heteroactivist stances reflect local historical and social circumstances, yet are undeniably nationally and transnationally constituted, aided by (but not beholden to) globalisation processes including colonialism, travel and technologies (see e.g. Aggleton et al., 2012; Binnie, 2006; Nash and Gorman-Murray, 2019). In order to understand heteroactivist resistances, we need to consider the specificities of place in relation to networks and connections, including transnational divergences and cohesions (see e.g. Binnie and Klesse, 2013a, 2013b; Massey, 1994, 2005).

In modelling accounts of anti-gay movements and political ideologies and action on the US historical experience, there is a tendency to view contemporary resistances as an 'export from the United States, overlooking the home-grown roots of the phenomenon' (Paternotte and Kuhar, 2017: 254). Place-specific analyses are also insufficient, and we agree with Paternotte and Kuhar (2017) that explaining phenomena only in national terms overlooks transnational and global factors and influences. Thus, developing a critique of the so-called globalisation of the Christian Right is crucial in reconsidering the circulation of ideas and the formation of ideologies and activisms that cannot be bounded within nation-states, nor can it be presupposed that the Christian Right is being exported and globalised (Butler, 2006), in ways that presume the 'locations of homophobia' in the Global South (Brown et al., 2010; Lalor and Browne, 2018; Rao, 2015). For example, anti-gay activism on the African continent is often attributed to the US Christian Right in ways that deny both agency and the nature of local politics (see Browne et al., 2015; Rao, 2015). Therefore, a nuanced transnational geographical lens is required as heteroactivism is inherently geographical.

Transnational

Contemporary transnational scholarship focuses mainly on 'transnational flows of migrants, labour, diaspora, communities, commodities and cultural products' (Nash and Browne, 2015: 563; see also Crang et al., 2003 and Massey, 1994) and shared activisms (Binnie and Klesse, 2013a, 2013b). In this research, we specifically focus on the transnational through an understanding of the 'dynamic networks that exchange ideas, values, cultural practices and information across national borders' and how this can constitute places and social relations within complex relational geographies (Valentine et al., 2012: 51; see also Adey, 2006; Jensen, 2011; Massey, 1994; Olsen and Silvey, 2006). Place then is understood as a momentary consolidation, however unstable or uneven, and as locations that are always open and fluid (Gregson and Rose, 2000; Massey, 2005; Rose, 1999). Geographically, scholars argue places are constituted in and through these dynamic networks where the movement of people, goods and knowledges reworks both material and ideological relations (Gorman-Murray and Nash, 2014; Jones, 2009; Rose, 1999; Valentine, 2002). It is these relationships that are the focus here, and our transnational perspective explores how heteroactivism operates across unstable and uneven networks made up of a variety of organisations that increasingly operate across national borders and whose objections are shaped and formulated within these multi-scalar systems of meaning.

Transnational perspectives can illuminate resistances that are developing through fragmented and unstable engagements. These work across multiple scales and they are interactive engagements in and through distinctive geographies. Because of this, a transnational perspective underpins our conceptualisation of heteroactivism where the movements of ideas, tactics and support are critical to national and local oppositions to sexual and gender equalities, but these flows do not determine the forms that heteroactivisms will take in any one place. This is not about the diffusion of state process through internationalisation (Weiss and Bosia, 2013). Our conceptualisation does not suppose a 'spread' or a 'flow', but rather an engagement across nations in ways that connect and share. Thus, the transnational approach does not suggest that we should take for granted that 'norms' develop in or emanate from a 'centre' and then move to the periphery. Instead, what our research shows is that alongside national contestations regarding, for instance, same-sex marriage, are grassroots mobilisations and the emergence of key flashpoints, or contestations regarding, for example, sexual education in schools, or employment requirements. These can feed into broader national debates, as well as draw on and feed into transnational discussions, movements and contestations. What is clear is that as ideas, tactics and activisms travel, they touch down in specific contexts. They are reworked in relation to that context, to historical norms and to relations of power. This reworking is transnational, and the movement is mutual, reconfiguring the 'origin' from where they emanate, as well as where they 'land'. This questions the idea of 'a centre' from which ideas/tactics/activisms originate and instead insists on engagements with local contexts that recreate 'the global' (Massey, 2002, 2005). Heteroactivist resistances, understood through this transnationalism lens, can thus be understood as travelling in ways that do not neglect the social, cultural and economic conditions of their production in *that* place, at *that* time.

Building on these transnational understandings, our work also contests what Rao (2015) terms the 'Locations of Homophobia', namely as located in the Global South but emanating from the Global North. Following legislative advances, and particular nationalist representations of 'tolerance' and 'inclusion', homophobia is often located outside of the 'progressive Global North' and in the backwards Global South (Browne et al., 2018; Lalor and Browne, 2018; Oswin, 2006). As Sabsay (2012: 606) argues, this justifies 'the current re-articulation of orientalist and colonial politics' as part of a sexual rhetoric that 'functions today as a marker that distinguishes the so-called advanced western democracies in opposition to their "undeveloped others"' (see also Browne et al., 2019). Western democracies are then created as spaces of inclusion, tolerance and acceptance in contrast to the vilified, exotic other who is backward and homophobic (Banerjea and Browne, 2018; Kulpa and Mizielinska, 2011; Oswin, 2006; Puar, 2007).

Placing 'homophobia' in the Global South, including Eastern Europe, creates a specific geographical imaginary that has effects for the Global North, as well as the Global South. To date, these effects have been predominantly understood through this conceptualisation of the Global South. Nevertheless, critique of these specific geotemporalities of 'progress' have been critiqued and rewritten (Kulpa and Mizielinska, 2011; Kulpa and Silva, 2016; Oswin, 2006). Yet, these imaginings serve to presume that contemporary experiences of LGBT lives in places like the UK and Canada are 'fine' and 'sorted' and any deviation from this is an individualised issue. It also reorientates sexual politics in the Global North towards 'other places' who have it 'worse', because for LGBT people the world is 'won' (Banerjea and Browne, 2018; Browne et al., 2018; Lalor and Browne, 2018; Oswin, 2006). These presumptions have been extensively critiqued by those who examine sexual and gender normalisations and exclusions within these supposed utopias and find ongoing marginalisations (see e.g. Browne and Bakshi, 2013; Duggan, 2003; O'Brien, 2008; Podmore, 2013). Our work on heteroactivism also questions these distinctions and the assumption that resistances have, or soon will, die out.

It is not just the Global South that is represented as homophobic and backward but also bodies and religions that are placed outside of 'progressive nations'. These bodies are marked by race or religion as 'not British' (or Irish or Canadian), and thus outside the 'world we have won' (see e.g. Boulila, 2019; Haritaworn, 2015; Kuntsman and Miyake, 2008). As Boulila (2019) notes, homophobia is 'naturalised in association with some bodies and spaces whilst being completely divorced from other contexts and subjects' (Boulila, 2019: 105). She contends that in Europe (and we might also include Canada), homophobia is attached to racialised groups. Thus, as we will see in Chapter 2 on education and schools, some bodies, ethnicities and racialised groups are marked as 'inherently homophobic' in places such as Canada and the UK (for discussion on homophobia and Russia, see Edenborg, 2018 and on Indonesia, see Boellstorff, 2004). Their portrayal as such stands in marked contrast to those who (pro)claim the return to British/Irish/Canadian values within whiteness and heterosexuality. Our research seeks to flesh out these complications and move away from a strict focus on the predominantly white British, Irish and Canadian groups that variously co-opt or ignore Brown, Black and ethnically marginalised people. Whiteness is often central to the ways these groups speak for 'the other side' (i.e. against LGBT equalities) in ways that centralise them in the UK, Ireland and Canada. It is also key to these groups claiming they are not homophobic, irrational or hate-filled (see Chapters 1 and 4) but properly situated within the white Christian state. These groups, and individual activists, are often regarded as benign, in contrast to the racialised, homophobic other (Haritaworn, 2015). That said, these lines are messy, and as we will see in Chapter 2, heteroactivist discourses are deployed by racialised (Muslim) parents, who can be supported by (mostly white) Christian groups. This contests any firm boundaries between homophobia/heteroactivism, as well as unsettling the white Christianity of heteroactivism.

Studying Heteroactivism: Transnational Methodologies and Flashpoint Methods

Given the transnational conceptualisation of heteroactivism, our data collection and analysis focus on the overlapping and networked flows of norms, values and ideas that are traded or exchanged across multiple scales by those opposed to sexual and gender equalities. Such an approach highlights shared, and locally specific, developments, strategies and approaches as they are deployed in various locations, not only nationally or transnationally, but also in particular locations, such as schools or workplaces. It does not negate local specificities, and throughout the book we understand a transnational approach as enabling analyses that recognise local specificities, as well as transnational formations. Taking a transnational approach moves away from the comparative. Comparative approaches seek to compare various contexts, identifying similarities and differences. This can result in hierarchising them on the basis of various criteria (Browne et al., 2015, 2017). The comparative presumes a bounded differential unit that can easily be compared to a similar bounded unit and these are usually geography, city, nation and so on. A transnational approach, in contrast, rejects the premise of bounded comparative units and instead understands place as formed in relation to other places through networks of interconnection (Massey, 1994). Thus, the methodology that emerges from transnational studies can note the connections and overlaps, without negating local contexts or specificities (Browne et al., 2017).

In undertaking a transnational approach, we focused specifically on Canada, the UK and Ireland. These contexts are important locations to consider opposition or resistance to LGBT equalities as they are often regarded, and in fact portray themselves, as inclusive and supportive of sexual and gender equalities.[6] All three have had coincident, but very particular historical trajectories in instituting legislative and social change for LGBT people, including through the enactment of human rights protections, partner recognition and open participation in the institutions of citizenship including military service (which we outline in the next section). For many activists, the pinnacle moment for LGBT inclusions was the institution of same-sex marriage by legislation in Canada in 2005; in the UK in 2013 and in Ireland, by referendum, in 2015 (see Chapter 1). Heteroactivist organisations are present in all three countries, are often local or national, but also work within and across national borders, within transnational networks (including through international conferences, reporting on and learning from heteroactivist organisations in other national contexts).

Strategically, heteroactivists employ myriad strategies including media engagement, policy engagement and lobbying, legal action, online activism (including petitions, social media, blogs and publications), large-scale protests, conferences, online publications and workshops. In order to understand the manifestations of heteroactivism, we collected data over the period 2015–2018. In particular, we focused on those moments or 'flashpoints' where contestations over the impact of LGBT equalities were vigorous, public and widely reported, in other words, those high-profile moments (which could vary between days, months and years) where specific issues gained attention either in the broader media or within the organisations themselves. Flashpoints then are public, spatialised battles fought over the implications of LGBT equalities in particular locations such as public schools or state institutions. These flashpoints are emergent, related to specific national contexts, but as we show here, have transnational resonances. These flashpoints constitute the organising structure of this book which considers con-testations around same-sex marriage, freedom of speech claims, objections to trans rights, LGBT visibility in public schools and state support of LGBT equalities.

In our data collection, we focused specifically on those organised groups publicly opposing LGBT equalities in one form or another and regardless of whether those groups where large or small, long-standing or short-lived. Some of these groups had clearly stated religious affiliations (e.g. Christian Concern in the UK). Yet while these groups often had religiously grounded arguments against LGBT equali-ties these were often quite muted and our main focus is on the secular positions that most groups deployed in public debates. Some of these groups reflect grassroots activism such as activism objecting to school curricula incorpo-rating LGBT families or 'trans' issues, while others are well-funded, powerful, political, activist organisations with strong socio-political agendas. We were interested in cap-turing groups' public statements and arguments around a particular issue and how they framed their opposition. For this reason, we do not focus specifically on any particular group or organisation, nor do we delve into groups' organisational structures, membership or funding. We are focusing on the major themes that arose at various flashpoints that work across and through different geographical contexts. As we note, these heteroactivist groups are not homogeneous, and such groups may have contradictory or incommensurate positions within different flashpoints. Finally, we are not examining any counterarguments or contestations made to heteroactivist opposition to LGBT equalities. Our interest is understanding and detailing the nature and substance of these objections.

Beginning in 2015, we began collecting information on oppositional groups in Canada, Ireland and Great Britain as they surfaced in key flashpoints. We systematically gathered data from publicly accessible websites where material (blogs, commentary news releases, newsletters, posters and so on) was downloaded and saved. Data was collected using web software such as DevonAgent and DevonThink to gather, collate and organise information. We also collected data from public comment sections, blog posts, newsfeeds, chats, email lists and listservs etc. We followed a variety of social media to collect data and observe activity on these various sites and social media platforms.

We also attended conferences, meetings, protests and other events, undertaking participant observation, taking handwritten notes and pictures where appropriate. Such research was largely covert in that researchers did not identify themselves as such but did register under their real names and used their own email addresses. Such research was often emotionally difficult as such groups spoke often in disparaging ways about one's friends, colleagues and families (see Maguire et al., 2019). We did not attend any private events, only events that were open to the public and had registration forms that were freely available or had no registration requirement. Appropriate Research Ethics Board clearance was obtained from participating universities. This process gathered a significant amount of data in the form of online content and researcher notes.

Focusing on flashpoints enables an exploration of the types of issues that gain traction and where heteroactivists are targeting their efforts as well as the particular arguments and discussions that emerged. They also show the main priorities for the groups themselves, where they want to target their efforts as well as what they neglect. This focus offers insights into their specific interests and how they wish to engage with broader sexual and gender politics. Therefore flashpoints offer insight into contemporary 21st-century sexual and gender politics for those who are opposed to the impacts of LGBT equalities. The focus on flashpoints also allowed us the dexterity to follow the ideas and discussions as they unfolded. We coded the materials gathered across a broad range of sources but focused on those produced by heteroactivists within specific national contexts. Using our databases, we delved into specific issues (e.g. around sexual education, Chapter 2) as well as broader areas (e.g. free speech, Chapter 4) which surfaced across various flashpoints. We found that social media was less helpful in providing insight and depth of understanding of the debates and key issues and we focused on heteroactivists' more formal public statements found in newsletters and website materials created by the groups expressly for this purpose. We supplemented the focus on heteroactivist groups' materials, with webscraping software that focused on mainstream reporting which, at times, was reproduced on heteroactivist websites. However, our main concern was on how heteroactivist groups understood themselves and their resistances.

We coded these data using open coding to identify key themes, argumentations and points for discussion. Following this broad mapping, we investigated in depth the ideologies and discourses being deployed within various flashpoints, using an analysis of how the arguments are constructed and made. We used this to develop insights into the broader systems of meaning that heteroactivists are developing. This allowed us insights into how they interpret and understand specific events, and their tactics of resisting LGBT equalities.

We coded materials in Canada separately from the UK and Ireland, and we also differentiated material from Ireland and the UK. In the same-sex marriage chapter, we use material from Canada to discuss the passing of same-sex marriage in the UK, but in general we focus on heteroactivists in these specific contexts discussing the issues and their tactics. We did not include material from the USA, as this has been extensively explored and is different from discussions within Canada, the UK and Ireland. Although we coded these national contexts separately, we then analysed the data together, bringing these into conversation with each other. This allowed us to explore both similarities and divergences, as well as seeing connections and discursive alignments in order to understand how the ideas were moving, without presuming that ideas are adopted/adapted. Instead, the analysis holds to the nationally and locally specific manifestations of discourses and ideologies as they travel or not. Throughout the chapters, we integrate our discussions of each place, focusing on particular themes, and taking time to describe a specific place/case/argument in some depth. At other times we work across these data to consider similarities in discussions and argumentation, as well as how specific issues that both emerge and are resisted.

Following our conceptualisation of transnational movements, this transnational methodology and analysis does not seek to compare different nations, finding 'winners' and 'losers' or asserting some form of hierarchy (see Browne et al., 2015). Instead, in both respecting national and local specificities, and working across these borders, we created a methodology that was diverse and agile in exploring specific issues when and where they emerge. This geographically informed process then refuses both national myopias that neglect transnational networks and connections (Kuhar and Paternotte, 2017a), and also the hierarchisations of national contexts, alongside presumptions of global sameness or diffusion from a centre to periphery (Kulpa and Mizielinska, 2011; Oswin, 2006). There are limits to this method: for example, it does not allow insights into the experiences of everyday lives within these discourses beyond what is presented by heteroactivist groups. However, it does allow us a starting point to delve more deeply into these issues through other methods and methodologies, as we discuss in the conclusion. We turn now to outline the contours of LGBT rights in each place in this study in the 21st century.

Contexts

In this book we draw predominantly on Canada and the UK to explore discourses of heteroactivism. This is because much of what we understand as heteroactivism, we have identified in the post-marriage-equality timeframe – in Ireland marriage equality was achieved in 2015. In this section, we briefly outline the broad contours of sexual and gender rights in each nation in order to give an overall understanding of the LGBT rights contexts in which heteroactivists are contemporaneously operating.

Canada

In Canada, the institution of LGBT equalities has been a slow, uneven and difficult process with more formal activism beginning in the mid-1960s when the first LGBT political organisations emerged to object to both the criminalisation and medicalisation of same-sex behaviour (Kinsman, 1987; Nash, 2006; Warner, 2002). By 1969, homosexuality had been decriminalised, in part, and the age of consent set at 21 years for anal sex between men. Across Canada, LGBT groups, newspapers, social clubs and community centres flourished under the careful scrutiny and often aggressive monitoring of police, municipalities, churches and community groups (e.g. Nash, 2006). However, other basic rights such as military service, pension and healthcare benefits, family benefits and marriage would be fought for in the courts across the country for the next 40 years. The passage of the Charter of Rights and Freedoms (enacted 17 April 1982)[7] prompted a series of court cases which gradually effected changes in the law at both the provincial and federal levels. The case of *Egan v. Canada* in 1995 was a significant decision with the Supreme Court of Canada 'reading in' sexual orientation into section 15 of the Charter even though it was not expressly listed as an excluded ground for discrimination.[8] Provincial human rights protections were enacted piecemeal across the country beginning with Quebec in 1977 with such legislation being fiercely debated throughout the 1990s (Herman, 1994; Smith, 2007;

Warner, 2002).[9] Scholarship today continues to document the diverse experiences of LGBT Canadians particularly with respect to race, colonialism and religious belief (e.g. Braun, 2017; Chin, 2019; Diaz, 2016; Hunt and Holmes, 2015; Kojima et al., 2017).

A series of court cases in the early 1990s provided the momentum for the legalisation of same-sex marriage on 20 July 2005, although in 2006, the Conservative government under Stephen Harper tabled a motion to reopen the same-sex debate which was ultimately defeated by a vote of 175 to 123. Since then, LGBT activist focus has been on issues such as bullying, LGBT content in public schools, student-run gay–straight alliances, queer immigration and more recently, trans rights. In 2016, the federal government passed Bill C-16 which included gender identity and gender expression as a prohibited ground of discrimination in the Canadian Human Rights Act.[10] As we discuss here, this legislation prompted considerable opposition which remains ongoing. On 28 November 2017, the Canadian Prime Minister formally apologised to members of the LGBT community for the 'state-sponsored, systematic oppression and rejection' they experienced and expressed the country's 'collective shame' for the mistreatment they suffered (Harris, 2017).[11]

United Kingdom (UK)

The United Kingdom is made up of England, Wales, Scotland and Northern Ireland. Wales, Scotland and

Northern Ireland have various levels of devolved powers, but the UK is predominantly read through England and the actions of the Westminster (London) government. The UK decriminalised homosexuality in 1967 and through-out the late 20th century political organisations pushed for legal protections and cultural change. This was resisted by the government which, in 1988, introduced section 28, which prohibited the 'promotion of homosexuality'. Yet, there can be little doubt that the UK saw rapid socio-legal change around sexualities and gender rights in the 21st century. From the imposition of 'section 28', which for-bade the 'promotion' of homosexuality, and numerous civic and legal exclusions (see Bell and Binnie, 2000; Stychin, 2003), a New Labour government in 1998 began to shift the discourses and policies around LGBT rights (Browne and Bakshi, 2013; Richardson and Monro, 2012). There were key employment protections put in place in 1999, in 2002 lesbians and gay men were permitted to adopt and in 2004 the Gender Recognition Act was passed allowing people to legally change their gender with the approval of gatekeepers including psychologists. The Criminal Justice Act of 2003 allowed for tougher sentences to be given for hate crimes and in 2004 civil partnerships were introduced without much public resistance. In 2010, the Equality Act consolidated protections for LGBT people for sexual orientation and gender reassignment and included ant-discrimination legislation around the provision of good and services. The Government Equality Office produced associated guidance for the public sector (see Chapter 6) and exemptions to the law included religious positions, such as nuns, priests and rabbis.

Although the Equality Act covered the entire UK, there are different legislative regimes with various levels of devolved power in Scotland, Northern Ireland and Wales. Much of the activisms we discuss in this book emanated from England and relate to legislation that covers England and Wales. However, the same-sex marriage chapter refers only to Great Britain, because there was no provision for same-sex marriage in Northern Ireland until October 2019 as we finished drafting this book. Thus, it is only briefly mentioned in Chapter 6 and the Conclusion. Nonetheless, in the majority of the chapters, we have chosen to retain the UK, because of key events in Northern Ireland, such as Ashers Bakery, which refused to bake a cake supporting 'gay marriage', which we discuss in Chapters 4 and 5. Scotland's consultation around Gender Recognition is also covered in this book (Chapter 3). However, the book is limited, and these are very specific legal and cultural contexts, which are not fully addressed in these pages. We did not, for example, look explicitly at Northern Ireland as the legislative context as well as the social and cultural conditions differ from Ireland and England, or Scotland and Wales. Moreover, although Great British heteroactivist organisations often understand themselves as British, their focus is predominantly England. We use the term British to reflect this but recognise that more work is needed to understand the geographies of English/Northern Irish/ Scottish/Welsh sexual and gender activisms. We hope these arenas will be taken up and developed in future work.

Republic of Ireland

The Republic of Ireland consists of 26 counties which were given independence from the UK in 1922. Following this, the 1939 constitution and subsequent governments closely tied the state to the Catholic Church throughout the 20th century. Imaginings of 'new Ireland' driven by the 'Celtic Tiger' in the early part of the 21st century also included a social and cultural element that saw the progression of LGBT rights gains. Within a generation, Ireland has moved from a country controlled by the Catholic Church where same-sex relations were only legalised in 1993, to voting for same-sex marriage in 2015 (McAuliffe and Kennedy, 2017; O'Carroll and Collins, 1995; Ryan-Flood, 2015; Smyth, 1995; see Chapter 1). In 2011, civil partnerships were introduced in Ireland, and since 2015 Ireland has had more progressive and coordinated gender recognition legislation than Canada and the UK, which allows self-identification in the changing of official documentation, such as passports and birth certificates. There is, however, no hate crime legislation in Ireland, and same-sex parenting legislation passed in 2015 has yet to be enacted. Although not addressed here, in 2018, in a referendum Ireland legalised abortion (see Browne and Nash, 2019), which was seen as a key moment in the changing face of Ireland. Throughout we refer to Ireland as shorthand for the Republic of Ireland, recognising that there is a need for all-island discussions, which is beyond the scope of this book.

Chapter Structure

Heteroactivism enables an examination not only of how the centrality of normative biological sex, 'traditional' gender roles and heteronormativity are 'best' for society is claimed, but also of the challenges to parental rights and concerns about the welfare of children, trans rights, academic scholarship, universities, freedom of speech and religion.[12] We begin this book by exploring same-sex marriage which we identified as the location of emerging discourses contesting LGBT rights, without overtly vilifying lesbians and gay men (see also Browne and Nash, 2014; Nash and Browne, 2015). We then go on to explore how heteroactivism seeks to reiterate heteronormativities in a range of arenas and through discourses that might at first seem tangential or even unrelated such as freedom of speech or parental rights claims.

In Chapter 1, we discuss the implementation of same-sex marriage as a key and pivotal battleground for LGBT equalities in all three countries (e.g. Browne and Nash, 2015; Kitzinger and Wilkinson, 2004). While there have been extensive queer critiques of same-sex marriage (e.g. Bell and Binnie, 2000; Calhoun, 2000; Sullivan, 1995), this chapter focuses on exploring how new resistances to same-sex marriage emerge where social, cultural and legislative contexts make overt hostility to same-sex relationships ineffective. We consider the recent same-sex marriage debates in Great Britain and Ireland, with a particular focus on the underlying heteroactivist arguments used to undermine support for same-sex marriage. In both debates, opponents drew on claims about the negative impacts of same-sex marriage for heteroactivists in Canada as a reason to vote against same-sex marriage. While same-sex marriage may have been the impetus in Ireland and Great Britain for the formation of oppositional organisations, it is the legal, social and political consequences of same-sex marriage that has sparked considerable heteroactivist activism.

In Chapter 2, we consider the battles in both Canada and the UK around the inclusion of references to LGBT and queer people in school curricula, including in sex education materials. Within nationalist discourses supporting LGBT equalities, schools and educational facilities become central to the transmission of national 'values' and 'norms' (Andersen and Fetner, 2008b; Johnson and Johnson, 2016; Thiem, 2009) that may be in conflict with those who oppose certain forms of human rights or the religious precepts of parents (Wainwright and Marandet, 2017; see also Callaghan and van Leent, 2019). This chapter investigates how schools have become a key site for heteroactivists in Canada, the UK and Ireland in their opposition to LGBT equalities (Nash and Browne, 2019; Rassmusan et al., 2016).

While heteroactivists are careful not to overtly object to the inclusion of LGBT people and families in the curriculum, they frame their objections around claims about parental rights and claims that these curricula reflect personal agendas. The chapter explores the racialisations of heteroactivism and how objections to state-based initiatives that seek to normalise same-sex marriage and LGBT rights as part of national values are contested by those who understand themselves as defending 'the nation' and 'our children'. The implicit whiteness of Britishness, and the co-option of Canadian immigrants of colour by oppositional groups, points to how heteroactivism can pass as benign in comparison to the protests of 'Muslim' others who are regarded as inherently dangerous (Haritaworn, 2015).

Gender transgressions and trans equalities are increasingly a lightning rod for heteroactivists and gender transgressions has long been a concern of those opposed to expressions of sexual difference (Kollman and Waites, 2009; Kuhar and Paternotte, 2017a; Kuhar and Zobec, 2017). Now, instead of focusing on the potential homosexuality of children who are gender non-conforming, the key perceived danger has turned to questions of disruptions to seemingly stable man/woman divides. Chapter 3 considers in more depth heteroactivists' objections to how understandings about 'gender' and biological sex are being reworked. For heteroactivists, trans people's existence and support for their gender choices is read as 'denying reality', 'ludicrous' but also 'dangerous' for trans people themselves, as well as 'our' (read heteronormative) children. We will consider how trans people's rights are rejected and resisted in ways that seek to undermine equalities agendas under the guise of 'protecting children and women'.

In Chapter 4, we untangle some of the complex debates where heteroactivists claim that their (and everyone's) freedom of speech is under threat. Beginning with a discussion of how heteroactivists resist accusations of bigotry, homophobia and transphobia, we then explore how claims about free speech challenge 'shutting down debate' because of accusations of harm. Equating harm and abuse, with upset and dissent, this reflects claims about the ability to argue in favour of heteronormative views on marriage and the family. We see claims grounded in freedom of speech arguments gaining ground, particularly in universities in the UK and Canada through government responses and changes in funding regulations. Heteroactivists argue that freedom of speech includes the right to contest LGBT rights. In doing so they contend that any attempt to restrict debate is the imposition of 'totalitarian' regimes that seek to exert control in problematic and anti-democratic ways. It is clear then that heteroactivists in legislative and cultural contexts where hate speech, discrimination and violence against LGBT people is prohibited have to work hard to create space to challenge LGBT inclusions.

In Chapter 5 we consider heteroactivist activism focused on the transformations appearing in the public sphere because of LGBT equalities. We consider the place and importance of religion in public and how Christianity in particular is set up in opposition to LGBT equalities. This includes workplaces, as well as broader public places. We show how the workplaces have been used as a location of contestation. This is because heteroactivists argue that religious employees who, for example, view marriage as only between a man and a woman are unable to express these views without facing hostility and potentially losing their job. Our consideration also includes broader heteroactivist concerns about the place of religion in public debates, as well as their concerns about the inclusion of LGBT equalities in public life around issues related to foster care, adoption and state documents such as passports and driver's licences. The threat posed to religious people is a central theme as well as the risk that LGBT equalities present for children and families in these contexts.

The Concluding Considerations discusses what the book has done: examining the 'dangers' of LGBT equalities that heteroactivists argue are undermining their rights and foundations of the family and society. We also consider the transnational considerations, as well as the place of white Christianity in heteroactivism in Canada, the UK and Ireland. Our conclusions also identify areas not covered, including abortion/broader gender rights, class, the effects of heteroactivism on everyday lives, the counter arguments/discussions and the geographical limitations of the book. We finally speculate on where we see heteroactivist resistances moving in the future, contending that scholarship and activism in this area are pressing and important alongside other considerations of LGBT equalities and their limitations.

Conclusion

Heteroactivist interventions challenge the notion that progress in sexual and gendered equalities is inevitable and the battle has been 'won' in countries often lauded for their progressiveness. This book seeks to understand debates regarding sexual and gender politics in the 21st century through understanding how oppositional organisations articulate their ideologies, particularly around specific sites and moments where their oppositions are highlighted. We interrogate how the implementation of LGBT equalities is resisted as they are perceived to transform social relations, reformulating political and legal relations at the state level as well as transnationally. This allows us to examine how LGBT equalities reshape socio-spatial relations by challenging the heteronormativity of spaces that were previously deployed to constitute heteronormative subjects. Taken together, a geographically centred, heteroactivist approach encourages analysis of how society, social life and political activism are being reworked through emergent resistances to LGBT political, legislative and social equalities.

1

Same-Sex Marriage: Supporting 'Heterosexual Families'

Introduction

Same-sex marriage played a key role in LGBT activisms in Canada, the UK and Ireland in the 21st century. Same-sex marriage equalities were the result of innumerable legal and social contestations in all three locations. The battle over same-sex marriage was not only 'intensely political' for society at large was but was also vigorously and sometimes acrimoniously debated within LGBT and queer positionings (Kitzinger and Wilkinson, 2004: 132; see also

Bell and Binnie, 2000; Browne and Nash, 2015; Warner, 1999; Weeks et al., 2001). Less attention has been paid to contemporary oppositions to same-sex marriage outside the US. This chapter explores how heteroactivist arguments develop in those legal and social contexts where gay men and lesbians no longer cause moral, religious, legal and social outrage in society at large. Thus, contemporary heteroactivist arguments against same-sex marriage (and its implications) need to find alternative grounds to support their opposition other than the vilification of LGBT 'lifestyles'. Here, we investigate heteroactivist opposition to same-sex marriage as it emerged in Ireland and Great Britain. In both these instances, oppositional arguments both resonated with, and departed from, arguments made by defenders of heteronormative marriage in Canada some 10 to 15 years earlier. Throughout the chapter, we show that heteroactivists largely moved away from arguments about the moral turpitude of gays and lesbians and focused on claims that hetero- and gender normative marriages were best for society, and in the best interests of biological children. The figure of the child introduced here is critical to heteroactivist discussions and is an underlying heteroactivist theme we explore throughout the book.

We begin this chapter with a brief discussion of debates in Canada in the early 2000s about same-sex marriage before we then introduce the British and Irish contexts. The chapter primarily considers the activities of heteroactivists in the 2014 debates in Britain regarding same-sex marriage and the 2015 Irish referendum on gay marriage. At the end of the chapter, we discuss how opponents in the British 2014 debate in particular, detailed the supposedly negative impacts of same-sex marriage on Canada in an attempt to influence the British debate. In examining these British and Irish marriage debates, we detail the key tenets underpinning heteroactivist ideologies that we explore throughout this book. These include: the figure of the child in trans or gender 'ideologies' and the undermining of Western social mores (Chapters 3 and 5); parental rights (Chapter 2) and the potential exclusion of 'traditional Christians' and other heteroactivists from the public sphere (Chapter 5). Overall, we contend that heteroactivist objections to LGBT equalities, including same-sex marriage, have to grapple with new legal and cultural contexts in the 21st century, where overt vilifications of LGBT people, relationships and lives are both unproductive and potentially illegal.

Canada, Great Britain and Ireland: Same-Sex Marriage and Heteroactivist Resistances

Same-sex marriage was formally instituted in Canada in 2005. For a decade, there was little overt or public mainstream difficulty around LGBT equalities until about 2015 when the events discussed here began to generate greater opposition around certain flashpoints such as sexual education and gay–straight alliances in public schools as well as questions about trans rights (Nash and Browne, 2019).[1] Those objecting to same-sex marriage in Great Britain and Ireland made arguments similar to those made in Canada in the early 2000s. That said, how these arguments were taken up and elaborated on demonstrates distinctive contextual differences between countries. In this section, we outline several key points arising in the Canadian debates on same-sex marriage before considering the British and Irish conversations. These national contextualisations highlight the transnational formulation of heteroactivist ideologies as they travel, merge and diverge across places and illustrate the transnational processes we discuss in the Introduction. This transnationalism is central not only to our engagement with heteroactivism but is critical to understanding heteroactivism itself.

Canada legally recognised same-sex marriage in 2005, after several decades of court cases and legislative actions that, in a piecemeal fashion, incorporated same-sex couples and their children into family legislation. Opponents of same-sex marriage in the early 2000s focused almost exclusively on the rights, needs and welfare of the child. Heterosexual (married) parents, it was argued, provided the most nurturing environment: 'By their sexual difference, they provide their children the full range of human nurturing that comes by being raised by a mother and a father' (Henry, 2006: para. 7). Ethicist Margaret Somerville claimed that children's rights include the experience of living in a procreative family unit held together by heterosexual marriage and enabling access to the biological mother and father (Somerville, 2010). This focus on heterosexual marriages claimed that children raised by married, male same-sex couples would be denied their inherent rights to their biological mother, and thus would be rendered 'motherless' – an unfair and troubling result (Nash, Gorman-Murray and Browne, 2019). Heteroactivists therefore contended that the best interests of the child could only be met within the heterosexual procreative unit, rendered stable by the institution of heteronormative marriage, and as the best model of proper gendered and sexual roles (Browne and Nash, 2014). Although criticism was not directly or overtly aimed at single or divorced parents (men or women), these arguments constituted an implied criticism of unmarried, separate or divorced heterosexual parents, as well as adoptive and foster families or those turning to reproductive technologies. Those failing to meet this ideal standard of child-rearing were seen to be deficient in their role as both partner and spouse. Enshrine Marriage Canada argued, for example, that 'Marriage is a child-centred, not an adult-centred, institution. No one has the right to redefine marriage so as intentionally to impose a fatherless or motherless home on a child as a matter of state policy' (quoted in Nash, Gorman-Murray and Browne, 2019: 4). Linking the public/private, state/ home creates the presumption of the good of the 'nation' being located within a heteronormalised trajectory that makes home lives and personal relationships a public good and public goods. As we show throughout the chapter, and the remainder of the book, state policy is positioned by heteroactivists as protecting the child. Thus, the risk of same-sex marriage is not only a privatised one for the child, but also a public one that undermines the underpinning foundations of heteronormative nations and societies (and at times Western civilisation).

As we detail throughout this book, arguments about the superiority of normative heterosexual and gendered marriage have become a central plank in heteroactivist arguments. However, these are not uniform as they travel and touchdown in ways that recreate the arguments, activisms as well as legal landscapes. As we show at the end of this chapter, the Canadian experience of same-sex marriage was portrayed as creating serious problems and was deployed by heteroactivists, particularly in Britain in 2014, to warn of the key 'dangers' of implementing same-sex marriage.

Same-sex marriage was legalised in Great Britain in 2014 after the initial implementation of same-sex civil partnerships in 2005 (see Barker and Monk, 2015). Debates about instituting same-sex marriage in 2013 were met with considerably more opposition than for civil partnerships in 2004. While groups opposed to LGBT equalities had operated for some time, new groups were founded to specifically combat the proposed same-sex marriage legislation (e.g. Coalition for Marriage). In other cases, existing organisations refocused their activism to more fully encompass objections to same-sex marriage. The Society for the Protection of Unborn Children (SPUC), for example, publicly opposed same-sex marriage despite not having campaigned on same-sex issues since the 1990s. Thus, in Great Britain, when the possibility of same-sex marriage arose, organisations were created, gathered and refocused their collective opposition which had, to that point, opposed LGBT equalities through individual court cases largely based on questions of religious freedoms (see Cooper and Herman, 2013; Cooper, 2019). With the specific focus on opposition to same-sex marriage, heteroactivists shifted how their resistances were framed, including drawing on transnational alliances and interconnections. It is important to note that while civil partnerships extended to Northern Ireland, same-sex marriage did not. We therefore refer to Great Britain throughout this chapter. Same-sex marriage was put into place in Northern Ireland in October 2019 by the UK Westminster parliament. Same-sex marriage and abortion are powers that were devolved to the Northern Irish assembly; therefore this was only possible because the Northern Irish parliament (Stormont) has not been in place since January 2017. The move was opposed by some parties in Northern Ireland, but they could not stop it due to the lack of a sitting parliament (see also Chapter 4).

The newly independent Ireland of the 20th century gave 'pride of place' to the heterosexual reproductive married family unit as constitutive of the Irish nation (Greene, 1994: 357). Not only did British colonialism reject homosexuality from the national body, so too did Irish 20th-century nationalisms (Conrad, 2001, 2004). Given that the Irish constitution of 1937 incorporated an explicit reference to man/woman marriage, any amendment to include same-sex marriage required a referendum with Ireland becoming the first country to hold such a referendum in 2015 (see Ryan, 2015 for full constitutional details). In this referendum, 62.07% voted Yes (1,201,607 people) and 37.93% voted No (734,300 people) (Referendum Results, 2015). There were official and unofficial No to same-sex marriage campaigns, with numerous organisations arguing for a No vote. The rules on referenda in Ireland meant that equal airtime on mainstream media was given to both the Yes and the No campaigns with extensive coverage given to both sides of the debate (Mulhall, 2015). Public spaces throughout Ireland were dominated by posters for both sides, appearing on lampposts across the country. We use these posters to explore key elements of the No campaign and how they sought to work against the emergence of a 'New Ireland' that would vote to accept same-sex marriage (see also Browne et al., 2018).

We now turn to key debates in the Irish and British discussions regarding same-sex marriage. These both reiterate and move away from key elements noted in the Canadian arguments in the early part of the century. One key difference to which we now turn, was the existence, in Ireland

and Great Britain, of civil partnerships, which influenced how equality could be claimed by heteroactivist groups.

Beyond Bigotry: Supporting Civil Partnerships to Contest Same-Sex Marriage

In Canada, Britain and Ireland, heteroactivist groups and commentators sought to distance themselves from accusation that their objections were based on personal and specific opprobrium towards LGBT people (see also Chapter 4). For example, the Campaign Life Coalition, a Canadian organisation, argued that being labelled 'homophobic' was an 'anti-Christian slur', and one that could not be 'farther from the truth' (Campaign Life Coalition, 2012, Canada, as quoted in Nash and Browne, 2015: 567). Similarly, at the Lumen Fidei conference in Ireland in 2018, John-Henry Westen (editor of *LifeSite News*) asserted that the 'usual tactic' of those promoting the LGBT 'agenda' was to call an opponent 'a hater and a bigot because of [their] stance on same-sex attraction' (Browne, fieldnotes, Lumen Fidei conference, August 2018, quotes are approximate). As we argue more fully in Chapter 4, heteroactivists claim their views are not homophobic (or transphobic or indeed bigoted) and that any attempt to paint them as such is designed to silence them. In this section, we explore how they worked to deflect these accusations in the same-sex marriage debates in Ireland and Great Britain. In particular, heteroactivists worked to develop arguments that did not vilify homosexuals and could not be portrayed as anti-gay. Instead, they developed alternative arguments that valorised the heteronormative family as best for society and children while simultaneously claiming that same-sex marriage and families are inferior, but not (necessarily) wrong.

In their arguments to retain marriage as only for heterosexual man/woman relationships, heteroactivists appeared to support a form of LGBT equalities while at the same time arguing against same-sex marriage. In the same-sex marriage debates in Ireland in 2014, for example, posters such as Figure 1.1 argued that LGBT people were already protected within civil partnerships. Therefore, in their terms, 'traditional' marriage, understood as being between a man and a woman could be maintained. The use of the word 'already' is indicative of something that has happened and that is enough, asking for more is unnecessary, and an indulgence that does not need to be granted. Ireland, as a nation, is already accepting and progressive. We have already achieved love for all and love for all looks different for different people. Thus, equality is already achieved, and in this presentation, the harm that same-sex marriage will bring by devaluing and disrupting heterosexual marriage.

Similarly, in the British debates in 2014, a number of heteroactivist groups supported civil partnerships but not same-sex marriage. Such groups pointed to their lack of objection to the passing of civil partnerships in 2004

Figure 1.1 'We Already Have Civil Partnerships. Don't Redefine Marriage'. Poster from the Irish Same-Sex Marriage Referendum

as evidence of their 'support' of LGBT relationships. In November 2012, David Coburn of UKIP's National Executive Committee contended:

> UKIP's stance on gay marriage is simple: we entirely, wholeheartedly support equal rights for couples regardless of their sexuality and we believe this has been achieved through the introduction of civil partnerships, which UKIP supported. (UKIP, 2013, quoted in Browne and Nash, 2015: 73)

This argument was also reproduced in 2012 to support Green Party Councillor Christina Summers who had been expelled from the party for opposing same-sex marriage. She asserted she was not a 'bigot' for holding 'the orthodox Christian position that marriage should be between a man and a woman', because she 'has no fundamental objections to the equality agenda':

> She has not spoken out against gay people. She supports civil partnerships. She believes that same-sex-couples should have the same legal rights as heterosexual couples ... She didn't campaign, she didn't 'preach hate', she wasn't 'homophobic'. Rather, she articulated what she believed, why she believed it, and then voted on the basis of personal conscience rather than party policy. (Spencer, 2012: paras 4 and 7)

The existence of civil partnerships for those in same-sex relationships allowed UKIP and Summers to espouse support for some form of legal 'equality' for LGBT people, while simultaneously opposing same-sex marriage. By maintaining this ostensible 'support' for LGBT equalities, heteroactivists could shield themselves from accusations of homophobic bigotry and simultaneously position themselves as victims who are being attacked for their own identities and beliefs. Indeed, as Spencer (2012) argues, this is not 'hate' or 'campaigning', because Summers supports civil partnerships; instead it is a matter of 'personal conscience'.

For heteroactivists, the man/woman complementarity (and the heteronormativity it represented) justified these differential legislative provisions that were not then 'unequal' because they were different. This enabled heteroactivists to logically support essentially the same legal protections provided by civil partnerships, while simultaneously contesting what they termed the 'redefinition of marriage'. Nevertheless, claims about the equality and parity of civil partnerships were contested by this very same assertion of difference. For example, the Christian Medical Fellowship maintained that marriage and civil partnerships were made for different relationship types 'and should be kept distinct' (Christian Medical Fellowship, 2012: para. 6; see also Browne and Nash, 2015). Using these differences to justify the distinction between marriage and civil partnerships highlights how the possibility of same-sex marriage in Great Britain resulted in the rise of a heteroactivist resistance that was not as apparent with the passing of civil partnerships. Thus, Lord Singh, head of the Network of Sikh Organisations, said in 2012 that he had 'respect for gays and lesbians' who have 'everything they need', but also saw same-sex marriage as an 'assault' on religion (Ross, 2012, quoted in Browne and Nash, 2014). Singh expressed 'delight' at civil partnerships, contrasting this with the 'attack' posed by same-sex marriage on heteronormative values. As we discuss in Chapter 5, while our focus and the focus of most heteroactivist arguments in the three countries are secular, religion still had an import. Heteroactivism at times referenced religion as the foundation for heterosexual marriage, but more often framed arguments outside of religion including in terms of the best interests of society. Here, religion and same-sex marriage are framed in opposition because heteronormative marriage has been based on the intersection, and alignment, of religion and the state. Redefining marriage undermines this connection extending the separation of church and state and in particular, the state support.

This opposition was also apparent at the Lumen Fidei conference in 2018. The organiser and chair, Anthony Murphy, said that in speaking the 'truth' about marriage, heteroactivists could reclaim the 'rightful place' of the (heteronormative) family in Irish society:

'A Bishop said that the WMOF [World Meeting of Families, happening at the same time] was not meant for traditional families, but for all families'

[The audience gasp in disbelief/shock]. He says that this is not about traditional marriage and that other forms of relationships are placed 'on the same level. This is nonsense and against God's plan' ... 'There have been calamitous events in Ireland brought through the popular vote. People choose to defy God, and got same-sex marriage'. (Anthony Murphy, Browne fieldnotes, Lumen Fidei Conference, August 2018, quotes are approximations)

The heteroactivist narrative about 'traditional', 'real' and proper families is positioned against those that are not 'on the same level' and marks a distinction between this discourse and the overt vilification of gay men and homosexuality. The use of common-sense claims seeks to challenge the establishment of new forms of common sense, where theirs is the 'natural truth' about the structure of society and human relations to the exclusion of all others. This reframes the referendum results in Ireland (and the passing of same-sex marriage in Great Britain) as 'calamitous', a loss of and for Ireland as well as for the nation and Irish people. It also historicises these relationships as 'new' and outside of historical inferences of 'the traditional'. Heteroactivists, as we now turn to argue, in framing certain familial forms as 'best for society', are arguing that these relationships are deserving of recognition through marriage, as the sole kinship familial structure that should be formally validated and recognised by the state through marriage.

Best for Society

The potential redefinition of marriage and the resulting loss of male/female complementarity as the defining feature of marriage was portrayed by heteroactivists as fundamentally detrimental to the optimum operation of society (a heteroactivist assertion that re-emerges across chapters). They argued for the superiority of heteronormative gender relations and heterosexual marriage as the foundational building blocks for a stable and healthy society and as the 'best' (and ideally only) location for the birth and nurture of children (Browne and Nash, 2014, 2017; Nash and Browne, 2015). Heteroactivists pointed to the historical importance of the role of the 'natural family' (defined in terms of two opposite-sex parents, and children). This is understood across all three contexts as 'central to a healthy, stable society' (e.g. Real Women of Canada, 2013) and 'is therefore in everyone's interest' (Society for the Protection of Unborn Children, 2012: 1, Britain). Opponents claimed that their opposition went beyond moral disapproval of homosexuals to highlighting social concerns of importance to 'everyone' (including homosexuals). Strong societies are apparently only achieved through longitudinal heterosexual commitments that are formulated through particular versions of the 'family' that are morally superior and ahistorical. This supersedes contemporary ideals or possibilities and would be undermined or weakened, they claimed, by including homosexual couples in the institution.

Heteroactivist organisations and think tanks worked to produce and/or reuse studies to demonstrate how the so-called 'decline of heterosexual marriage' offers explanations for the ills perceived to be befalling Canadian and British society (this is less a feature of Irish heteroactivism, which tends to draw on studies from elsewhere). In Canada, this includes claims that child poverty, boys' deteriorating academic performance, the coming 'demographic winter' (i.e. population, read white population, decline) and a declining labour force are all due to a decline in long-term, heterosexual marriages (Browne and Nash, 2014, 2015). In Great Britain, the Christian Medical Fellowship argued:

> Stable marriages and families headed by a mother and a father are the bedrock of society and the state has a duty to protect the uniqueness of these key institutions. There is considerable evidence to show that marriage leads to better family relationships, less economic dependence, better physical health and longevity, improved mental health and emotional well-being, and reduced crime and domestic violence. Same-sex marriage, in comparison with marriage, is an unproven and experimental social model. (Christian Medical Fellowship, quoted in Nash and Browne, 2015: 566)

The claim that the 'people of Britain' (and Canada) have 'enjoyed' the 'vital role' of marriage is also supplemented by 'studies' and reports produced by pro-family think tanks and policy institutes (e.g. Cardus in Canada). While not directly attacking same-sex marriage, these groups continue to build a case for privileging heterosexual marriage over all other forms of state-sanctioned relationships and infer that same-sex marriage will undermine heterosexual marriage. In this way, research is utilised to support a claim for 'special privileges' to be given to those who are married in ways that are to be celebrated by the nation and recognised by the state:

> [T]here are some commitments which are so crucial to the common good that everyone is obliged to recognise and celebrate them. Heterosexual marriage is the most important of these. Without it, none of us would even exist to begin with, and there would truly be no such thing as society, because there would be no human beings on the planet, no families to form the basis of wider society. Such a commitment, therefore, has special privileges (such as the right to share a double room in a hotel). (Thomas More Institute, quoted in Nash and Browne, 2015: 567)

In arguing against same-sex marriage equalities in Great Britain, same-sex relationships were once again positioned as 'different' not only because of the importance of gender complementarity but also as a less appropriate location for reproduction and the raising of children. In these discourses, marriage equality is not possible because heterosexual marriage has distinctive purposes and responsibilities grounded in historical 'fact' and biological imperatives. These biological imperatives focus on sex and the absence of 'natural' procreation which proves that same-sex relationships do not deserve the privileges of marriage and that such denial is good for society as a whole. This allows opponents to also make the argument that LGBT activists agitating for same-sex marriage are being selfish in putting the desire for marriage and children ahead of the rights of children themselves. Therefore, this special role assigned to heterosexual marriage justifies discrimination against others and deflects accusations of homophobia given it is critical of non-married heterosexuals as well (see e.g. Kathy Faust https://them beforeus.com).

Seeing same-sex marriage as detrimental for society, and families constituted outside of heteronormative marriage as somehow less or inferior, creates discourses that do not necessarily vilify gay men and lesbians directly because this critique can also be directed at unmarried heterosexual couples, the divorced and single parents. The figure of the child clearly plays a central role in these arguments and for the position of heteronormative marriage heteroactivists are seeking to reclaim for married, procreative, heteronormative families. As we show in the next section (and Chapters 3 and 5), LGBT equalities pose particular 'dangers' to children, which is a central heteroactivist claim.

Best for the Child

The figure of the child operates as a key theme in heteroactivist discourses. Heteroactivists use the figure of the child to juxtapose equalities claims for LGBT people against claims for the rights of children in the face of the harm 'the LGBT agenda' poses to them. The arguments heteroactivists have developed about the superiority and centrality of the 'traditional' and 'natural' family, centralises the child as not only the desired product of marriage, but as the feature that sets heterosexual marriage apart from, and as better than, other relationships, including unmarried heterosexuals and non-heteronormative couples. The key distinction made between 'traditional marriage' and same-sex marriage is the possibility of procreation through 'natural' sexual relations. This special position afforded to heterosexual, procreative relationships moves 'private' domestic life into the public/state sphere. The public/private differentiation that animated conversations about 20th-century homosexual immorality and disease is redirected to focus on the 'natural' and 'fruitful' sexual acts of heterosexual coupling, which '3rd parties' have a vested interest in supporting (Thomas More Institute, n.d.). Marriage then is 'primarily about the generation of children and is not just about the couple themselves' (Evangelical Alliance, as quoted in Nash and Browne, 2015: 571). This requires the state to focus on the 'best possible arrangements for raising children' (Evangelical

Alliance, quoted in Nash and Browne, 2015: 571), which, during both the Irish and British campaigns against same-sex marriage, is clearly and unequivocally the procreative heterosexual male/female household.

In Canada, Great Britain and Ireland, heteroactivist organisations argued that the 'complementary sexual difference' underpinning heteronormative marriage not only supports the essentialist biology of procreation but is also key to the 'healthy upbringing' of children (see also Browne and Nash, 2014; Nash and Browne, 2015). Thus, regardless of the merits of the parent:

> no woman can be a father and no man can be a mother. As family law recognises, the interests of children should be paramount. Those interests require the traditional definition of marriage to be kept as it is. (Marantha, n.d., Britain, quoted in Nash and Browne, 2015: 572; see also Marantha, 2012)

The 'natural family' then is positioned as the proper place for the rearing of children, where they will apparently 'thrive' within specific sets of gender/sex norms (that also set up the 'truths' of sex/gender for trans people, see Chapter 3). The 'fact' of procreation and the 'proven' benefits of heterosexual marriage, as established through a body of 'global research', is contrasted with the 'experiment' of same-sex marriage (Christian Medical Fellowship, 2012). These discourses stop short of suggesting that same-sex parenting is 'wrong' or immoral, focusing instead on the ideals of heterosexual coupling in marriage as the 'gold standard' (see Christian Concern, May 9a, 2019).

In the same-sex marriage debates in Ireland and Great Britain, the adult figure evoked as unsuitable for parenting and thus undermining the case for same-sex marriage was not the 'dangerous and degenerate' homosexual of old, but instead the selfish adult who puts their desires over the needs of a child for their mother and father (Browne et al., 2018). Assumptions regarding the protection of the figure of the child relates not only to their conception, but also to their place of nurture. 'Children's rights', properly nurtured and protected through male/female, mother/father relationships are understood as necessarily superseding adult rights in order to be a 'civilised society'. Heteroactivist groups thus assert that the 'natural order' and 'society' are negatively affected through the creation and raising of children in ways that privilege adult (non-heterosexual) desires over those of the 'rights' of children. The emphasis is not on deviancy but on the 'good of society' (Browne and Nash, 2014; Nash and Browne, 2015). The focus on biological procreation does more than simply elevate opposite-sex marriage by placing it within the realm of the 'natural', it also enables a protective stance to be adopted towards children in fighting back against same-sex marriage (or as we see in Chapter 3 towards trans kids who need 'help').

Heteroactivism is concerned for the future as it is constructed, or in their terms 'destroyed', through present decisions regarding LGBT rights (see also Chapters 3 and 5). These concerns go beyond women's bodies as needing protection from 'fathers, husbands and the (national) state' (Mostov, 2000: 91), to specifically seeking protections for heteronormative families that are formed through biological bonds and linked to reproductive futures. The figure of the child, central to heteroactivist discourses, fits the futurity envisaged by some theorists (Edelman, 2004). While the child as a queer figure in need of 'straightening' has been discussed extensively by queer theorists (see e.g. Bruhm and Hurley, 2004; Stewart, 2019; Stockton, 2009, 2016), Edelman's figure of the child arose from his critique of the US Christian Right. When examining same-sex marriage, in Canada, Great Britain and Ireland, the child is constructed as needing 'proper' (read heteronormative) parents in order to develop appropriately. Throughout the book we explore the supposed dangers posed to children, including the primary school child who requires protection from sexual education and same-sex relationships (Chapter 2). In Chapter 4, we also examine how university students can be seen as requiring protection from 'silencing' as well as from academics who are unduly influencing them. In this book, the child needing to be protected emerges not only in education, but also as both the threat, and the threatened in the context of the 'the transgender child' (Chapter 3). Here, we further interrogate the interrelations of proper parent and safe/appropriate childhood through the Vote No campaign in the Irish same-sex marriage referendum. These incorporated the 'need for a mother', and the spectre of the dangerous gay man who pursues children through fatherhood.

The Homosexual Spectre: Children Need a Mother (and a Father)

Whereas in Great Britain, the Evangelical Alliance (2013, quoted in Nash and Browne, 2015) argued that same-sex couples 'can never produce a baby – a fundamental fact not altered by the possibility of adoption or artificial insemination for which special legal rules apply', in Ireland the spectre of surrogacy and the absence of the mother was a key argument for the No campaign during the 2015 referendum (Browne et al., 2018). Those who sought a No vote included a group called 'Mothers and Fathers Matter', implying the need for both in bringing up a child. In Ireland, as with Great Britain, access to adoption and reproductive technologies were not included in the same-sex marriage bill but were covered under separate legislation. Nonetheless the focus was on the need for children to have opposite, normatively sexed/gendered parents. In opposing same-sex marriage then, the argument was that allowing same-sex marriage would undermine the Irish 'traditional' family in ways that were detrimental to the child, the nation, society and the 'common good'.

A key means of engaging in the referendum debate in Ireland was the use of posters which were ubiquitous in public spaces (see also Browne et al., 2018). Figure 1.1 shows one example of these. The use of the Irish child in posters such as these creates a specific pictorial and textual discourse that seeks to position heteroactivists as protecting Irish children through guarding the experiences of Irish childhood. These experiences are only ever properly located within male/female married relationships. Thus, in Figure 1.2, children *deserve* a mother and a father. The visual discourse is of the three figures recreating a unit, joined through kissing parents. It is implied that heteronormative parentage is a child's right that will apparently be removed by same-sex marriage, reiterating the need for a specific, 'proper' family form as something that children 'deserve'. Thus, the life of a child outside of the heteronormative married family unit is 'less' than, and inferior to, childhoods within heteronormative marriage, the validity of which is evidenced by the presence of biological children.

There is a circularity to this, that is, the child makes heteronormative marriage superior and the presence of the child requires heteronormative marriage. In this understanding, society and the state through legislation cannot and should not make room for families that have two mothers or two fathers. This hints at the fundamental failings of lesbian and gay male parenting, which some heteroactivists have labelled 'child abuse' (Browne, fieldnotes, The New Normal Conference, 2015). As Ryan contends, Irish legal precedent suggests that while:

one Irish mammy [is] firmly embedded in the bosom of the home [and] is self-evidently integral to the common good ... the prospect of two women raising a child together falls outside the constitutional confines of family life. (2014: 425, as quoted in Browne et al., 2018; Ryan-Flood, 2005)

Lesbian parenting and lesbian mothers were rarely mentioned in the debates regarding same-sex marriage. When lesbian/female parents were discussed, the focus was on children who are portrayed as searching for a father (Mothers and Fathers Matter, 2015; O'Brien, 2015). This presumes a particular form of reproduction, ignoring, for example, home insemination and known donor relationships. Finding 'real', genetic parentage in 'other' places, because the sperm used in clinics in Ireland can be located in Denmark and the US, implies that these children are 'only half' and therefore 'not fully' Irish. This then breaks Irish national identities and seeks to reconstitute a form of genetic-place-kinship connectivities (Nash, 2005). Where Irish nationhood cannot be explicitly denied on the basis of sexuality, the reproduction of 'half Irish' children indicates that these are not 'real' families and that the children's conception outside of married intercourse is inferior. This improper relatedness contests heteronormative genetic constructs of 'real' Irishness based in cultural connectedness to place through the route of biological parentage (see also Browne et al., 2018).

The dominant figure in the representation of same-sex parenting during the Irish referendum was 'two married men'. Their representations focused on the dangers of their potential parenting and procreative routes. Surrogacy was evoked (again often ignoring other routes to parenthood) as representing an 'attack' on the mother and 'child's right to a mother':

> Even if a future court does not find that two married en have a right to have children through surrogacy, any Government which permits opposite-sex married couples to use surrogates will be bound by the Constitution to also allow two married men to use a surrogate, which once again is a deliberate attack on the child's right to a mother. (Mothers and Fathers Matter, 2015, as quoted in Browne et al., 2018: 534)

Fathers were often mentioned in the Irish same-sex marriage debate in the dyad of mother and father. Yet, as the above quote illustrates, the rights of 'two married men' and their relationship with children was an important focus. Whereas posters focused exclusively on children needing 'a mother', such as those from the Iona Institute, there were no posters that specifically and emotively pointed to the absence of the father. This gendered form of hetero-activism reflects more broadly the ideals of women and men in heteronormative relationships, and the patriarchal constructs of the nation that demonises non-hegemonic forms of heterosexual masculinities (Conrad, 2001).

What remains unsaid in the poster in Figure 1.2 and in other posters is the emphasis on surrogacy as creating an absent mother highlighted by the line 'She needs a mother for life not just 9 months' (see Browne et al., 2018: 533). While single mothers can be accepted, it is only in very rare cases (death or similar), that fathers should be enabled to have children, especially female children, 'alone'. Essentialised genetic roots underlie heteroactivist arguments, while here the supposedly fixed biological sex of woman/female renders men unfit parents without the presence of the mother. This points to the supposed risk of a child having two male parents, not only in terms of what is lacking, but also the dangers they apparently pose to 'vulnerable women and children'.

Speaking specifically about surrogacy rather than broader fertility treatments not only points to a male homosexual lack, but also to a desperation on the part of 'predatory men' who seek 'defenceless' children. This is a familiar trope, that of the predatory gay man, although in this case it is two gay men, looking to exploit vulnerable women who will bear their (deliberately motherless) children. Women's bodies become 'wombs for rent' for these predatory gay men (Nast, 2002). Through this discourse, Irish heteroactivist groups tacitly aligned themselves with certain feminists who also protest the classed and racialised

Figure 1.2 'Children Deserve a Mother and a Father'. Poster from the Irish Same-Sex Marriage Referendum

exploitation of women's bodies through surrogacy. This echoes the 'pro-woman' and compassionate Christian rhetoric that surfaces in both the US and Canada (Saurette and Gordon, 2013; Burack, 2014b).

Given that men cannot biologically reproduce without access to eggs and uteri, the discourse of surrogacy and the naming of men who seek it as predatory seeks to prove the unnaturalness of surrogacy in order to point to, but not explicitly name, the unnaturalness of same-sex marriage. The risk of gay male parenting hints at a much more sinister mythology about the predatory gay man as paedophile. This dangerous predatory gay man is the mostly unnamed spectre regarding the importance of male/female married relationships as the 'best for children'. Bringing the predatory gay man into the debate subtly is crucial. The discursive tactic is to vilify gay men without suggesting that they are all 'deviant', instead focusing on 'prospects' and potentials for an Irish childhood without a mother. These discussions about children, parenting and families in the same-sex marriage debate were predictions about the future of Ireland and Great Britain if same-sex marriage were approved. However, at the time same-sex marriage was approved in Ireland and Great Britain, same-sex marriage had been in place in Canada for over ten years. We finish this chapter by exploring the transnational warnings to the British that emanated from Canada about the implications of legalising same-sex marriage.

The Canadian Example: Predicting What Is to Come for Those Who Oppose LGBT Rights

The British and Irish examples in this chapter focus on the arguments that were made before the passing of same-sex marriage in Great Britain and Ireland. In these debates, heteroactivists drew on claims about the dangers of same-sex marriage, which illustrates how some transnational networks can operate. Canadian authors spoke directly to British (and subsequently Irish) audiences to alert them of the consequences of same-sex marriage. To illustrate, we consider an article published on 24 February 2013 in *The Interim*, 'Canada's Life and Family Newspaper', by Rory Leishman (see also Nash and Browne, 2015). This article offers insight into key themes that re-emerge throughout the book. The article gives an explicit warning to Great Britain, arguing that implementing same-sex marriage would mark the 'onset of a new age of religious persecution in Britain' (Leishman, 2013: para. 1). As we discuss explicitly in Chapter 5, LGBT rights are often placed in opposition to religious, particularly Christian rights, and in this article, Leishman specifically points to same-sex marriage as a key moment in this process. However, the article goes well beyond the site of the church as a place where same-sex marriages might take place, to explore the multitude of spaces (schools, work, public spaces) where Canadian examples 'prove' that the British heteroactivist fears are also well founded. Leishman's arguments, while focused on religion, go far beyond theological arguments. Instead both he (and Somerville, who we discuss below) offer insights into heteroactivist concerns about the impact of same-sex marriage. More than this, as the rest of the book shows, many of Leishman's 'predictions' were correct in that heteroactivists have grappled with and resisted many of these same issues.

Leishman focuses on schools as employers and argues that teachers who object to same-sex marriage might find their employment in jeopardy. There is a grave risk, in his view, to teachers, for example, who refuse, on the grounds of conscience to teach that heterosexual and homosexual marriage are of the same 'moral equivalence'. As evidence, Leishman discusses the case of a British Columbia schoolteacher who wrote letters to a local paper in opposition to LGBT equalities and was disciplined by the local school board, who found his comments discriminatory and as creating a hostile environment for LGBT students. In his discussion, Leishman utilises a very specific rendition of events to imply that the issue was the teacher's objections to same-sex marriage. However, the series of letters were written in 1997 and a complicated series of disciplinary actions and appeals unfolded before same-sex marriage was made legal in Canada in 2005. Nonetheless, this example is used to point to potential dangers to employment for those who are opposed to same-sex marriage (and LGBT equalities more broadly), which we examine in Chapter 5.

Leishman goes on to warn about LGBT equalities as a threat to parental rights and specifically a threat to the ability of parents to withdraw their children from classes that might conflict with their religious beliefs. He uses several court cases related to both public and Catholic schools. In several court decisions in Quebec, the court held that parents did not have the right to withdraw their children from a 'world religions' course nor did schools have the right to avoid teaching the mandated 'World Religions' course. The question of same-sex marriage had little to do with whether students should take a mandated, secular course on world religious but the link between religion and specifically Christianity and its opposition to same-sex marriage was implied. In the next chapter, we consider in more detail, claims about the need to protect parental rights around determining a child's education and the implications of this for home and family relationships. In Chapter 5, we discuss the counterposing of sexual and gender rights and religion as a key binary through which British and Canadian heteroactivists create and operationalise their oppositions to LGBT rights.

Here however it is important to note that Leishman's discussion highlights the transnational nature of heteroactivist discourses around children's and parental rights that were visible across Canada, the UK and Ireland at the time we undertook this research (Nash et al., 2019). Margaret Somerville (2010), who was a law professor at McGill University in Montreal and is now a bioethicist at

University of Notre Dame Australia, offers further insights into these transnational connections.[2] Glossing over specific state nuances, Somerville asserts what she perceives as unproblematic parallels between nations adopting same-sex marriage, asking:

> Are we repeating in a new context and in new ways the terrible errors and grave injustices that occurred with Australia's 'stolen generation' of aboriginal children, the United Kingdom's 'home children' sent to Canada and other British Commonwealth countries, and the 'scoop' of native children from reserves into Canadian residential schools and white adoptive homes, all of which deliberately separated children from their biological families? (Somerville, 2010: 43)

The superiority of normative heterosexual and gendered marriage has become a central plank in heteroactivist arguments. However, the assertions are not uniform as they travel and touch down in ways that recreate the arguments, activisms as well as legal landscapes. Here Somerville equates sexual and gender rights with removing children from their families as part of colonial projects in Australia and Canada – a set of circumstances considerably different from the current debates about same-sex marriage and parenting. In equating this to same-sex marriage, Somerville is attempting to predict what she understands might be the historical legacies of same-sex marriage by drawing on disparate and unrelated events.

Much like Leishman, Somerville is suggesting some form of universal danger circulating transnationally because of LGBT equalities. In a similar way, and referencing schooling, parental rights and the passage of same-sex marriage in Canada in 2004, Leishman argues that same-sex marriage will create significant social division and is something other nations might be subject to despite historical and geographical differences – a claim that in many ways has proven somewhat prescient, although as we show the focus of their activisms to realise these claims have shifted (e.g. from children in same-sex relationships to trans children as disrupting heteronormative gender alignments and configurations). While the impact of same-sex marriage is extensively debated by sexualities scholars with respect to the life and health of LGBT people (see e.g. Auchmuty, 2004; Harding and Peel, 2006; Warner, 1999), discussions of the perceived impact of same-sex marriage, and the associated activisms by heteroactivists, has not received the same attention. Heteroactivists in the early part of this decade were predicting specific 'dangers' that would emerge as a result of heterosexual marriage no longer being positioned as superior to same-sex marriage, and as we will show they have turned their attentions to agitate around some of these issues.

Conclusion

Canada, Great Britain and Ireland all legalised same-sex marriage in the 21st century. These legal moves faced opposition and resistance that cannot be equated with the forms of homophobic challenges that dominated legal and cultural landscapes in the 20th century (see Bell and Binnie, 2000; Binnie, 2006; Stychin, 2003). Not only are the discourses secularly orientated, rather than privileging theological and religious argumentation, in the new cultural and social landscapes of the early 21st century Ireland, Canada and Great Britain, heteroactivism operates in ways that do not overtly vilify the 'unnatural' gay man or lesbian while still formulating objections to the impact of LGBT equalities.

When contesting same-sex marriage then, key tactics that heteroactivists employ include distancing themselves from accusations of bigotry and prejudice, in part through ostensibly supporting civil rights and equalities in the form of civil partnerships. They focus on the 'naturalness' of procreation that reasserts heterosexuality as different to other relationship forms, and as better for society and children, in the form of a mother and a father. Because these arguments do not overtly demonise lesbians and gay men, and indeed support 'equal rights', they argue that they could not be bigoted. What is also important is what is left unsaid – the spectre of the gay man who might be a danger to children is rarely overtly stated, instead it is implied *without* labelling 'unnatural' desires and 'immoralities'. How heteroactivists make their arguments is also important. Same-sex/gay marriage is an impossibility in heteroactivist epistemologies. This is marked linguistically by the use of scare quotes around gay marriage to indicate their scepticism regarding the concept itself. Civil partnerships do not need such grammatical additions, because they are seen as different to, and distinct from, same-sex marriage.

Heteroactivist arguments against same-sex marriage contest the changes they perceive these equalities are having on society, as well as themselves. Same-sex marriage in Canada, the UK and Ireland can be seen as fixed, 'normal' and lasting yet the heteroactivisms we consider here contest the presumptions that LGBT equalities are stable and unassailable. The danger to Irish (and British) children in the future as well as the detrimental implications of same-sex marriage on society are, and continue to be, key themes for heteroactivists. A meme that circulated during the Irish referendum campaign said, 'don't want same-sex marriage, don't have one'. The presumption underlying this is that same-sex marriage only affects those who choose to engage in it. What Leishman highlighted is the ways that same-sex marriage creates cultural shifts that can displace certain heteronormativities at school, in the workplace and in public places. For heteroactivists, the figure of the child is critical to a broad range of heteronormative rhetoric which we explore in Chapter 3 on trans or gender 'ideologies' and the undermining of Western social mores (Chapters 3 and 5). Concern about defending certain children is also grounded in heteroactivist claims about parental rights (Chapter 2) and the participation of 'traditional Christians' and other heteroactivists in the public sphere (Chapter 5). Throughout, the figure of the child re-emerges in relation to the dangers posed by LGBT equalities. We now turn to explore this through discussions regarding education and schooling that contest the inclusion of LGBT people, sexual education and same-sex relationships.

2

Schools: Challenging the Inclusion of LGBT Lives and Families

Introduction: Heteronormative Schools

Schools have become a critical location for heteroactivists, given the public educational system is designed to reflect approved national values and interests, which over the course of our work began to include LGBT equalities, starting with same-sex marriage. Schools are locations where children are separated from their parents for much of the day and as a result become key sites for learning potentially alternative values and norms from those of their parents or community in more privatised spheres (Anyon, 2005; Holloway and Jöns, 2012; Wainwright and Marandet, 2017). When national values are unsettled, schools can become central sites of contestation (Barker et al., 2010; Brooks and Waters, 2015; Waters, 2017). The ostensible legitimisation of some LGBT people as full and equal citizens in places like Ireland, Canada and the UK constitutes a 'new national value' incorporated into the school system as part of diversity and inclusion policies (Stella and Nartova, 2015: 18; see also Neary et al., 2017; Rayside, 2014).[1] Those objecting to the implementation of LGBT equalities must now renegotiate their place within these new national values, including how they are manifest through state apparatus such as schools.

Binnie (1997: 223) argues that spaces (including schools and classrooms) are not 'naturally or authentically "straight" but rather are actively produced and heterosexualised'. This 'straightness' is challenged when social and political changes place LGBT people and their families on an equal footing with heterosexuals. The inclusion of LGBT people in the school system through the curricula and diversity and inclusion policies can breech the home/school, public/private boundaries. Thus, while LGBT youth continue to experience difficulties in school spaces given the embeddedness of heteronormativity (DePalma and Atkinson, 2009; Epstein and Johnson, 1998; Herriot et al., 2017; Neary et al., 2017), new values and norms that embrace LGBT inclusion can conflict with the values and attitudes of parents fostered in the private spaces of the home and within broader kin groups/communities.

In this chapter, after introducing the key flashpoints in both primary and secondary school education in Canada and the UK, we show how particular heteroactivist contestations about LGBT inclusion in schools moves between local flashpoints to regional and national discourses, illustrating the multi-scalar creation and movement of heteroactivist resistances. The spaces of education, particularly those of state-operated schools, have become a key battleground for the implementation of LGBT equalities legislation. We begin by considering heteroactivist arguments about parental rights in relation to so-called state 'indoctrination' of LGBT equalities. We then turn to what heteroactivists argue are the dangers posed to children by the inclusion of same-sex issues in the school curriculum, including material on gender identity. Finally, we begin to tentatively consider how the intersections of ethnicity, race and religion are deployed by heteroactivists to make claims about 'conservative immigrants' in Canada and Muslims in Britain who oppose same-sex relationships being taught in schools. In doing so, we contend that schools are a key site of contestation for heteroactivists, which need to be defended from incursions by LGBT equalities. We also highlight more broadly how heteroactivism is racialised in ways that are not uniform. Indeed, as we have noted, heteroactivism is neither uniform nor unified, and is marked by numerous divisions, divergences and contestations.

Outline of Context and Education Flashpoints

This chapter is focused on the UK and Canada, where heteroactivist oppositions have emerged to school inclusivity of LGBT lives and reference to same-sex marriage as well as the presence of trans children in primary and secondary schools. In Ireland, there is discussion of a new sex and relationships curricula, and our data show that there is some disquiet regarding this, but at the time of writing in early 2019, this had not emerged fully. Observation at key Irish events, however, also indicates an unhappiness with the guidance for religious education in Irish primary schools (entitled 'Alive') that is currently used in schools, and broader internal battles regarding Catholicism in the curriculum which are beyond the scope of this research. We do discuss key Irish issues arising from the Irish conferences we attended, but do not focus on any specific Irish issue in this chapter.

In the UK, opposition to sex education and LGBT inclusions in schools has been gaining momentum over the course of our research in compiling this book. Since 2017, there has been a rise in mainstream reporting on issues related to trans children in school. In 2019 a series of protests arose around primary school lessons and specifically the 'No Outsiders' programme which includes teaching regarding sexuality and gender (https://no-outsiders. com/). It was written by Andrew Moffat, the Assistant Head Teacher at Parkfield Community School where he started this programme (see www.parkfield.bham.sch. uk/About-the-School). Parkfield is a primary school in

Birmingham, UK catering for children ages 4–11 and is identified as being predominantly Muslim. In early 2019, the school became the focus of media attention when parents who identified themselves as Muslim withdrew their children from the school to protest the inclusion of same-sex and LGBT relationships in the No Outsiders programme. They, and others, began weekly protests outside the school. The school suspended the lessons, subject to further consultation with the parents, and in July announced that they would be reintroduced under the title 'No Outsiders for a Faith Community'. The protest spread to other schools who also saw themselves and their schools as Muslim. Here we discuss the Parkfield protests to offer insights into key arguments regarding LGBT inclusivity in schools and also to tentatively introduce the racialised ways that heteroactivism is constructed. In showing how Muslim heteroactivists have to align with 'British values', we explore how some predominantly white Christian groups reconstituted the Muslim other, through ostensibly supporting the protestors.

We also examine the representations of the Rowe family, in the UK, who withdrew their children from their Christian primary school because a child in the class presented as a boy or a girl on different days. The Rowe family were supported by Christian Concern and appeared on numerous media outlets discussing their issues with how gender diverse children in primary schools are supported in ways that they see as detrimental to 'our children'.

In Canada, we consider heteroactivist opposition to the province of Ontario's Health and Physical Education (HPE) curriculum. This new curriculum was introduced late in 2014 by Premier Kathleen Wynne's (an out lesbian) Liberal government and was met with considerable backlash (we discuss Wynne's personal positioning below and in Chapter 5). While the new curriculum updated a wide range of health and physical fitness issues, major objections were raised to sex education provisions. Opponents objected to the inclusion of what they labelled radical and inappropriate gender and sexual material that included discussion of LGBT relationships and families, same-sex marriage, gender identity and expression, and sexual orientation and sexual practices. As with the UK example, the racial and/or ethnic identities of those opposed to the HPE became important within a Canadian context that both legally and culturally supports particular forms of multiculturalism and diversity.

Parental Rights

Parental rights are central in heteroactivist framings of opposition to LGBT visibility and inclusion both in school curricula and in the material spaces of the school itself. In the cases we examine, heteroactivists are generally opposed to the introduction of LGBT equalities in schools, including sex and relationship education, arguing that parents have specific rights and responsibilities over their child's

education which should supersede or override public man-
dates. This, as we will see, challenges state and national
authority over public education, with parents claiming
they are the 'first educators' of their children. As such, parents are presented as having a right to be consulted about
what is taught and these consultations might result in the
removal of what they determine to be 'offending material'
or enable parents to remove their child from the class.

While in Canada and the UK, claims about 'parental'
rights might have little *legal* traction, it is an important unifying strategy for heteroactivists. Claims to parental rights
are used to leverage a unifying political and social discourse
across schools, school boards and state jurisdictions. In
these arguments, the right of the child is subservient to
the right of the parent, mirroring arguments about 'selfish'
LGBT people seeking to reproduce to satisfy their own
desires. This once again centres on the 'best for children'
argument (see Chapters 1 and 5). The presumption is that
parents (heterosexual, married parents in particular) know
what's best for their children and have the right to teach
their children their own moral values. This right is seen as
under threat from the state, for example in the UK:

The might of the political and educational establishment has closed ranks against these parents ...
I'm beginning to see a pattern here. Parents who
dare to challenge the new orthodoxy in relation
to relationships, marriage and family are intolerant,

narrow-minded and cannot be trusted to educate their own children in these matters. So-called big-oted parents are now the killer argument to justify teaching children in England about any aspect of sex, in lessons from which, after September 2020, their parents cannot withdraw them. And worse, the state truly believes that they own our children. (Tully, n.d.: paras 2–4)

Here, Tully draws on fears of the loss of parental control and how the potential labelling of some parents as 'big-oted' is used to close down discussion. Fears of being regarded as bigoted are seen to work to silence parents from speaking their concerns and heteroactivists defend against accusations that they are bigoted, homophobic or transphobic (see Chapters 1 and 4). They claim this 'killer argument' undermines parental rights and enables schools to teach about 'any aspect of sex' without consideration of parental rights or age appropriateness.

Claims about parental rights include a demand to be consulted regarding lesson content and teachings related to sexuality and gender. In the UK Rowe case, Sally Rowe argued that 'other parents' should have been consulted about another child's gender presentation. She noted 'One day a boy, next day, girl, no consultation' (Eli, 2017: para. 4). Similarly, the 'lack of consultation' was cited in the Parkfield protests in Birmingham in the UK where beliefs were portrayed as being 'imposed' on children and parents.

Although parents were invited to community meetings, they were not given the right to exclude their children from lessons or to have references to same-sex relationships or gender identities removed from the teachings that their children received. In Canada, Premier Wynne and the liberal government were accused by parents opposed to the HPE of introducing sex education without sufficient parental consultation. The subsequent Conservative government under premier Doug Ford, whose election campaign promised to repeal the curriculum, was also accused by heteroactivists of 'broken promises', because of his perceived failure to take parental opposition into account when his government was making, what could be seen as 'minor', revisions to the HPE (Freiburger, 2019; Granic Allen, 2019).

Central to the parental rights argument is a sense of ownership, that is, that parents, not the state, 'own our children'. It has long been contended that the nation by default, is heterosexual (see Bell and Binnie, 2000; Duggan, 1994; Richardson, 1998; Warner, 1993). However, for heteroactivists, contemporary state support of LGBT equalities through legislative and judicial enactment means both the state and associated schooling has been 'politicised'. In the Rowe case, the school presented acceptance of gender non-conforming children as an unassailable given and that 'equality law meant that they had to accept the child's wishes' (Christian Concern, Nov. 2, 2017). This implies that had the equality law not forced the school's hand, the wishes of the gender-non-conforming child would not (and should not?) have been taken into account (in Chapter 3 we discuss this in relation to those who are supportive of their children's gender transition and those who are not). Opponents read this as the imposition of a 'political agenda' in what parents and the school claim is 'neutral' school space, again, ignoring how schools have historically acted to create national citizens joined by a common set of norms and values (Nash and Browne, 2019; see also Evans, 2016; Johnson and Johnson, 2016; Joshee et al., 2016).

Indeed, these claims extended to understanding schools and the state as 'totalitarian regimes' that 'indoctrinate children' against their parents' will:

> The first thing that a totalitarian regime tries to do is to get to the children, to distance them from the subversive, varied influences of their families, and indoctrinate them in their rulers' view of the world. Within limits, families must be left to bring up their children in their own way.

> As we approach September 2020 when Relationships Education becomes a compulsory subject in all schools in England, parents are becoming more and more concerned about how they will protect their children. The Big Brother nightmare will then become a reality for all parents who will not be allowed to withdraw their children from these lessons, no matter what is being taught.

The Government is determined to trample over the rights of parents to bring up their children in line with their own values. And it's not just parents with a religious faith who will [be] undermined. You don't have to have a religious faith to want to protect your child against inappropriate teaching on intimate matters about sexuality and relationships. (Society for the Protection of Unborn Children, 2019: paras 6–8)

In Canada, similar heteroactivist claims about the broader 'LGBT agenda' infiltrating public education surfaced, particularly within those heteroactivist organisations with a long history of opposing LGBT equalities. Inclusion of same-sex relationships, marriage and discussions of gender in school education is, for these groups, another example of forcing the acceptance of LGBT 'lifestyles' on children. For example, Campaign Life Coalition (CLC), a long-time opponent of LGBT equalities, argued that the 'gay-lobby' had been making 'slow, subtle inroads into educational curriculum and text books under the guise of euphemisms like "equity" and "diversity"' (Campaign Life Coalition, n.d.b: para. 4; see also Rayside, 2014). Here the 'LGBT agenda' is portrayed as all powerful and pervasive, rather than a set of equalities that are legislatively enshrined and require enactment. As 'an agenda', these equalities become something that parents must 'protect their children' from.

Parent groups in Canada, the UK and Ireland reason they need to fight back, in the courts and through protest, against what the Canadian group, Parental Rights in Education Defense Fund, calls a 'belligerent government ideology' bent on 'indoctrinating children in the classroom with philosophies that undermine the religious beliefs of their parents' (Interim, 2011: para. 10).

Many organisations sought to present their objections as encompassing more than religious precepts. Tully, speaking for the Society for the Protection of Unborn Children, for example, in the quote above, sought to frame their arguments as more broadly applicable than just 'religious' and as a call to all who see relationship and sex education as 'inappropriate' and to those seeking to 'bring up their children in their own way'. The compulsory nature of sex education is the focus and the inability of parents to withdraw their children is a key contention in the claim of 'totalitarian', 'belligerent' governments.

Opponents of the required HPE curriculum in Ontario protested what they regarded as state indoctrination of the children. Such indoctrination was against their parental 'values' and constituted what they termed 'sexual abuse':

> To manipulate a child's mind and coerce them into believing that it is permissible and acceptable to do something which is against their parent's beliefs is reprehensible. [The school board's equity policy

represents] sexual abuse in the first degree. (Klaas Detmar, public trustee, Hamilton-Wentworth School Board in Craine, 2010: para. 2 and title)

Across the UK and Canada then, heteroactivists argued that the government is forcing young children to accept concepts that their parents consider offensive and morally questionable. This both forces the child to learn something that heteroactivists understand as morally 'wrong' and also supposedly interrupts the parents' right to teach. *LifeSite News* for example, claims that the Ontario HPE curriculum creates conflicts between home life and school lessons and is designed to separate children from their families. Ontario school curricula represents for heteroactivists an 'ideological colonisation' seeking to 'liberate' children from the perceived 'repressive moral and religious beliefs of their parents' (Laurence, 2016, June 30). The state is presented as a 'foreign occupier' breaking through what should be the protective boundary around private family life (Nash and Browne, 2019).

In contrast to the state as the educator, then, parental rights arguments position parents as the 'first educators' of their children. It is parents' responsibility to engage with 'sensitive topics' (such as sexuality), and schools should focus on 'English, maths and science'. Teaching students about same-sex relationships or 'homosexuality' was 'unnecessary' (Preece, 2019) and being 'drummed' into children (Stonestreet, 2019). In Canada, Premier Wynne's Conservative political opponent (at the time), Patrick Brown, argued that 'teachers should teach facts about sex education, not values ... Parents teach values' (Campaign Life Coalition, 2015a). In this way, parents can ensure a child's education, specifically around relationships and sex, aligns with parents' positions (Jones, 2016).

The border between the classroom and the domestic and private spaces of the home is portrayed as perilously permeable. What is discussed or taught in the classroom might lead to the promotion of the homosexual agenda in domestic life (and places of worship) (LifeSite News, 2010, Canada). Heteroactivists regard the sanctity of the home as foundational to the natural family and the rights of parents to instil in their children their own beliefs and values. This is challenged by school spaces and nation states that do not allow for the removal of children from particular classes. Challenges to the legal right of parents to remove children from lessons has largely failed in Canada, although such a determination will continue to be made on a case-by-case basis.[2] In the UK, relationships and sex education (RSE) will become compulsory in September 2020, with no right of removal for parents. At the time of writing, Ireland continues to consult on relationship and sex education curricula, but it is expected to be compulsory. The absence of the legal right to remove children from certain lessons is central to heteroactivist oppositions and the compulsory nature of these curricula has given rise to heteroactivist claims about LGBT and state authoritarianism that leads to the 'indoctrination' of children, who need to be protected.

Protecting Our Children

The figure of the child, which we introduced in the last chapter, is also key to heteroactivist educational discourses. Important here is the construction of children as innocent absorbers of knowledge. Children, in this view, require singular and unified information and moral guidance, particularly in relation to religion and sex, lest they become 'confused', indoctrinated or reject parental values that oppose gender non-conformity and hold same-sex relationships to be inferior. What is at stake for heteroactivists in both Canada and the UK is the ability of parents to protect their children from the idea that same-sex marriages are 'normal'. Parents and children who hold 'traditional values' will be marginalised, and children might perceive their parents as 'bigots' or 'homophobes' leading to conflict within the home and in the relationship between parents and children. The idea of private space to deal with private issues was a feature of the Rowe case in the UK, where the Rowes called for the 'young transgender boy' to be helped in a 'private space', rather than in the sphere of a primary school environment (Nash and Browne, 2019). The primary school and its classrooms are portrayed as neutral places, ignoring that heteronormativity is, until recently, the default normative value operating in that place.

By implication, the state, as the protector of the heteronormative order, is supposed to protect this space and to make it 'safe' for those who seek to protect 'vulnerable' children from harmful sexual and gender 'ideologies' and gender confusion (see Chapter 3). Schools in this rhetoric become 'battlefields' (Farley, 2017) when they challenge or redefine heteronormative values. The potential for danger and harm relates to the assertion that children are too young to understand certain materials, that LGBT-related teaching is not age-appropriate, that all children are heteronormative and that not all children mature at the same rate. Parents, therefore, are the best arbiters of what is best for their children to learn. Age-inappropriate materials covering gender and same-sex relationships are presented as confusing and upsetting, and children 'need to be allowed to be children rather than having to constantly think about equalities and rights' (Klett, 2019: para. 24).

At the Lumen Fidei conference in Dublin in 2018, numerous speakers argued that sexual and gendered equalities pose a grave threat and that these equalities need to be opposed in order to 'protect' *their* children. Protecting their children, and not all children, relates to how heteroactivists feel that they have lost control of Irish national morals, as well as the perceived loss of Catholic schools to secular agendas. Primary schools, in particular, were seen as the places experiencing the biggest threat because young children are seen not only as vulnerable but as impressionable to the detriment of their moral development:

The worst snares are laid for children. Books in primary school – 'Tale of two dads' [said in a mocking tone with a faux US accent], Heather has two mums, Mama, mummy and me. The Heather book defies biological facts – she does have a daddy. [Audience titters]. He derisively reads the blurbs of various books: 'This is used in primary schools to poison the image of marriage in children. It upsets children and confuses them. He said that a 5-year-old asked their parents if it is ok to have two mummies'. It turns out that the '5-year-old was afraid because Daddy would have to leave, if it was ok to have two mummies'. (John Lacken, Browne fieldnotes, Lumen Fidei conference, quotes are approximations)

In this quote, John Lacken sought to denormalise that which is made normal through children's books that encourage inclusion and acceptance not only of LGBT people, but also of difference more broadly. This is read as a 'poison', a threat not only to children's safety, but to their moral fibre through the destruction of the traditional and sanctified 'image of marriage'. The supposed confusion and upset in children who no longer have the stability of their truth is presented as arising from a loss of parental control and the absence of a (heteronormative) moral state. The threat here is not predatory gay men, but the equivalence of same-sex marriage that leads a 5-year-old to believe that it is compulsory for all.

Protecting Children from LGBT Activists

Heteroactivists battling against the inclusion of sex and relationship education also claim that these inclusions reflect the 'personal agendas' of those seeking to implement them. As Rosky (2012) argues, there is a fear of indoctrination through the active recruiting of children into the queer lifestyle. Children might learn to identify with (and enter a queer lifestyle) through exposure to influential LGBT people including teachers and prominent cultural figures. This argument often emerges as a personal attack on high-profile LGBT individuals who are accused of promoting their 'lifestyle'. In Canada, it was intimated that the sexual and gendered aspects of the HPE were driven by Ontario Premier Kathleen Wynne's sexuality and her supposed personal desire to corrupt children as part of the wider LGBT 'agenda'. Opponents argued, for example, that the HPE curriculum contained a 'not-so-hidden agenda coloured by homosexuality' (Baklinski, Mar. 12, 2015: para. 2).

In the UK, the Assistant Head Teacher Andrew Moffat's sexuality was continually made an issue. Parents claimed that teaching about equality and same-sex relationships in the school was actually the desire of this teacher to promote his 'personal preferences', and that he was actively '"brainwashing" their children by promoting homosexual and transgender lifestyles' (Christian Institute, Mar. 15, 2019: para. 15). Parents sought to draw a line between accepting that some people will have a different lifestyle and belief system to them, to being asked to affirm that this lifestyle/belief system is something which they should positively agree with and that it should be promoted as an option for their children. (5 Pillars, 2019: para. 6)

Such a position could appear to be a direct attack on the character and professionalism of individuals involved in the school system. Heteroactivists recognised that such attacks could be regarded as homophobic and sought to deflect such criticisms. Parents opposed to the HPE curriculum in Ontario claimed, for example, that they were 'not homophobic, not concerned Premier Kathleen Wynne is a lesbian [or that] she's not conservative' (Warmington, 2015: para. 2). In the UK, the fact that Andrew Moffat was appointed to his position was used to counter the accusation of homophobia. Miriam Ahmed, a parent opposed to the school's sexual and gender equalities teaching said, 'If we had a thing against being gay then we would have campaigned when Mr Moffatt was appointed four years ago' (Matthews, 2019: para. 11). The problem, they claimed, was that 'his [Moffat's] only focus is on gender reassignment and homosexuality, that's all the guy is focusing on' (para. 12). The spectre of the over-sexualised gay male was subtly evoked, while resisting accusations of homophobia (see also Chapter 1):

They are trying to radicalise and reengineer our beliefs and they're saying if you don't support us, then you must be a homophobe and you must be a radical. It's just not true.

…

He is bringing gay celebrities into assembly, and showing pupils pictures of his partner. There was a gay author brought in during World Book Day.

…

We have no issue with Mr. Moffat as a person at all. He's homosexual, that's fine. We don't have an issue with that. But his sex life needs to be left in his bedroom. (Matthews, 2019: paras 10, 13, 16)

The separation of LGBT people and the public is crucial to the argument regarding the inclusion of LGBT people in schools. Gay men must keep their 'sex life in the bedroom' thereby reducing understandings of their identities, lives and relationships to gay male sex. Bringing in 'gay celebrities', showing pictures of a partner and discussing gay authors is not to be located in the public sphere of the school, but in the privacy of the bedroom. The bifurcated spatialisation of the public/private enacted through these representations of school spaces is central to understanding how school spaces are contested. Public displays of sexual identities and relationships can only be implicitly and explicitly heterosexual. Other sexualities and relationships should be privatised, 'left in his bedroom'.

White Nations: Co-opting and Coping with 'Others'

Any discussion of religion and the racialisation of heteroactivism must be located within considerations of whiteness. A full discussion of this is beyond the scope of this book, although we introduce some key ideas in order to support their development beyond these pages. Here we consider how whiteness and Christianity are read as part of 'British/ Irish/Canadian values', such that heteroactivist groups are seen as benign and are ignored or rendered invisible (Boulila, 2016, 2019). In both the UK and Canada, some heteroactivists made much of the seemingly multi-denominational resistances to LGBT equalities, although we have identified important distinctions about how this unfolded across places, as well as between heteroactivist groups within the UK.

Co-opting 'the Other': Multicultural Canada

In Canada, organisers such as Campaign Life Coalition and the Parents Alliance of Ontario called their resistance a 'rebellion', 'led by families from ethnic communities that include Chinese, Muslim, South Asian, eastern European as well as some African and Latin American immigrants'. Included were 'a variety of Christian denominations, protestant clergy, Catholic laity and the non-religious' (LifeSite News Apr. 21, 2015). Such representations sought to downplay the role of more 'traditional' (white) Christian groups in opposing LGBT equalities in favour of claiming a more diverse constituency. This also marks the rather complicated tensions between LGBT equalities as 'Canadian' values and Canada's commitment to multicultural diversity and tolerance, as well as links to colonialism, abortion and forced sterilisations (Kwak, 2019; Ley, 2010; Westlake, 2018). In the case of sex education in Ontario, what was represented as uniting people across these disparate groups was the universal position of 'parent', which compelled these groups to take action because of the supposed threat that the HPE curriculum posed to their children (Campaign Life Coalition, 2015a). Of course, this notion of 'parent' did not include LGBT families and children.

Representing these groups as multi-ethnic or multicultural is critical in Canada given the legal and cultural landscape. Several Supreme Court of Canada (SCC) *Charter of Rights and Freedoms* (1982) cases made it very unlikely that court challenges based on 'Christian' or 'religious' values would support parents removing children from classroom instruction because of the contents of the HPE curriculum (although distinctive facts might change this outcome). Therefore, it was important for heteroactivists to emphasise that their objections were not based on religious grounds but on the fact that cross-culturally, all the objectors were parents with similar concerns.

Gathering around the shared experience of parent, the argument became about being stripped of their rights to parent. This repositioned the dialogue from one about increased rights for LGBT people, to the seemingly rapidly decreasing rights of those who opposed LGBT equalities. This is highlighted by the fact that despite the historic centrality of Christianity in Canadian national life, a series of SCC decisions stripped away what it termed 'Christian historical privilege in public schools', naming this privilege an underlying source of injustice given Canada's multicultural heritage (Seljak, 2016: 546). In a pivotal case, SCC Chief Justice McLachlan noted that many parents with strong religious beliefs might disapprove of different family types and that children might experience some form of 'cognitive dissonance' if exposed to such family models. Nevertheless, she asserted that such cognitive dissonance is 'neither avoidable or noxious' and that 'experiencing alternative views is part of growing up in a diverse society'. McLachlan contended that children can be expected to encounter difference in a diverse state school system and must learn that their values are not necessarily shared by others in a country such as Canada.[3]

This legal (and political) landscape offers a partial explanation for why grassroots organisations emphasised their multi-ethnic and multi-religious membership, organised around the universal role of 'parent'. So, while organisations claimed religious and ethnic diversity, they also positioned themselves as supporting more universal,

'traditionally principled' families across religious and ethnic lines. Such a diverse opposition supposedly 'exemplifies
the emergence of new Canadians [a term for new immigrants to Canada] as a socially conservative, non-partisan
political force especially on family values' (Weatherbe,
Mar. 19, 2015: para. 1). The provincial Conservative Party
in Ontario, in particular, remains opposed to the HPE policy as a strategy designed to make inroads into immigrant
communities – communities who Conservatives claim
are more likely to hold conservative beliefs and could
be mobilised to vote against the Wynne government in
the 2018 elections (Campaign Life Coalition, 2015b).[4]
Heteroactivist arguments, then, operate across and within
diverse racial, ethnic and political (e.g. left/right) boundaries in ways that cannot be predicted beforehand and that
have a distinctive geography.

Hateful Others: Muslims in Christian Britain

Similar to the presumption that Canada's immigrant communities are inherently 'traditionally minded' and conservative
and thus opposed to LGBT equalities, the Parkfield protests
were also framed as led by immigrants and in particular by
'Muslim Mums' (and at times Muslim parents). The idea
that immigrant communities containing 'hateful others'
opposing LGBT equalities feeds into nationalistic discourses
about who 'belongs' in Christian Britain. As Haritaworn
argues, Muslim immigrants to Europe are often framed as
'figures of racialised homophobia and transphobia' (2015: 3)

and names these perspectives as 'Muslim Homophobia', which needs to be understood within particular racist and colonial histories.

Parkfield's parents, in contrast to the unity around parenthood we see in the Ontario example above, were *Muslim* parents. They were marked by their religion and an associated form of racialisation. This was apparent throughout the coverage of the protests. The parents involved in the Parkfield protests, as well as the media, described the protests as reflecting a direct conflict between Islam and 'homosexuality'. Thus, their heteroactivist arguments were racialised through a religion that is often perceived as other to not only the nation-state, but also to LGBT equalities (see Haritaworn, 2015; Puar, 2007). Thus, to resist LGBT equalities they had to work to create a link to Britishness, or at least reject their presumed otherness to 'inclusive' national values. One parent, Fatima Shah, was quoted as saying:

> It's inappropriate, totally wrong. Children are being told it's OK to be gay yet 98 per cent of children at this school are Muslim. It's a Muslim community.
>
> …
>
> We believe in fundamental British values and believe gay people should be treated with mutual respect and without prejudice or discrimination just like any other human being. We respect the

Equality Act and believe it can be implemented without the promotion of homosexuality. (Shah, in Preece, 2019: paras 7–8, 16–17)

It is notable that Shah links their protests to British values,[5] because the Parkfield protests were not assumed to be defending British values. This is in stark distinction to other (predominantly white) heteroactivists who are clear in their invocations of protecting the nation through opposing LGBT equalities. Heteroactivist Muslim parents had to overtly articulate their alignment with British values, to challenge the erasure of their protests as simply 'not British'. Therefore, in seeking to align her Muslim values with perceived 'fundamental British values', Shah recognises the potential disconnect her position as a Muslim parent has from supposedly inclusive British society. This difference requires both a 'mutual respect', but also a distancing. In this discourse, Muslims are not gay, and should not be told that it is 'ok to be'. However, British values (and laws) are to be 'respected', by respecting 'gay people', but without the 'promotion of homosexuality' which is directly related to teaching acceptance of LGBT people and relationships. 'Accepting British values' points to the whiteness, and assumed Christianity, of Britain, where Muslim others cannot define the nation or protect its values through their religion. Instead they need to work to align their objections to 'fundamental British values'. Parkfield protestors as Muslim and Brown bodies are 'elsewhere' and 'not British'. The problem then becomes 'the' Muslim religion (and race categorisations which underpin this but are not overt in these texts).

The Parkfield Muslim parents who opposed LGBT equalities being taught in schools are navigating the figure of the Muslim Homophobe by trying to align with the discourses of a 'tolerant Britain'. This Britishness was then invoked through the law which accepts gay teachers and also through agreement with, and the support of, Christians. In the media, parents and others noted that a small group of Christian supporters attended one protest at Parkfield (Preece, 2019). This could be read as an effort to paint the overall opposition to LGBT inclusion in schools as 'really British' and to deflect critiques of Muslim values as fundamentally opposed to being 'gay' and as 'not British'. Linking Muslims with intolerance of 'British values' contrasts with the ways in which other (white) British heteroactivists, who draw on the same values regarding same-sex marriage, are not seen as opposing 'British values'. In particular, white Christian opposition can be read as benign, the 'other side of the debate', and defenders of the nation and society, whereas Muslim resistances to LGBT equalities are rarely read in the same way (Bhattacharyya, 2013; Boulila, 2016, 2019; Puar, 2006, 2007).

The danger of Muslims was a central theme, even where commentators supported their opposition to LGBT equalities. In the one Christian Concern email that spoke of the Parkfield protests, a point we address below, they quoted, and provided a link to, an article by the 'Rebel Priest', Jules Gomes (Mar. 12, 2019), saying:

> Muslims, promoting pansexuality to their children is like 'forcing their forefathers to chew pig fat', as happened with disastrous consequences in the 19th century. (Christian Concern, email Mar. 15, 2019)

The disgust that is evoked through the 'chewing of pig fat' is targeted both at LGBT people 'promoting pansexuality' and Muslims who object to pig fat. In his longer article, Gomes went on to argue that this forced engagement with pig fat came about because of its use on ammunition by the British Army, including soldiers from British colonies, in the 19th century. This, he argues, led to the 1857 Indian uprising against Britain and the murder of Muslims and the desecration of mosques. Gomes traces these forms of British colonialist violence and contends that they led to historical jihad against Britain, linking this directly with the contemporary Taliban. He therefore contends that because of historical British actions to suppress Muslim uprisings, Muslims in Britain are 'radical'. These are not 'British Muslims', they are Muslims in Britain, in other words, in these readings, Muslims can only ever have proximity to Britishness, they can never be British.

By putting 'Muslims', 'Jihad', 'radical' and 'the Taliban' adjacent to each other in the text, Gomes creates a stickiness between danger and Muslim (Ahmed, 2013). Thus, he contends:

[T]he government should not appease Islam or any other religion. At the same time, Britain's rulers and gay activists should avoid unduly provoking Islam. (Gomes, Mar. 12, 2019: para. 20)

The separation of Britain from Muslims is matched by also separating Muslims from 'British rulers' and 'gay activists'. This is a warning for those who are now seen as 'in power' (rulers and activists) to avoid 'provoking' Muslims – indicating the inherent danger and violent assumptions of 'Islam'. Gay activists, in Gomes's reading, have become linked to 'the state' and historical state oppressions through their placing alongside 'British rulers'. Both 'Britain's rulers' and 'gay activists' are under threat because of Muslims in Britain, who are linked to the Taliban.

These discourses of Muslim, gay activists and British rulers evoke specific spectres of Muslim (who cannot be gay) *and* gay others (who cannot be Muslim and also never referred to as British), both of whom are threats to Britain and reiterate the import and centrality of (white) British heterosexual cultures. Therefore, in condemning 'gay activists' and 'British Rulers', Gomes creates Muslim protestors as belonging elsewhere, and a dangerous force that might be unleashed. In doing so he portrays (in a generous reading) some Muslims as always potentially violent and always at war in Britain, and always a threat, potentially violent against 'the British'. He does this by *supporting* their cause against the No Outsider's programme, suggesting that it is about 'teaching gay sex', which is abhorrent to them, and equating this with the violent and bloody repressions of the colonial era. While, as we will see in Chapter 4, heteroactivist groups work hard to distance themselves from the accusations of hate, here Muslim heteroactivists (although they sought to move away from accusations of hate) are often repositioned in proximity to it. The hateful others remain 'hateful' towards Britain, and 'other' to it.

However, in other readings of the Parkfield protests, it is 'liberal elites' that, it was argued, created the hateful 'Muslim other'. This is supported by the literature, and as Haritaworn (2015: 9) notes, liberal inclusions can construct a 'new regime of diversity racism' which positions 'Muslim' bodies as 'repositories for sexism, homophobia and anti-Semitism'. Further, 'gays, trans and queers are recruited as "symbolic border guards" (Yuval-Davis, 1997) and as a key part of constructing Muslims as "hateful Others"' (Haritaworn 2015: 10). Blogger and pastor David Robertson suggested that the 'left' cannot be tolerant of both diverse sexualities and also include Muslims into British society. His contention was that the inclusion of diverse sexualities and of Muslims are at odds with each other. For Robertson, this meant that that LGBT activists and 'tolerant modern British liberals' had to choose whether to support 'Muslims' or same-sex marriage. They could not be inclusive of both, or indeed be both:

It is taken as a given [in the media] that teaching primary school children about same-sex marriage is a good thing. It is also assumed that the Muslims are at best culturally ignorant or at worst a bunch of ignorant religious fundamentalists in conflict with tolerant modern British liberals.

…

I must admit that I too bought a little into 'the Muslims are narrow religious bigots' narrative and wondered why Christians were also not taking a stand on this issue (it turns out that many are but this is not being reported – largely because of the liberal bias of many of the mainstream established churches). But having read and listened to the Muslim spokespeople, I have to say that I have generally been very impressed. (TheWeeFlea, 2019: paras 3–4)

In his blog TheWeeFlea, Robertson's readings of Muslims as 'ignorant' and in conflict with 'liberals' presumes that all Muslims do not support same-sex marriage and cannot occupy the position of a 'tolerant modern British liberal'.

His presumption is that all Muslims oppose same-sex marriage and thus, when he heard 'the Muslim spokesperson' presumably speaking in ways that he would agree with (and was suitably 'impressed'), he revised his position, critiquing those who would vilify Muslims as 'ignorant religious fundamentalists'. Robertson's critique reflects Haritaworn's assertions of liberal inclusions, while also reiterating Muslims as other to the 'British', 'liberal' and 'modern'. Reading Muslims as dangerous heteroactivists and Christians as benign points to how racialisation and religion create specific forms of heteroactivism. These are often unnamed and presumed, particularly when they read themselves in terms such as defending the nation. Even where 'Muslim parents' are supported by Christian heteroactivists, they remain other to the nation, and not central to its defence.

Refusing Homogeneity: Differences within Heteroactivism

Christian heteroactivist groups in the UK took a number of distinctive stances towards the Parkfield protests, demonstrating ideological heterogeneities among heteroactivists. For example, the organisation Anglican Mainstream adopted a supportive position towards the Parkfield protestors, despite the protestors' opposition being based on Islamic religious understandings. This was very different from the response of Christian Concern, who sent just one part of one email (usually they would send several messages for Christian parents that they offer support to, as they did with the Rowe family). It was not a 'top story' for them but was buried in the email highlighting a *lack of engagement* with this issue. Parkfield received extensive mainstream media coverage, and yet Christian Concern did not put themselves forward to support those who sought to contest LGBT equalities by offering legal support, media support, calls for monetary support and so on (as they usually do).

It is important to note that Christian Concern understand themselves as defending the Christianity of the nation (United Kingdom) which they purport is under threat. They are seeking to be a 'a strong Christian voice in the public sphere'. They 'engage on a broad large range of issues, including abortion, adoption and fostering, bioethics, marriage, education, employment, end of life, equality, family, free speech, Islamism, religious freedom, the sex trade, social issues and issues relating to sexual orientation' (Christian Concern, n.d.). The use of the term 'Islamism' is important as Christian Concern actively campaigns against 'Islam in Britain' seeing it as detrimental to British society. The lack of attention given to the Parkfield protests by Christian Concern might infer that the focus on Islam and 'Muslim mothers' conflicted with their ethos, despite the opportunity the situation and the parents offered for promoting their anti-sexual and gender equalities causes. Thus, as Boulila (2019) argues, we cannot understand sexuality and gender outside of race (see Crenshaw et al., 1995; Ferguson, 2003, 2019; Haritaworn, 2015; Puar, 2007). Here this is shown through manifestations of heteroactivism, where religion, race and sexualities interlock to create divergent paths for Christian heteroactivist organisations that are vehemently opposed to 'Islamism'. This religious difference between those who would oppose same-sex relationships being taught at schools, also points to the schisms within heteroactivisms. This refusal to understand heteroactivism as uniform affords it a complexity and coherence that is often overlooked in discussions of those who oppose or resist LGBT equalities.

Conclusion

An analysis of heteroactivism enables an understanding of activists who resist LGBT equalities in schools as grounded in particular racial, gendered, sexual, religious, classed and nationalistic moments as well as broad transnational and historical contexts, including colonial relations. Schools have become a key site of contestation for heteroactivists who argue against the inclusion of same-sex marriage, discussions of gender identities and the positive representation of LGBT lives in schools, particularly primary schools. Once again heteroactivists seek to go beyond the vilification of homosexuals as morally repugnant and to frame their resistances to issues such as state-mandated relationship and sex education as concerns about parental rights and consultation. They argue that the seeming politicisation of education (that is assumed to be neutral when focusing on heterosexuality) created potential harm and confusion for children while they make accusations about the personal 'agendas' of teachers and politicians that seek to 'brain-wash' children. Heteroactivists argue that the privatised space of the home is being invaded by the state through children's education and is reconstituting the private/public divide around issues of sexuality, gender and childhood (Nash and Browne, 2019). Throughout this chapter, it is clear that the spaces of the public education system are understood as (re)created in and through national values and legislations and require defending. These intertwined scales of home, classroom, school and nation are variously evoked to resist teaching same-sex marriage as morally equivalent or to even mention that there are families with 'two mummies and two daddies'.

The place of the state and the nation has also been brought into view through these debates around questions of 'Britishness' and 'Canadianness', immigration and colonialism. In these tentative steps towards exploring the racialisation of heteroactivism, we showed that the focus on 'hateful others' (Haritaworn, 2015) meant that in Britain attention was paid to Muslims, and their religion, *as those* who might be regarded as transgressing British values. By contrast, in the attention and coverage given to Christian organisations, these groups were presented as merely giving 'the other side' to debates but as operating within understood Britishness and whiteness. Thus, heteroactivists can at times use 'diversity' as a means of emphasising that their arguments are progressive and inclusive (rather than bigoted and homophobic), as we saw in the case of the 'parents' in Canada. In the context of Parkfield, the shared cause of objecting to same-sex relationships in schools was not enough for racialised and Islamic communities to be included by some well-established heteroactivist groups. Consequently, heteroactivism is racialised in different ways, through white Britishness that sees threat in the Muslim who is in Britain, but not of Britain, but also through Muslim parents who have to align with 'British values' in order to have their resistances to LGBT equalities heard. Heteroactivism then is inextricable from the politics of race and in this chapter, we have pointed to both the continuing demonisation of Islam and the use of 'diversity' as a productive and beneficial presentation of inclusion. However, as we note in the conclusion, this is only a start in discussions of the racialised ways in which heteroactivism is manifest, there is far more to be done.

Even between UK organisations that are ostensibly aligned ideologically and racially, we see multiple and conflicting reactions to the visibility of LGBT equalities in schools in relation to ethnicity and religion. In Canada, immigrants were specifically presumed to be conservative and 'traditionally minded' and thus 'naturally' opposed to LGBT equalities. They were targeted for activism around school curricula and for votes in the 2018 Ontario provincial election. Moreover, the Canadian legislative and cultural focus on multiculturalism means that the inclusion of 'ethnic communities' lends legitimacy to Canadian heteroactivisms. Yet, as we have indicated here, hetero-activism is not uniform and has internal divergences. It unfolds in distinctive geographical ways that cannot be predicted, but nor are they necessarily cohesive. Affording heteroactivism this complexity requires further investigations into how heteroactivisms are manifest because the composition of such groups politically (e.g. left/right) and their ideological bent based on religious or cultural constitution cannot be used to define them. We now move to examine how transgender identities and gender non-conformity are resisted and challenged by heteroactivists.

3

Trans: Resisting Gender Ideologies and Trans Equalities

Introduction

Transgressions of normative gender identity and expression have long been a concern of heteroactivists and surfaced in the same-sex marriage debates in Canada (early 2000s), Ireland (in 2015) and the UK (in 2014) (see Chapter 1, e.g. Browne and Nash, 2014; Nash and Browne, 2015; Kuhar and Zobec, 2017).[1] Initially, the argument in these debates broadly revolved around the centrality of 'sexual complementarity' in the heteronormative[2] definition of marriage. This was underpinned by the so-called 'natural connections' between gender identity, sex characteristics and gender expression in normative opposite-sex relations. The heteronormative family was portrayed as central to the raising of biological children and understood as forming the backbone of society. Heteroactivists argue that any reworking of this understanding would lead to the breakdown of the family and society (Browne and Nash, 2014; Nash and Browne, 2015). As we note here, while heteroactivists continue to assert various forms of biological essentialism as the foundation of heteronormative marriage (Chapter 1), contemporary contestations arise around trans equalities legislation and the wider social and cultural acceptance of variances from a normative man/woman binary in gender identity and expression.

At the time of writing, heteroactivist opposition was erupting in the UK and Canada around the passage of legislative protections, for trans people although specific cultural distinctions can be discerned.[3] This chapter explores how dominant oppositional arguments are being formulated in these varying contexts. We begin with a review of heteroactivist arguments focusing on readings of sex as unchanging and essentialised biological 'truth', rendering any deviation from sexed binaries 'lies' and 'against reality' (Westen, 2018). We then consider heteroactivist perceptions of the so-called dangers of trans ideology; in particular, we focus on the perceived threats of global trans activism, the dangers posed to trans people and trans children by such activism, and finally the push to defend and protect 'our' women and children. This chapter underpins discussions of trans and gender non-conforming rights for the remainder of the book.

The selected Canadian, UK and Irish trans flashpoints discussed here illustrate how heteroactivists frame their concerns about trans visibility and equality in public debates. In the UK, we draw from a series of examples sparked by debates about gender identity and trans inclusion that fed into an ongoing national debate from 2017 (see Barker, 2017). This includes contestations around trans healthcare and trans rights in schools, institutions and professional associations. We include some individual cases that received national attention from heteroactivist groups. In Canada, we focus on the debates surrounding the passage of Bill C-16, federal legislation that added non-discrimination provisions and protections based on gender identity and gender expression to the *Canadian Human Rights Act*, and also made related amendments to the *Criminal Code*. Trans issues have been less prevalent in Ireland, perhaps reflecting the lack of attention paid to the passing of gender self-identification in 2015, at the same time as the same-sex marriage referendum (2015; see Chapter 1) and the focus on the recent abortion (2018) referendum. However, it did emerge in the conferences that we attended, which we discuss here.

Trans as a Lie: Redefining Reality

Despite work from the late 20th century contesting the fixity of gendered bodies (see e.g. Butler, 1990), claims about essentialised, fixed, sexed bodies continue to ground heteroactivist arguments. In the UK, Canada and Ireland, heteroactivists objected to claims that sex or gender could be understood as anything other than biologically certain and constituted as a 'natural' binary. While heteroactivists acknowledged the existence of intersex people, they largely represent intersex people as a 'legitimate' biological anomaly while, as we discuss here, contesting various aspects of medical interventions and assessments of trans people (see e.g. Zelikovsky, 2019). Binary, gendered normativities that recreate heterosexuality are central to heteroactivist conceptualisations of sexualities and genders (Browne and Nash, 2014; Nash and Browne, 2015). This rigid understanding renders the possibility of other gendered identities unthinkable and to suggest anything to the contrary is an 'attack' on the normative gender binary. John-Henry Westen, a Canadian editor of *LifeSite News*, was an invited speaker at the Lumen Fidei conference in Dublin in 2018: He argued:

'Being transgender is ludicrous ... Human sexuality is binary, women are XX, men are XY. There are genetic markers for female/male. It is binary and this is a rule, and self-evident'. Westen argued that identity is not in our bodies, it is in our thoughts, but a fixed false belief means you are mentally ill. 'If I insist that I am Margaret Thatcher or a cat, I will be told that I am mentally ill and delusional. Trans is civil rights for mental illness. Did you get that?'

Audience: 'Yes'. (John-Henry Westen, Browne fieldnotes, Lumen Fidei conference, quotes are approximations)

The 'ludicrousness' of transgenderism for heteroactivists is based on supposedly self-evident rules grounded in biological essentialism. Lumen Fidei, as a Catholic organisation, positions their arguments within the unalterable truths of the Bible. The affirming response of the Lumen Fidei conference audience to the comment above approves of both Westen's articulation of 'science', 'truth' and 'fact', and the differentiation of 'them' from 'us'. The state, through its normalisation of gender fluidity, causes suffering for both trans-identified individuals and for those (such as the members of Lumen Fidei) who are being forced to respect trans people's civil rights (see also Christian Concern, Nov. 29, 2018).

In Canada, the introduction of Bill C-16 galvanised heteroactivists who vehemently oppose anti-discrimination legislation aimed at protecting trans people. While some groups referenced religious beliefs about gender and sexuality as the foundation for their objections, almost all groups also asserted various scientific grounds for their opposition. The Association for Reformed Political Action (ARPA), for example, while acknowledging that bullying and harassment are wrong, argue that 'as Christians':

We simply cannot affirm that everyone 'has the right to define their own gender identity' and to

have others affirm them in that. We do not consider 'behaviour that reinforces traditional gender
norms' (leaving out bullying and other cruel treatment) to be ignorant or confused ... We cannot set
aside the truth that people are male or female. It
would be unloving to do so. (ARPA, Nov. 9, 2016)

For ARPA (and other groups such as REAL Women of
Canada), while their religious arguments were important,
they framed their main arguments for a secular audience
within particular strands of scientific and psychiatric literature
(e.g. Landolt, Nov. 2, 2016). As we discuss in Chapter 4,
many of these groups echoed Jordan Peterson who, in his
testimony before a parliamentary subcommittee against Bill
C-16, argued that, for example, provincial human rights policies protecting trans people's existence were simply wrong:

[The Ontario Human Rights Commission argues
that] sexual identity, biological sex, gender identity, gender expression, sexual proclivity all vary
independently, and that's simply not the case. It's
not the case scientifically. It's not the case factu-
ally. (Standing Senate Committee on Legal and
Constitutional Affairs, 2017: para. 12)

For heteroactivists, Bill C-16 risked enshrining the unsci-
entific 'social science theory of social constructionism as the
legally sanctioned scientific doctrine of the land', thereby

supposedly allowing ideology to prevail over science (Plett, Mar. 2, 2017: section 1500). Further, as REAL Women claimed, Bill C-16 'is based purely on politically correct ideology, not facts or evidence and is being rammed through Parliament in a highly undemocratic manner' (Landolt, Nov. 2, 2016: para. 10; see also ARPA, Nov. 9, 2016).

For heteroactivists, the possible existence of gender-variant individuals is based on 'a lie' demonstrated by an apparent lack of scientific research and on suspect ideologies driven by political activism. Heteroactivists worked to shift the argument away from claims that could be perceived as a direct attack on trans individuals while at the same time making claims that undermined trans people's very existence by reasserting essentialised man/woman distinctions. They argued that these 'gender ideologies' existed in opposition to 'the truth' which excludes the possibility of gender transgressions and fluidities. Accordingly, these 'gender ideologies' are positioned as harmful for society, for 'our' children and (normative) women and girls as well as to so-called trans people themselves.

The Dangers of Trans Ideologies

Global Activism

Heteroactivists often denied the existence of transgender people while asserting claims that the experiences of trans people were the result of perverse ideologies. These ideologies, they argue, besides being detrimental to trans people themselves, are also dangerous to the health of nations, and Western culture as a whole. In the UK, heteroactivists went so far as to claim that trans activism represented a 'global movement' seeking to undermine normative heterosexual relations and gendered binaries to the detriment of society, the family and children. Some commentators suggested that the debates against trans equalities were part of a larger battle by ordinary people 'unhappy with … the socio-economic agenda' pushed by 'political and intellectual "elites" in Western society' (VandenBeukel, 2016). Resistance to trans equalities is then framed by some as part of a wider global resistance movement reflected, for example, in the Brexit vote, the election of Trump and the backlash against 'progressivism, feminism, environmentalism and globalism' (VandenBeukel, 2016).

UK heteroactivists, pointing to the supposed existence of a 'global transgender activist movement' (Transgender Trend, May 22, 2019: para. 6), also noted a nationally 'impending cultural collapse' (Christian Concern, Oct. 19, 2018: para. 10) because of the impact of trans ideologies on the nation-state. Heteroactivists argued that trans activism, which pushed human rights claims and social acceptance, reflected a homogenous and dangerous 'transgender agenda', one that would allow transgender activists 'to take over and redefine reality according to their own propaganda' (Moseley, Sept. 12, 2018: para. 3). The so-called 'transgender lobby' was framed as a poison to 'Western nations' injected not only through the passage of legislative amendments, but more importantly, through the cultural changes, driven by a 'biased' media promulgating a 'harmful' and 'experimental' agenda (Christian Institute, May 5, 2017). The use of the singular 'transgender lobby' is important here as trans groups, activists and trans people, as well as allies and supporters, are represented as powerful and united and thus a serious and credible threat. For UK heteroactivists, 'the' global movement is portrayed as 'one of the major defining issues of our time' and one that cannot be 'conveniently ignored or avoided simply because only a small number of individuals claim to be transgender' (Moseley, Nov. 16, 2017: para. 2).

Trans political activism is seen as suspect not only because of its ideological claims and its enforcement through political correctness but also because it reflects the desires of only a minuscule portion of the population. Canadian Professor Gad Saad argued that Bill C-16 reflected the 'tyranny of the minority', forcing '99 percent of the population' to appease a few individuals who were 'declaring victimhood through identity politics and intersectionality for sympathy' (Luetke, 2017: para. 4).[4] This perception of being 'forced' to accept these circumstances as normal through state intervention is a pivotal point across both Canada and the UK. As Carys Mosely from Christian Concern argues:

> We are being forced by the law, governments and transgender ideology rolled out across the public sector to accept the notion of 'gender identity',

to accept that it is normal for a person's gender identity to differ from their sex, and to prioritise a person's self-identified gender identity above their sex at all levels of legislation and public policy. Those who disagree are increasingly being attacked as 'transphobic' and 'bigoted' and accused of hate speech in the press and on social media. This hostile and punitive attitude is a problem across the western world. People have been harassed, abused, lost their jobs, prohibited from public debate, been kicked out of coffee shops for debating trans issues, and one has even been the victim of attempted murder for challenging or seeming to challenge transgender ideology. Enough is enough. (Moseley, Nov. 16, 2017: para. 18)

State support for trans equalities is portrayed as fomenting 'hostile and punitive attitudes' towards an 'us' who are merely defending 'reality', and as something occurring 'across the Western world'. In Canada, Jordan Peterson argued that trans activism 'is a vanguard issue in a kind of ideological war ... an ideological variant that is rooted in what has become known as post-modernism, with a Neo-Marxist base' (Standing Senate Committee on Legal and Constitutional Affairs, 2017: paras 82–83; see also, Campaign Life Coalition, May 3, 2017). For the UK's Christian Concern (May 28, 2019), focusing on a smaller scale than the 'civilised Western World', trans inclusion in schools is equated with forcible education, similar to Communist authoritarianism. Celebrating trans identities as a 'natural variant' is presented as 'ridiculous to most people', therefore teaching acceptance in primary schools is a form of 'indoctrination' that violates the 'truth'. Similarly, sowing gender confusion through such policies as the Ontario Health and Physical Education curriculum (HPE, discussed in Chapter 2) also reflects strategic state 'indoctrination' to ensure the next generation believes that 'transgenderism/transsexualism is an innate, genetic characteristic just like skin colour or race' (Campaign Life Coalition, n.d.a). By linking trans activisms to authoritarian states that are portrayed as anathema to 'Western civilisation', heteroactivists challenging trans inclusions present themselves as both upholding and fighting for Western civilisation itself.

The supposed 'state imposition' of the 'transgender agenda' through equalities policies and legislation is strongly opposed by heteroactivists. They paint themselves as 'normal' and 'ordinary', but as oppressed both by the state and by others, including by trans support in the media, as well as by broader cultural changes. Thus, Christian Concern argues, heteroactivists experience violence, abuse and incoherence in their everyday spaces, including work and public spaces because these spaces increasingly reflect values and norms different from their own (see Chapter 5). In the UK, heteroactivist claims about the power of the 'global transgender movement' go well beyond the impacts on individuals, and this is portrayed as 'dangerous' to broader society and Western civilisation.

Dangerous to Trans People and Trans Children

In the UK and Canada, heteroactivists seek to oppose trans inclusions, while attempting to present a caring attitude towards trans children (Christian Concern, Nov. 29, 2018). The approach of some groups was to profess concern about the mental health of trans people dealing with gender 'confusion', arguing that the role of the state should be to assist individuals in embracing 'the bodies they were born with' (Christian Concern, Nov. 29, 2018). Such a stance allowed these heteroactivists to oppose the 'delusion that they are trapped in the wrong body' but to argue that the delusion 'deserves compassion' (Christian Concern, Nov. 29, 2018). In taking this approach, heteroactivists seek to deflect accusations of bullying and discrimination of trans adults and children.

In focusing on trans children, heteroactivists argue that such children are being harmed through supportive institutions (such as schools) and through social and cultural transformations that do not challenge their 'delusions' but, in fact, encourage them. Prevalent arguments in Canada and the UK focus on the so-called harm being done to trans children and 'our' (cis-gender) children, in the name of what they understand as a misplaced compassion and understanding for trans children. For heteroactivists, then the 'trans lobby' has been successful in ways that are

damaging not only to society but to trans people themselves. The Christian Institute argues, for example, that

> instead of providing transgender people with the
> support they need to help them embrace the bod-
> ies they were born with, society is compounding
> their confusion, with damaging consequences.
> (Christian Institute, n.d.: para. 5)

Heteroactivists argue that gender fluidity is a form of mental illness and that trans ideologies provoke confusion in
children. If this is the case, supporting trans children could
be understood as a form of child abuse (Moseley, 2017,
Nov. 16 and Dec. 15). While opposition to Bill C-16 did
not expressly make claims about how trans ideologies were
a danger to children, this is in contrast to the battles over
Ontario's sex ed curriculum as discussed in Chapter 2 where
opponents argued that radical gender ideology would cause
confusion and anxiety, violating children's innocence. Such
a course was a reckless, 'morally offensive and dangerous
sexual agenda' (Weatherbe, Mar. 19, 2015).

In his speaking engagement in Ireland, John-Henry
Westen (cited above) argues that challenging 'self-evident
reality' constitutes a 'false belief' that makes you 'mentally
ill'. That trans identities are based on a lie is a critical point,
because teaching this lie to children then is constituted as
unthinkable and confusing. In Christian Concern's words,
'suggesting to six-year-old children that they can change

gender is unkind and irresponsible' (Christian Concern, Nov. 2, 2017). Christian Concern (Nov. 29, 2018) suggests that all children in the UK are being asked in school, 'do you want to change gender'? This, in their view, leads to 'confusion' and an increase in children referred to Gender Identity Clinics.

In Canada, opponents of Ontario's HPE argued confusion and anxiety would result through the introduction of a 'radical gender ideology'. Heteroactivists also drew on research claiming that so-called gender confusion is something children would 'outgrow' or was 'transitory'. ARPA (Dec. 16, 2016) argued that efforts to reinforce 'gender identity disorder is confusing to a child and greatly increases the likelihood of a life of emotional and psychological suffering'. Thus, those who seek help to resist their children's feelings should be supported, in contrast to those who 'celebrate' their children's mental illness.

As gender binary structures are seemingly questioned more widely, through broader social and cultural changes in Canada and the UK, the existence, and 'celebration', of trans people is perceived by heteroactivists as increasingly dangerous. Heteroactivists positioned the figure of the trans child within the global trans agenda. As Transgender Trend (2019, reproduced by Anglican Mainstream) argues, the figure of the child is central in:

the context of the current worldwide cultural obsession with 'gender identity', driven by a global transgender activist movement. Labelling children 'transgender' politicises the child. Whereas a child with gender dysphoria may be helped and supported, the 'transgender child' becomes an emblem of a social justice movement and may be used to provide 'proof' of an ideology in order to further wider political goals.

…

This has nothing to do with helping children but everything to do with using them as a propaganda tool to further the radical agenda of those who wish to do away with the precious distinctions between men and women. (Christian Institute, July 30, 2019: para. 9)

Transgender Trend (May 22, 2019) contends that while children with 'gender dysphoria' might be 'helped and supported', trans children are political pawns for a global movement. This reiterates a distinction between 'science-based' gender issues that can be 'supported' such as 'gender dysphoria' and those based on gender ideologies propagated by trans activists. This suggests that the child, already innocent, vulnerable and cis-gendered, is 'labelled', and subject to 'propaganda' in ways that need to be addressed in order to restore gender norms. These norms are simultaneously evoked and reiterated through the marking of the 'child with gender dysphoria' as needing help and support in ways that are denied by 'a global transgender activist moment'.

In the UK, considerable attention has been paid to the increase in referrals to gender identity clinics. Interventions into 'sexed-based' realities are considered harmful, and the antithesis of professional medical practices. Concerns regarding these clinics and how they operate are used to suggest that trans children (in particular) should not be treated as they are currently being treated. Medical interventions supporting transition are read as permanent, harmful and thus subject to transition regret. This is despite the assertion that 'virtually 100% of children put on puberty blockers go on to transition' (Christian Concern, Nov. 29, 2018), which would be read by others as affirming this is the correct course of action. Hormone blockers leading to transition means that young people who choose to use these blockers are using them to understand their gendered identities and work towards their gendered futures. For Christian Concern, this shows instead that there is 'no way out', and that puberty blockers and other interventions are seen as causing harm and regret:

> He [James Caspian, 'a psychotherapist who special-
> ises in working with transgender people'] says that
> UK policies are moving towards this affirmation
> model and he is concerned that some young peo-
> ple might be making permanent decisions about
> their body that they will later regret … There are

people who feel damaged by what they have been through. Although the principle of all therapy and medical practice is to do no harm, people are saying they have been harmed.

There are legitimate questions to ask about people who regret transitioning. There are also questions about the long-term effects of hormone therapy. Trans activists, however, don't want these discussions to take place. They don't like the fact that someone like Stella,[5] who used to identify as a boy and now enjoys being a woman, exists. Nor do they like the fact that there are many who regret transition. (Christian Concern, Nov. 29, 2018: paras 10–14)

Heteroactivists read the permanence of hormone blockers as reiterating the inability to reverse the effects and the 'regret' that 'someone like Stella' feels, because 'she now enjoys being a woman'. The 'they' here is again homogenised and 'trans activists' who are assumed to be refusing 'legitimate questions' (see Chapter 4) that Christian Concern believes undermines the case for hormone blockers and associated support for young people.

For Christian Concern (Nov. 29, 2018), research on the long-term effects of hormone blockers is also being prohibited by trans activists to the detriment of children. Conversely, the idea of de-medicalising transition is also opposed. Trans people are seen as mentally ill, and requiring mental health support not physical interventions:

> those presenting with gender dysphoria are more likely to experience mood disorders, anxiety disorders, autism and attempt suicide. We would be concerned that the proposed changes would make trans people less likely to seek medical attention. They would also undermine the pain experienced by those who experience gender dysphoria ... The proposal to remove any legal and medical steps from the process underestimates the seriousness of what is involved. There are significant safeguarding concerns that the most vulnerable will be put at risk by moves to self-identification. (Evangelical Alliance, Oct. 18, 2018: para. 14)

The concern of Evangelical Alliance is with trans people's need for medical help and their pain, because of the presumption that 'gender dysphoria' leads to other issues (see Johnston, 2018). The seriousness of changing gender, for Evangelical Alliance, needs to be preserved and which, if lost, puts vulnerable trans people at risk. These 'concerns' highlight a compassion which is focused on the dangers for trans people and the supposed need to protect them from themselves by medical professionals, law makers and those who would 'safeguard them'. In Canada, for example, Michele Sirois, president of Québec Women's

Rights Association in her representation in opposition to Bill C-16, objected to the medicalisation of treatment for children including 'mutilation' such as mastectomies and the use of hormone blockers as evidence of the medical risk to children (Standing Senate Committee on Legal and Constitutional Affairs, 2017).

Other conversations around the claimed long-term harms arising from forcing children and young people to live in their assigned sex at birth are dismissed or minimised. Discussions of suicide in particular can be seen as 'tactics' used to 'bully' heteroactivists and others:

> They (Mermaids)[6] have taken on a bully pulpit to strike fear and moral shaming into school staff telling them that if they do not do exactly what gender confused children want of them, or follow the exact letter of what those children's parents are telling them to do, these children will commit suicide, the staff member could lose their job or the matter might even become more serious than that. (Kriska, 2019: para. 4)

While trans people might be at risk for suicide, in Kriska's terms, it is the staff who are under threat for being blamed for causing a trans person's suicide. This puts their jobs in jeopardy as a result of failing to follow parental dictates. A child's suicide is also seen as less than the loss of a job or 'the matter' becoming 'more serious'. 'Children' here are 'gender confused' and parents are 'telling' staff what to do, which is not acceptable. Parental concerns regarding suicidal ideation are dismissed. Where parents are seeking to resist trans and gender-non-conforming identities, behaviours and support, they deserve compassion, advice and support. In contrast, where parents support their trans and gender-non-conforming children, parental rights, so fiercely sought in relation to LGBT education in schools (see Chapter 2), are superseded by the 'truth', staff members' jobs and 'more serious' implications.

In this critique, heteroactivists distinguish between parents who support their children by accepting their trans children from those who do not – a position also taken up by heteroactivist groups in Canada. However, in Canada, this approach was used to highlight how parents are supposedly being socially pressured into supporting transition for their children. In the Canadian Bill C-16 debates, it was contended that the apparent already-existing pervasiveness of the term 'gender ideologies' was having an impact on how parents were able to handle their potentially trans children. During the parliamentary hearings, Senator Plett, citing Dr Alice Dreger of Northwestern University's Feinberg School of Medicine, argued that with the normalising of trans ideologies, parents who encourage their children to change genders 'are socially rewarded as wonderful and accepting', while parents who try to take it slow 'are seen as unaccepting, lacking in affection and conservative' (Plett, 2017).

The dangers of a 'global transgender movement' were portrayed differently in Canada than in the UK, but nonetheless, all sought to refute challenges to the 'natural' gender binaries regarded as fundamental to Western civilisation. Such dangers, it is argued, are not simply confined to broad social and political impacts, but also have detrimental effects on trans people themselves. At times, heteroactivists in the UK, Canada and Ireland strive to take a compassionate approach that celebrates resistance to sexual and gender diversity while condemning any support for non-conforming, LGBT or queer lives (see Burack, 2014b). This is perhaps because trans people are increasingly read as marginalised individuals, protected by equality and hate crime laws, rather than through frames of 'abominations'. Thus, trans people cannot be read as dangerous simply for rejecting gender conformity. For heteroactivists, one way of resisting trans rights in these contexts is to encourage support of trans people's 'ill health' and to deal with gender 'confusion' by assisting individuals to embrace 'the bodies they were born with' (Christian Institute, n.d.). Such a position allows activists to oppose the 'delusion that they are trapped in the wrong body' but to suggest it 'deserves compassion'. In taking this approach, heteroactivists are seeking to avoid accusations of bullying trans children. Instead, they suggest that trans children are being harmed through supportive institutions and cultures that do not challenge their 'delusions'.

Protecting 'Our' Women and Children

Heteroactivist resistances that question the possibility of a 'transgender child' or that claim gender fluidity is an ideology deployed for political purposes, underpins the claim of the harm of 'the trans agenda'. These claims insist that this harm is inherent when trans identities are affirmed, and they are dangerous to *both* them (trans kids in particular) and us (presumed heteronormative families and children). Thus, harm extends beyond trans children, to 'our children' (who are presumed cis-gender and heterosexual) and calls up a specific duty of care by public bodies, such as schools, in terms of the 'welfare of children' (Moseley, Dec. 15, 2017). 'Our' children then are central to trans conversations and the potential harm of 'gender ideologies'. In a UK example, the Rowe parents removed their child from his school because another child was presenting alternatively as either a boy or a girl. They argued that transphobia and bullying would be weaponised against their child as well as them as parents, where 'our son might be disciplined as a bully simply because he thinks that a boy really is a boy, and a girl is a girl' (Christian Concern, Nov. 2, 2017).[7] For the Rowe family, the ideals propagated in the private places of the home came into conflict with trans-inclusive school spaces that seek to protect and support vulnerable young people. Here this discourse is turned on its head, with heteroactivists and their children positioned as victims and the implication that an 'innocent' (and 'natural') 6-year-old's beliefs would be disciplined and labelled as 'bullying', clearly delineating the threat trans ideologies pose to 'our children'.

In Canada and the UK, not only were children supposedly placed in danger because of trans ideologies, heteroactivists also raised concerns about the danger posed to women and girls because of transgender activism. Specifically, heteroactivists made claims about the potential presence of 'men' in women's and girls' spaces including bathrooms and changing facilities, women's shelters and clubs. Scholars have written extensively about the problems experienced by trans people around single-sex spaces (e.g. Cavanagh, 2010; Doan, 2010; Halberstam, 2005; Johnston, 2018), but heteroactivists argue that women and girls are most at risk if trans women (who they read as men) use women's spaces.

In Canada, legal scholar Brenda Cossman (2018) argues that objections to trans rights legislation based on anxieties about cis-gender women's spaces had largely disappeared but these concerns did (re)surface in several representations made against Bill C-16. For example, Diane Guilbault, Vice-President, Québec Women's Rights Association argued that Bill C-16 would allow men who identify as women to use spaces designated for women. Their concern was grounded in the undisputed existence of male violence and the need for protections for women in the face of this violence. The spaces in danger include women's changing rooms, bathrooms, businesses and women's shelters.

In the UK, these debates have been central to recent discussions on gender inclusions, setting up a binary between women's rights and trans rights. Panics regarding the 'dangers of men' are linked to biological assertions that trans women are men. These men are inherently and 'naturally' dangerous to women and girls, in their potential occupation of 'female-only spaces'. Using the Girl Guides as an example, Christian Concern argues:

> [S]ince updating Girlguiding's equality and diversity policy last year to include a 'transgender policy', the Guides have allowed adults and children who 'self-identify' as female to be leaders and members, despite still having male bodies. On trips away, the children can share bathrooms and bedrooms. The policy states that leaders are not permitted to tell girls or their parents if their daughter's leader, or fellow member, is transgender. Helen Watts, one of the expelled leaders, said that girls had a right to 'female-only spaces'. She said: 'I am very upset and I am also really angry. We had some serious concerns about a policy that ignored basic safeguarding principles'. (Christian Concern, Sept. 27, 2018: para 2–4)

Invoking safeguarding principles, as Helen Watts does in the quote above, paints trans people as dangerous and unfit to be around children. Drawing on child protection policy language implies that there is a failing in 'basic' care by trans adults and children in providing respect for their legal right of gendered history non-disclosure. Parents of cis-gender children are read differently from the supportive parents of trans children (above) who were seen as overly forceful and as costing people their jobs or being duped into supporting their children by external forces. Here, parents have a 'right' to the intimate and gendered histories of leaders and other children (see also Chapter 2). The privacy they might expect for their own children regarding their genitalia, for example, is not to be afforded to trans children or Girl Guide leaders.

The supposedly inherent danger of heterosexual men is seemingly addressed through 'female-only spaces', including toilets, bathrooms and changing rooms. These spaces apparently protect girls and women from abuse and create spaces where 'they can feel safe from men' (Christian Institute, Feb. 6, 2018). This safety is apparently lost when trans people are allowed to self-identify but have 'male bodies'. The dangers go beyond potential harm caused by heterosexual men to also risking 'retraumatising vulnerable and victimised women for the sake of ideology' (Christian Institute, Feb. 6, 2018). Self-identification of gender then needs 'checks and balances' particularly for dangerous trans women (who are read as heterosexual men and thus inherently dangerous in women's spaces).[8]

Girls are specifically rendered endangered. Christian Today's (Feb. 2, 2019) discussion of Scottish school guidance around trans issues, for example, focused on the place of girls' bodies as sites to be protected in places such as changing rooms, toilets and overnight accommodation. Nudity is critical here and the 'healthy boundaries girls may have around who sees them undressed' would be contested by the presence of trans women (but trans men are not named as dangerous to boys and their 'healthy boundaries') (Christian Today, Feb. 2, 2019). It is presumed that healthy boundaries pertaining to women-only spaces are safe for all girls, and mixed spaces are unsafe. The 'dangers' of trans students to 'everyone else' sets 'girls' rights to privacy and dignity' in contradistinction to the 'fundamentally unreasonable requirements' that would include trans students (Christian Today, Feb. 2, 2019). In this way, heteroactivists have framed women and girls' rights as opposite to and against trans equalities. Deploying these equalities discourses has gained traction in contesting the rights of trans people and has vilified trans women as men (and therefore violent and dangerous).

Additional claims positioned within a 'rights of women' focus target the issues of sport and divorce and marriage. In Canada, Michele Sirois, president of Québec Women's Rights Association (Standing Senate Committee on Legal and Constitutional Affairs, 2017), in opposition to Bill C-16, argued that trans rights would conflict with women's 'hard-won rights' particularly in women's sports. Further, concerns for those married to individuals who transition was also raised. Discussing the Scottish government's consultation on the Gender Recognition Act 2004, Carys Moseley of Christian Concern argued:

> Less well-publicised but equally immoral is the fact that the Scottish government asks whether or not it should be 'possible to apply for and obtain legal gender recognition without any need for spousal consent' (Question 7).

> This would effectively force a woman married to a man who insists on legally becoming a woman to accept this change. Historically women married to such men have tended to divorce them, as these men violated the marriage covenant. A change in the law could mean that a woman who refused to consent could end up being divorced by the husband and punished by the law for standing up to this violation of marriage. This arrogant demand for absolute acceptance of transgenderism of course is what Stonewall's slogan 'Acceptance without exception' is all about: forcing everybody else to accept this on pain of legal punishment and social ostracism. (Moseley, Nov. 16, 2017: para. 13)

Forcing trans people to seek 'spousal consent' is tied to understandings of marriage as, in this case, a form of joint ownership, based on sexual difference and complementarity between men and women. This is breached by trans people who 'violate' marriage by rejecting the sexual complementarities inherent in the legal and biological definitions of men/women. Sexuality and gender are both in play in defining marriage in this way. Marriage is constructed as not only between a gender-normative man and a gender-normative woman, but also as the right to enforce these legal distinctions through a lifelong commitment. However, it is the loss to women that is highlighted. Women are 'punished' by the law for 'standing up to this violation of marriage'. They are again seen as vulnerable, as needing protection as well as empowerment, because they are at risk of their marriage being 'violated' without their consent. Trans men and their husbands are not mentioned or seen as vulnerable and needing protection in the same way.

In contrast to the focus on girls, boys are not seen to be at risk from trans men in toilets, changing rooms or overnight accommodation. This relates back to gendered understandings that place women and girls as inherently weak, vulnerable and needing protection. The gendering of the danger speaks to understandings of appropriate gendered binaries within normative man/woman sexual complementarities. These sexual complementarities understand trans women as dangerous to women, because it is argued that they are, and can only ever be, men and men are threatening in women's spaces. However, in claiming their transness, they become even more dangerous because they are 'mentally ill'. In these circumstances, not all men might be dangerous outside of women's spaces, only those who seek to enter women's spaces as women are read as such. This both reiterates heteronormative binaries and the dangers of trans people and 'the trans agenda', it also enables a protective heteroactivist (male) stance that specifically focuses on trans women, and 'not all men'.

Conclusion

[Tony] Blair's administration made it possible for same-sex couples to adopt children. Then Cameron and Clegg introduced same-sex marriage without any manifesto mandate.

...

This is despite the fact that on every metric, children do better in general where they are brought up in a home with a married mother and father ... The Gender Recognition Act takes this a stage further and undermines the very nature of humanity as being male and female ... This is despite the self-evident truth that people are created male and female, and that is immutable regardless of whether people have surgery to 'change their gender'. Yet now, to state the truth, to oppose the establishment's full-spectrum push to change the fundamental nature of gender in law, is to get you in trouble. (Kurten, 2017)

The perceived trajectory from same-sex marriage to trans issues is captured in this quote from Kurten (2017). The move from same-sex marriage to trans inclusions is pointed to as evidence of the existence of a 'slippery slope' that is posited as a ludicrous result as well as dangerous. Trans issues and gender ideologies form a key part of recent heteroactivist discourses. Similarly to the transgressions of heterosexuality caused by same-sex attraction, gender non-conformity can now no longer be represented or condemned as obscene, grotesque and dangerous (although, again, such views remain in some quarters). The term transphobia, and indeed anti-trans activism, falls short in conceptualising the underlying objections of these new resistances. Some heteroactivists argue for compassion to those who resist or question gender non-conformity, even as they struggle with it, reading this as a 'mental illness' that deserves compassion but also makes trans women even more dangerous (see also Burack, 2014b). In contrast, those who embrace any form of gender non-conformity, or in particular are seen as supporting trans children, are read as undermining not only the children's best interests, but also broader 'Western society'.

Trans and gender non-conformity is understood as a 'lie', and a mental illness that rejects the 'realities' of biological and essentialist understandings of sex. This means that trans people and gender-variant children are harmed through trans rights, legal protections, medical and state support. While suicidal distress is seen as a tactic to force compliance to what are seen as the new orthodoxies of gender, regret regarding transition is presented as prevalent and illustrative of the dangers of supporting trans kids with regard to access to hormones. However, it is not only trans children who are harmed. Trans rights are created in a binary that is opposite to, and incongruent with, women's rights, such that trans inclusions are read as in contradistinction to women's rights to safe space. Thus, trans women are not only 'not women', their rights also directly infringe on the rights of 'sex-based women' and make these women unsafe and retraumatised. In reading trans women (as mentally ill), and as dangerous to women in 'female-only' spaces, heteroactivist rhetoric claims to be 'protecting women'. Gender is crucial here. Across heteroactivist discussions, trans men, when they are mentioned, can be seen as dangerous to themselves, mentally ill, and in need of protection. Trans women are emblematic of a dangerous 'global transgender movement' that is portrayed as a danger to 'our children', and particularly women and girls, who are inherently vulnerable and need protection. A key discourse, that we now move to discuss is the claim that it is not possible to have a 'legitimate debate' regarding the dangers heteroactivists contend exist in trans and broader LGBT rights. Trans rights have been a key catalyst in the contention that free speech is under threat.

4

Freedom of Speech: Creating Space to Contest LGBT Equalities

Introduction

One of the central premises of this book is the argument that heteroactivism allows us to conceptualise resistances to LGBT equalities that are not captured by discourses of homophobia based in late 20th-century forms of anti-gay opposition which vilified gay men and lesbians. In the 21st century, while some groups still make personal attacks on LGBT people, there has been a shift in tactics in places where LGBT equalities are protected (Browne and Nash, 2014; Nash and

Browne, 2015). In the previous chapter, we argued that trans inclusions were seen by heteroactivists as 'ludicrous' and in Chapter 2, it was contended that LGBT inclusions in school spaces were indicative of a totalitarian state. Building on this, this chapter shows that central to resistances to LGBT inclusions are claims about violations of freedom of speech and freedom of expression. In speaking out against LGBT equalities, heteroactivists deploy free speech claims in a variety of ways, including as we will discuss, as a shield against accusations of hate speech or of homophobia.

Historically, LGBT activists made free speech claims to contest state discrimination and societal prejudices against sexual and gender minorities (Kinsman, 1987; Warner, T., 2002; Smith, 2007). In this chapter, we explore how freedom of speech claims are now a central and necessary tenet of contemporary heteroactivism in the UK, Ireland and Canada at the time of writing (mid-2019). Free speech claims are used to attack LGBT legislative and political equalities and to understand this, we focus on heteroactivist free speech claims as a key contemporaneous contestation of LGBT rights. Following an outline of the key contexts of free speech in Canada, the UK and Ireland, the chapter explores examples of heteroactivist free speech claims that are utilised against accusations of 'bigotry', 'homophobia' and transphobia and that are key to heteroactivists' attempts to make room for 'other arguments' and 'other sides' of the debate. We then explore how heteroactivists deploy claims about free speech to challenge what they understand as 'silencing'.

In particular, we examine how heteroactivists are creating key arguments about being forced or compelled to support LGBT equalities when such equalities are against their own values and beliefs. We consider their claims that debate is being 'shut down' in part by accusations that their speech is harmful, and their accusations about the problems that they are having in navigating 'murky' legal landscapes. We then move to investigate their arguments that LGBT equalities are actually 'ideologies' that are stifling free speech in ways that are detrimental to heteroactivists and to civil society. Because of these threats to their heteroactivist values and beliefs, they argue it is imperative to act, to resist and to 'fight' for free speech, not only for themselves but for the benefit of all, even those with whom they might disagree. In this chapter, we offer insights into how free speech claims are deployed as a tool for heteroactivists in places where there are legal limits to discriminations against LGBT people. Our contention is that discourses of freedom of speech are critical to heteroactivist resistances to new sexual and gender legislative landscapes that define contemporary political, social and legal landscapes in Canada, the UK and Ireland.

Contextualising Free Speech Discussions in Canada, the UK and Ireland

Canada

A central tenet in our argument is the importance of thinking about the multiple and varied geographies operative in heteroactivist oppositions. As we discussed in Chapter 3, Jordan Peterson's foray into trans oppositions began on the University of Toronto campus, and his arguments soon circulated transnationally, surfacing in the UK, Australia and elsewhere (Lynskey, 2018; Russell, 2018; Callaghan and van Leent, 2019). As we discuss in this chapter, Jordan Peterson's attacks on universities (the location where his original objections surfaced) opened up the campus freedom of speech debate in Ontario, and indeed, across the country. Up until Peterson's interventions and the Lindsey Shepherd incident at Wilfred Laurier University,[1] freedom of speech debates in Canada were relatively muted.[2] Peterson's initial notoriety emerged from his objection to using non-binary and trans students' pronouns, which he claimed was a form of 'compulsory speech'. His growing influence through social media and speaking engagements heightened his national and transnational visibility, including in the UK, and to an extent Ireland, and claims about 'compelled speech' figure prominently in debates regarding trans rights. In the fall, 2018, Ontario Premier Doug Ford, who defeated Kathleen Wynne in the spring of that year, passed legislation requiring all Ontario post-secondary institutes to introduce free speech policies by 1 January 2019, indicating, as we will argue, that there is significant traction to the claim or accusation that there is a shutting down of debate and a 'stifling' of free speech.

United Kingdom

In the UK, heteroactivist free speech arguments are much newer but are increasingly pervasive. Questions about free speech emerged in contestations over 'no platforming' at UK universities. This included those who argue their free speech rights are being infringed upon, including feminists and gay rights activists who believed it to be an infringement of their rights and earning potentials when they found themselves no platformed (see Nash, Gorman-Murray and Browne, 2019). Heteroactivist groups have supported some feminist and gay rights activists who were no platformed, such as Julie Bindel, Germaine Greer and Peter Tatchell. In 2018–2019, the Conservative government weighed in to support 'free speech' in university spaces and in 2019, the Equality and Human Rights Commission stated universities had a 'legal duty' to support free speech on campus. The Office for Students was given oversight of this area.

Conversely, speech is restricted in the UK for matters related to 'terrorism' and 'extremism'. In the late 20th century, the words of key Northern Irish figures were not allowed to be broadcast. Thus, free speech claims have to contend with this particular historical context and related discussions about what constitutes extremist language. The UK's Prevent Strategy defines extremism as 'vocal or active opposition to fundamental British values of law, individual liberty and mutual respect and tolerance of different faiths or beliefs' (UK Government, 2015: 2) and the associated guidance includes references to 'extreme right-wing' groups (UK Government, 2015). Heteroactivists have successfully challenged the Prevent Strategy in the courts, arguing that this 'vague' definition has serious implications for religious freedom. While fully supporting tackling 'radicalisation and terrorism' (read Islamic terrorism), this definition was seen as potentially rendering 'opinions which differ from current social norms' as extreme (including oppositions to sexual and gender rights) (Evangelical Alliance, n.d.). The meanings of 'British values' are contested as well as the point that questions of 'tolerance' also included tolerance of the Islamic faith. While not explicitly addressing sexualities and genders, these debates point to the interlocking constitution of gender, sexuality, race and ethnicities in the creation of the figure of the 'terrorist' as well as the 'homophobe' (see e.g. Puar, 2007; Haritaworn et al., 2018; Boulilia, 2019). Thus, the process of seeking to keep debates open in order to challenge LGBT rights is racialised as white, and often Christian (see also Chapter 5).

Heteroactivists have welcomed guidance from the government regarding free speech at UK universities (House of Commons and House of Lords, 2018) and, specifically, direction that universities not follow the National Union of Students and individual university student unions on 'no platforming'. As we argue here, trans issues play a central role in these debates, emerging in university contexts around the no platforming of feminism and gay rights speakers (see Nash, Gorman-Murray and Browne, 2019; see also Chapter 3). Challenges to same-sex marriage and relationships and family education also feature in hetero-activist discourses claiming such legislation restricts their free speech rights.[3]

Ireland

In Ireland, contestations framed as freedom of speech issues have not emerged as central heteroactivist arguments. However, as we discuss below, it was key heteroactivist commentators from the Iona Institute such as John Waters who sued the RTÉ (Ireland's national broadcaster) when Panti Bliss/Rory O'Neill, a guest on a chat show, implied that they and the Iona Institute were homophobic.[4] At the time of writing in 2019, there remained a platform in the mainstream Irish media for heteroactivist viewpoints, although it is clear that this is understood as diminishing and under threat. In all contexts, heteroactivist contestations against accusations of 'bigotry', 'homophobia' and 'transphobia' have been ongoing including in the same-sex marriage debates and trans rights debates. Across the UK, Ireland and Canada, heteroactivist resistance to trans rights has required heteroactivists to assert their 'free speech' is being abridged.

Free Speech: Not Bigotry or Homophobia

Homophobia in a broad sense can be used to name activities that foster discrimination against LGBT people in employment and housing as well as exclusion or denigration in more informal settings. This also includes activities supporting the denial of public services to LGBT people or the exclusion of LGBT people from key state institutions such as marriage or military service (Badgett, 2014 in Lamontagne et al., 2018: 967). However, despite these definitions, scholars have long acknowledged that the term and its definitions are inadequate given it 'foregrounds individual psychological processes rather than [acting as] a critique of social power' (Boulilia, 2015: 106; see also O'Brien, 2008; Bryant and Vidal-Ortiz, 2008). As we show below, heteroactivists claim that the label 'homophobe' is inaccurate because they are not afraid of homosexuals. In objecting to the accusation of homophobia, heteroactivists assert that their objections to things such as same-sex marriage (Chapter 1) or LGBT education in schools (Chapter 2) are not bigotry but reflect 'common-sense' positions about LGBT equalities (e.g. Baklinski, 2016; Carpay, Apr. 24, 2017). This, then, is not an attack on LGBT people but a reasoned *debate* about the nature of these institutions. These claims are used to create room to speak so-called 'truths' and to counter the dismissal of heteroactivist ideas as merely bigoted. In this section, we detail heteroactivist contestations of the term homophobia as well as accusations of transphobia and other pejoratives. We then examine the reclaiming of 'hate', before moving to offer a discussion of a wider set of arguments grounded in free speech and freedom of speech claims in the following sections.

(Re)Defining Homophobia

Heteroactivists seek to narrow the meaning of the term homophobia to only reference a personal dislike or 'fear' of LGBT people. For example, in the spring of 2017, John Carpay, the president of the Canadian organisation the Justice Centre for Constitutional Freedoms, argued that words like 'homophobia' are dangerous because they lack clear definition, are ambiguous and therefore likely to create uncertainty in debate. Nevertheless, Carpay goes on to define homophobia as 'an irrational fear of homosexuals or homosexuality' (Carpay, Apr. 24, 2017). He then argues that those who disagree with same-sex marriage or 'the gay agenda' are expressing a reasoned opinion which 'should be refuted by reason, logic and facts. Bullying and name-calling, through accusations of "phobia", are a poor substitute for the healthy debate' (Carpay, Apr. 24, 2017). This narrowing of the meaning of homophobia allows heteroactivists to deflect accusations that their opposition to LGBT inclusions is 'homophobic' (see discussion of trans people in Chapter 3).

Deflecting claims that heteroactivism is homophobic is politically and socially important for heteroactivist groups. When the Ontario Liberal government of Premier Kathleen Wynne, an out and married lesbian, introduced the updated Health and Physical Education curriculum, which included sexual education, opponents were initially labelled homophobic. In parliamentary debate, Wynne went so far as to call Conservative MP Monte McNaughton 'homophobic', given his objections based on concerns about age appropriateness (Morrow, 2015). McNaughton rejected this, arguing that calling someone homophobic was 'the lowest thing a premier could say about another legislator' (Canadian Press, 2015). Similarly, in late 2014 and 2015, the premier also suggested that protestors, largely consisting of parents' groups, were also homophobic in their objections. Opponents and commentators argued this claim was 'smearing her [Wynne's] opponents' and was a 'disgusting act' (Lilley, 2015; see also Canadian Press, 2015; Mann, 2016).[5]

In Ireland, heteroactivists sought to arguably limit 'free speech' by seeking legal and compensatory recourse against being labelled 'homophobic'. In 2014, Rory O'Neill (an LGBT activist and drag queen, Panti Bliss) labelled prominent Irish figures as 'homophobic', including an *Irish Times* journalists John Waters and Breda O'Brien. The Iona Institute threatened legal action against Ireland's national broadcaster (RTÉ) who aired the show (McGarry, 2014; Duggan, 2014). RTÉ apologised and paid compensation to those who were so labelled (RTÉ, 2014). Opponents tried to frame the label of homophobic as defamation. In their narrowed understanding, homophobia is only applicable to those who physically or verbally abuse people. Therefore, heteroactivists can not only distance themselves from the term (and associated terms such as transphobia, as well as 'bigot'), but can further claim that homophobia is an offensive label and a personal slight.[6]

In this context, those using the term 'homophobe' are framed as abusers, not as individuals exercising their free speech rights, which as we shall see below is called for in relation to rejecting the 'harm' of speech acts.

This tactic of redefining the accusation of homophobia as defamatory is an important heteroactivist tool. This is because the homophobe label can be a powerful one with particular weight in contexts where both culturally and legislatively, hate speech is prohibited. Heteroactivist groups are very aware of the power of these labels. They can work to avoid doing anything that might warrant labels such as homophobe/transphobe/bigot, and reject any association between these terms and their actions. For example, in Ontario, parents protesting in Ottawa about the sexual education curriculum were advised to 'avoid statements that would allow them to be portrayed by the news media as "homophobic"' (Weatherbe, Apr. 29, 2015). Parents needed to argue that 'they did not object to the program, just that it is "too risky" for children' (Weatherbe, Apr. 29, 2015). Similarly, in the UK, Parkfield parents railed against being called 'homophobic bigots' for their objections to a programme that included discussions of same-sex relationships (see Chapter 1). They said that they objected to the 'dangers' posed to children from this programme and were not against LGBT people as such. In this way, protestors in both the UK and Canada sought to present themselves as 'ordinary parents' and not '"homophobic bigots", as some would have you believe' (Blizzard, 2015).

Transphobia is also a term that heteroactivists reject for largely the same reasons. As we discussed in Chapter 3, heteroactivists often argued that admitting the existence of trans people was challenging 'reality' as well as the biological 'truths of binary sexes'. Heteroactivists argued these 'truths' as not 'transphobic', and that the term transphobia was too vague to be an appropriate descriptor. Maria Caulfield, a prominent UK Conservative MP, was quoted as saying definitions of what counts as 'transphobic' can be dangerously all encompassing (Christian Institute, Oct. 18, 2018). The term was being used, they asserted, to silence opponents on 'the altar[7] of extreme political correctness on which freedom of speech is being destroyed' (Kurten, 2017). Indeed, Christian Concern argued that 'If we want to know the truth, we must tolerate "political incorrectness"' (Christian Concern, Jan. 30, 2019). Setting 'political correctness' in opposition to 'the truth', paints those who label heteroactivists as transphobic as rejecting reality (see also Christian Institute, Oct. 18, 2018).

Despite protestors' claims that their opposition to the Ontario Health and Physical Education curriculum was not homophobic, a prominent opponent of the curriculum was removed as a 2018 Conservative Party candidate on that basis. Tanya Granic Allen was accused of making homophobic and anti-Muslim comments online several years before the run up to the 2018 election. Conservative Party leader, Doug Ford, dismissed Granic Allen as a candidate, arguing that the party 'is comprised of people with diverse views that if expressed responsibly we would respect' and that Allen's characterisation of certain issues (same-sex marriage) was 'irresponsible' (CBC, Apr. 10, 2018; Isai, 2018; see also Ditchburn, 2015). Granic Allen's removal shows that individuals in public office who may harbour anti-gay sentiments can be censured (as we will discuss in relation to workplaces in Chapter 5). In the UK, UKIP fired David Small, a newly elected local councillor, for racist and homophobic comments posted on social media.[8] Reprimanding some people as 'homophobic' allows others to claim they are 'not homophobic' and indeed groups, including political parties, can claim that they are 'dealing with homophobia' (see Ahmed, 2012). Again, this deflects criticism that commentary on, for example, the inferiority of same-sex families or the impossibility of trans women is homophobic or transphobic and asserts that such arguments are protected free speech.

Enabling Debate, Reclaiming Hate

Heteroactivists often argue that labels such as bigot and homophobe are used in an attempt to stifle debate. Kurten (2017, discussed in Chapter 2) contends that: 'if you dissent, you are a bigot to be fought and silenced'. Where homophobia is defined as a 'mental illness', opponents such as John Carpay (Oct. 17, 2017), argue that in order to shut down debate, all one has to do is 'accuse your opponents of being far right, racist, fascist, white supremacist, Islamophobic or homophobic' (Carpay, Oct 17, 2017) and 'calling someone a "racist", "homophobe", "Islamophobe" or other insult is a means of silencing opposition' (Campbell-Jack, 2018). In seeking to distance themselves from labels of 'hate', hetero-activists can then claim that they are exposing the bigotry of those who support LGBT inclusion because it is LGBT people who are intolerant of 'other views'.

As part of their work to avoid being labelled 'homo-phobic' and to work towards enabling a debate on their terms, heteroactivists can also seek to reclaim the term 'hate'. In Ireland at the Lumen Fidei conference (2018), John Lacken, a key organiser of the conference, suggested that the Catholic Church's sexual abuse issue is 'primarily a homosexual problem', but that clergy, church leaders and others are silent, 'perhaps because they fear to be called names such as homophobic and haters' (John Lacken, Browne fieldnotes, Luman Fidei Conference, 2018, quotes are approximations). Challenging not only the accusa-tion of bigotry, but also the need to 'hate' (sin and evil), reflected a key theme of the conference. The reclaiming of hate, in a context of love, they argued, is not as oxy-moronic as it might seem at first. John-Henry Westen, a Canadian and editor at *LifeSite News*, titled his presenta-tion: 'It's Hate Not to Tell LGBT Catholics Gay Sex Leads to Hell'. In reclaiming hate, while rejecting accusations of bigotry, he sought to create space to attack inclusion, spe-cifically from a position of 'love':

'The usual tactic is to be called a hater and a bigot because of my stance on same-sex attraction'. On a radio show he had argued 'I love my brothers, because it is hate not to tell them' ... He said that he was praying for hate – love what God loves, hate the things that God hates ... He suggests that the church needs more hatred ... It is hate *not* to tell same-sex attracted Catholics that gay sex leads to hell'. (John-Henry Westen, Browne fieldnotes, Lumen Fidei Conference 2018, quotes are approximations)

Westen names the ways that heteroactivists would argue that 'supposedly' tolerant, open and inclusive societies such as Canada, the UK and Ireland call those resisting LGBT equalities 'haters' and 'bigots'. Weston seeks to deride name calling while at the same time reasserting the importance of their own truth, which might be labelled as 'hate'. His argument is that their hatred of gay sex is done for love, because 'gay sex leads to hell'. Moreover, John-Henry Westen used studies from LGBT magazines such as *Xtra* in Canada to contend that LGBT lives are dangerous for LGBT people. He said that 'health issues are endemic to the [LGBT] community' and argues that people should 'believe the LGBT community. It harms your body, mind, heart and soul this lifestyle' (John-Henry Westen, Browne fieldnotes, Lumen Fidei conference 2018, quotes are approximations). Because of these dangers, he argued that it is 'hate' *not* to speak out against the risks of LGBT lives, because the research supporting the risks stems from, and is driven by, 'the' LGBT community.

Labels such as homophobia, transphobia and bigotry have been used to name discriminations against LGBT people. Heteroactivists opposing LGBT equalities seek to deflect this label by creating narrow definitions that serve their purposes. Heteroactivists employ tactics to avoid and reject these labels and to construct arguments that are not 'anti-gay' but are instead presented as pro-heteronormativity. However, in rejecting these labels, heteroactivists can still seek to discuss 'hate' with regard to LGBT equalities. Consequently, heteroactivists argue that it is 'hate' *not* to tell people about the purported dangers of 'this lifestyle'.

Free Speech, Not Forced Speech: Rejecting Gender Self-Identities

In contrast to seeking space to speak against LGBT equalities, heteroactivists argue that being required to respect LGBT equalities 'compels' them to speak in particular ways. This forced support of LGBT people, they argue, undermines their belief in the centrality of heteronormative societies. The argument about 'compelled' or 'forced' speech has become critical in the UK and Canada where it is contended that equalities initiatives can ask for adherence to, and the performance of, LGBT inclusions. For heteroactivists, these inclusionary requirements are 'unjust' and need to be resisted in order to protect 'freedom'.

The debate in Canada regarding freedom of speech was relatively muted until the very public objections by

Jordan Peterson at the University of Toronto in 2016 over the required use of people's pronouns (rather than those associated with their sex assigned at birth) in university class-rooms. Peterson was also a strong opponent of proposed federal human rights legislation (Bill C-16) that sought to protect people against discrimination on the basis of gender identity and gender expression. Peterson argued that Bill C-16 'requires Canadians to use a form of address that has particular ideological implications', which is unacceptable (Standing Senate Committee on Legal and Constitutional Affairs, 2017). As legal scholar Brenda Cossman (2018) suggests, these interventions by Peterson gained traction and claims about 'freedom of expression provided a new and legitimizing discourse for long-standing conservative opposition to trans rights' (Cossman, 2018: 2).

The debate about 'forced speech' in Canada focused on the required use of gender-neutral or selected pronouns through either legislative or criminal sanction (Standing Senate Committee on Legal and Constitutional Affairs, 2017). Such forced speech is portrayed as an 'egregious infringement of freedom of speech' by Bruce Pardy, because:

> [c]ompelled speech puts words in the mouths of citizens and threatens to punish them if they do not comply ... Forced speech makes people say things with which they do not agree. (Standing Senate Committee on Legal and Constitutional Affairs, 2017)

Claims for freedom of speech grounded in the rejection of 'compelled' or 'forced' speech are also prominent in the UK and to a lesser extent, in Ireland. In the UK, for example, concerns about so-called 'forcing' of speech surfaced when Dr Mackereth, a medical doctor, was classed as 'unfit' as a disability assessor. He said, during disability assessor training, that he would not accept a person's gender self-identification. The position he was training for deals with vulnerable individuals claiming disability benefits by 'proving' their disability and work capabilities. Although heavily critiqued as a punitive process for those seeking welfare payments and support, the training did include gender training to promote gender inclusivity within assessors. Mackereth claimed that obliging him to use pronouns that he did not agree with was 'forced speech', and an infringement of his free speech right. Simultaneously, linking to discussions of bigotry and transphobia above, he argued that his failure to use requested pronouns was not indicative of any bias against trans people, even if he might 'upset people':

> I'm not attacking the transgender movement. But, I'm defending my right to freedom of speech, and freedom of belief. I don't believe I should be compelled to use a specific pronoun. I am not setting out to upset anyone. But, if upsetting someone can lead to doctors being sacked then, as a society we have to examine where we are going. (Bird, 2018: paras 6–7)

Being 'compelled' to use a specific pronoun that contra-
dicts one's (in this case Christian) belief that sex is assigned
at birth is read as an attack on free speech. This minimises
the harm associated with these actions for those whose gender identities are not respected. The harm then is focused
on those who are 'compelled'.

The implications of trans lives and identities underpin
much of the free speech debate in the UK and Canada. In
unpacking these arguments about 'forced' or 'compelled'
speech, we return to several arguments discussed in the
previous chapter. There we contended that heteroactivists
regard trans political activism as working 'against reality' and
as counter-intuitive to the 'norm'. That 'norm' was understood as the position of 'the majority', who supposedly hold
that the binary gender system reflects 'common sense'. The
evidence that one is being forced or compelled to speak in
certain ways demonstrates that these ideas have to be forced
upon people because they are detached from reality. They
could not come into common use by themselves, because
gender transgressions are 'ludicrous'. 'Forcing speech' that
could not otherwise come into being, is positioned as one of
the hallmarks of a 'totalitarian state'. These state powers are
used in ways that are oppressive and deny the liberal freedoms
fundamental to the democracies of the UK and Canada:

> We sleep-walked into slavery, and it's in the domain
> of speech that the death of our freedom is most pro-
> nounced. We hate 'hate speech', but don't love free

speech anymore … Dr. David Mackereth, a physi-
cian with 26 years' experience in Britain's National
Health Service, was sacked because he wouldn't
refer to a hypothetical 'six-foot-tall bearded man' as
'madam'. (Gomes, Sept. 12, 2019: paras 3 and 7)

The death of free speech is linked to the 'hypothetical "six-
foot-tall bearded man"'. Trans people, in particular, are
positioned as detrimental to society and any attempt to
secure their rights will result in the killing of a freedom
because their inclusion is 'ludicrous' and has to be imposed
by a totalitarian state (a similar argument heteroactivists
made about LGBT inclusions in schools, Chapter 2). In
place of free speech will be compelled speech, as opposed
to 'hate speech'. The use of scare quotes indicates a disapproval of the term, and presses the reader to 'love free
speech' which has been 'lost'.

Challenging Compelled Speech: Winning Arguments?

Claims about compelled speech or forced speech have also
arisen in other instances. In Northern Ireland, the Ashers
Bakery case illustrates other dimensions of 'compelled
speech' arguments. Individuals, in asserting a right to
avoid compelled speech can also be understood as asserting the right to discriminate against LGBT people. As we
discuss here, the Ashers Bakery case is regarded as a victory
for freedom of speech well beyond those wanting to avoid
putting certain messages on cakes for religious reasons.

In contrast, the Supreme Court decision in the Trinity Western Case (see Chapter 5) is regarded as denying religious freedom through disallowing a religious institution the ability to establish its own internal policies that were arguably discriminatory or detrimental to LGBT students.

Ashers Bakery, owned by Daniel and Amy McArthur and Daniel's parents, Karen and Colin McArthur, was taken to court by the Northern Irish Equality Commission when the bakery refused an order for a cake with the message 'Support Gay Marriage', citing their religious beliefs. At the time, same-sex marriage had not been legalised in Northern Ireland (as it had in rest of the UK).[9] The McArthurs were initially found in breach of equalities legislation in the regional courts in Belfast, but the UK Supreme Court found that there was no breach, arguing the McArthurs' refusal was based on the message on the cake and not on the sexual orientation of the person requesting the cake. As Daniel McArthur claimed, 'we did not turn down this order because of the person who made it, but because of the message itself'. The victory meant that businesses could not be 'forced to promote other people's campaigns' (Christian Institute, Oct. 10, 2018). As we show in the next chapter, this move separated the message from the messenger in terms of discrimination, where a person could not be refused on the grounds of their sexual orientation, but the message can be.

Heteroactivist groups celebrated this decision as a victory for free speech. They claimed, 'the law says that the freedom to stand up for heteronormative marriage is worthy of protection in a democratic society' (Coalition for Marriage, Aug. 20, 2019). Heteroactivists could continue to argue for the 'protection of (man–woman) marriage' in places where same-sex marriage was not yet legalised. Some gay rights activists such as Peter Tatchell celebrated the decision as allowing for free and open debate (Coalition for Marriage, May 1, 2018; see also Nash, Gorman-Murray and Browne, 2019).

The case was also read as having implications beyond opposition to same-sex marriage and to allow for what Daniel McArthur called 'freedom of speech and freedom of conscience for everyone' (Christian Concern, Oct. 10, 2018). The idea of 'everyone' was elaborated on by the Coalition for Marriage, as ensuring a broader 'freedom to disagree':

> It is not merely a 'gay cake case' as the media puts it. What is on trial is our whole society's attitude to tolerance and the freedom to disagree.
>
> Will Muslim bakers be compelled to bake a Charlie Hebdo cake which ridicules their faith? Will lesbian T-shirt makers have to produce T-shirts saying 'gay marriage is an abomination'? Will Catholic printers have to print leaflets denouncing the Pope? Will feminist web designers have to produce websites which degrade women? (Coalition for Marriage, May 1, 2018: paras 4–5)

While Muslims, lesbians and feminists may well be read as opposed to heteroactivist aims, the purpose of this invocation is clear. 'All' are supposedly protected and 'tolerance' of 'disagreement' is expected.

The argument about the evils of 'compelled speech' has emerged as an important discourse in heteroactivist discussions in Canada, the UK and Ireland. This suggests that compelling speech is an infringement of free speech because it forces speech acts that might be against fundamental values, impacting on 'freedom' itself. This claim about the right to 'not support' LGBT equalities is often combined with assertions that the denial of service or the exclusionary practices are not bigoted, transphobic or homophobic and are instead a matter of freedom in liberal democratic society. When LGBT rights are embedded in the legal and social fabric of Canadian, UK and Irish society and are seen as offering inclusion for all, claiming 'freedom' is at risk is a careful calculation associated with being forced to do something against your will. 'Hate speech' then becomes something that is contested not only because LGBT 'lifestyles' are dangerous, but also, as we will now contend, because it is read as shutting down debate due to associations with harm.

Shutting Down Debate through Accusations of Harm

Arguments about the shutting down of debate because of the risk of harm for marginal groups has arisen in Canada and the UK. Heteroactivists have worked to narrow the understanding of the harm that exclusionary speech can do by claiming that the only harm that must be prevented is physical harm and not emotional or psychological harm. This has been particularly visible around so-called safe spaces on university campuses and in contestations about the harm certain speech acts can cause in their attacks on LGBT inclusions. Arguments about speech being 'compelled' or 'forced' is a critical point for heteroactivists, alongside claims they are also losing the right to dissent through being forced to say something with which they disagree. This arises not only when heteroactivists must conform to inclusive guidelines or laws, but also when their views are shown to cause harm through exclusions and discrimination. In challenging these associations and creating space to debate LGBT inclusions, they attempt to contest 'safe space' and to show that it is those who are shutting down debates who are intolerant. Here we outline heteroactivists' claims about the detrimental impact of protected university spaces which are seen to limit dissent and how they deflect concerns about the harms arising from unfettered free speech. Overall, in this section, we illustrate how heteroactivists seek to push for the possibilities of contesting LGBT rights through recourse to free speech.

Heteroactivists claim that Canadian and UK universities, in their creation of 'safe space' zones, have become places where 'political correctness has gone mad' (Carpay, Oct. 24, 2017; Everyday For Life, 2017; but see

Tabachnick, 2018 for an alternative view). Students are accused of 'hypersensitivity' and of bullying student bodies in order to censor unpopular views (Farmer, 2019). These safe spaces and associated speech restrictions are seen as problematic because they may 'specifically target those who believe in traditional marriage' (Coleman, 2016), as well as those who seek to debate trans rights (as well as other unpopular views such as abortion right or euthanasia). Moreover, people are supposedly regulated through being 'told' that 'hearing views that some students disagree with was a form of abuse, and that students needed campuses to be "safe spaces"' (Harris-Quinney, 2017). By conflating disagreement with abuse, heteroactivists understand the label of 'harm' to be attributed to alternative viewpoints that are then constructed as something from which students need to be protected. They contrast this harm with what they understand as 'actual abuse'. Thus, heteroactivists define 'safe spaces' as sites where there is an absence of alternative viewpoints driven by 'liberal' lecturers and a small group of 'militant' students (Harris-Quinney, 2017). The ability to question LGBT equalities is always implicit in these discussions. For example, in the case of the UK social work student, Felix Ngole, it was argued that his right to express 'Biblical beliefs' against same-sex marriage should not 'effectively be privatised to protect the feelings of others' (Christian Concern, Apr. 26a, 2017). This reduction of real harm to merely 'upset' feelings is critical in underplaying the impact of heteroactivist words and actions on LGBT people in order to make space for their arguments.

LGBT inclusions can lead to sanctions based on protecting people from abuse and harm, and through seeking to make campuses, as well as locations such as workplaces, safer. This includes social services dealing with vulnerable people, such as in medical professions and social work. Due to UK legislative changes around equalities, public sector workers began receiving compulsory training that challenged heteronormative worldviews. This also meant dismissal if you did not adhere to the requirements of LGBT inclusions. In the case of Dr Mackereth, he suggested that he should be able to 'upset someone' by not using their chosen pronoun (Christian Concern, July 13, 2018). Heteroactivists seek then to distinguish harm from 'upset' but also from disagreement:

> I hope we are all against ... 'speech that does harm' (or hate speech). The devil is however in the detail. I think liberal theology is harmful – does that mean I want liberal theologians silenced by the law? God forbid! ... To disagree with them [government committees and those who hold power and contain liberal and LGBT people from the church] is to be guilty of causing harm and hurt. (Robertson, 2019: para. 15)

Robertson, in redefining harm, separates it from 'hate speech' and instead associates it with theological disagreements. This is, in part, to combat accusations of abuse of

LGBT people by the church and the associated harms that are currently being identified under the rubric, 'spiritual abuse' (Sherwood, 2017). Countering the conceptualisations and experiences of LGBT exclusions in the church as spiritual abuse, Robertson specifically associates harm with inclusive liberal theologies that can welcome LGBT people. He then argues that disagreement is equated with 'harm and hurt' and silencing, which he would not impose on those with whom he disagrees. This both negates the experiences of abuse and works to create space to disagree with those who say that they have been subject to it. The use of abuse to describe LGBT exclusions is intensely problematic for heteroactivists and requires significant contestation because it implies illegality in some circumstances or might generate social or political backlash.

'"Murky" Legal Landscapes'?: Shoring Up Free Speech

There is considerable tension between seeking free speech and those specific legal restrictions around non-discrimination equality laws. In Canada and the UK, universities have been instructed to 'protect' free speech. In August 2018, the Ford government announced that Ontario universities and colleges had until 1 January 2019 to implement free speech policies, which must ensure that there is open and free enquiry and that students are not shielded from ideas or opinions they might find offensive. Further, these policies must direct that neither students nor faculty can obstruct others from expressing their views under threat of disciplinary action (Giovannetti and Hauen, 2018). Failure to introduce or comply with these new policies may result in funding cuts. In making this announcement, Ford argued that 'Colleges and universities should be places where students exchange different ideas and opinions in open and respectful debate … Our government made a commitment to the people of Ontario to protect free speech on campuses' (Office of the Premier, 2018: para. 2). In the UK, the university minister in 2018 was quoted as calling attempts to 'silence debate' 'chilling' and accused university student societies of being hostile to 'certain unfashionable but perfectly lawful views' (Bennett, 2018). However, in March 2018, a UK government report on freedom of speech did find universities were experiencing difficulties around 'no platforming' and regulatory guidance, but that these problems were not pervasive. The report was critical of safe spaces, but noted that equalities duties should not hinder free speech, while adhering to the law (House of Commons and House of Lords, 2018). Thus, in both the UK and Canada there are legal and political interventions into the free speech issues that might temper how resistance to LGBT equalities might be framed but in ways that are contextually specific to places with anti-discrimination (as well as anti-terrorist) legislation.

Under Ford's policies, free speech is protected speech as long as it does not include illegal speech which is captured under criminal or civil laws, which includes sanctions for speech that is threatening, defamatory, discriminatory, harassing, or is an unjustified and a substantial invasion of privacy and confidentiality or hate speech which falls under the Criminal Code or human rights legislation (Cossman, 2018). In the UK, regulatory provisions that limit free speech include fear or provocation of violence, acts intending to or likely to stir up hatred on specific grounds, including sexual orientation and encouraging or supporting terrorism (House of Commons and House of Lords, 2018). It is critical then for heteroactivists to distance their dissent, debate and different opinions from these legal confines. This is why separating their arguments regarding the importance of heteronormativity and 'hate', from homophobia, transphobia and bigotry, as we saw above, is so important. Thus, for example, Turner argues that 'we believe that in a free society, as long as no one is inciting violence, there has to be the right to be wrong' (Turner, 2019: para. 15).

How one is 'wrong' is critical given that being wrong against a secular and inclusive LGBT legislature might well be considered illegal, if those words are discriminatory. Yet focusing on incitement and keeping the definition of harm specific to physical violence ensures that heteroactivists can deny that their words, framed as 'reasonable', can be found to cause psychological or social harm. This harm is committed by 'extremists' (and not heteroactivists). Nevertheless, even 'no platforming' those who would incite violence with their words is questioned by some heteroactivists:

Most would agree that the National Union of Students are not wrong to implement a no-platform policy against al-Muhajiroun, the British National party, the English Defence League, Hizb ut-Tahrir, the Muslim Public Affairs Committee and National Action. The question, then, to those of us who agree with some attempts to no-platform participants but who disagree with the no-platforming of others, is what precisely are our criteria for curbing so-called 'free speech'? ... by failing to tolerate the intolerant one necessarily acts intolerantly and thereby does not oneself deserve to be treated with toleration. (Thomas More Institute, 2017: paras 4–5)

Pushing back against 'intolerance' challenges any criteria that might shut down 'free speech' and seeks to contest equalities legislation in the UK and Canada by pitting it against 'free speech'. This creates what Bennet (2018) calls a '"murky" legal landscape'. Accusations of intolerance are made against 'liberals' and universities because they are regarded as silencing debate. This form of silencing is deemed hypocritical because the inclusive ideals of human and LGBT rights ask for tolerance and celebration of diversity for all, while simultaneously becoming (see Chapter 5):

very unhappy if they hear anyone express a traditional view about marriage and family.

They can even accuse us of 'extremism' and 'hate speech' because we don't share their radical views, even though we only believe what everyone believed about marriage until the day before yesterday. (Coalition for Marriage, Aug. 29, 2019: paras 5–6)

This unhappiness is linked to mere emotional upset and denies accusations that these views might cause harm. The Coalition for Marriage (Aug. 29, 2019) argues it 'turns out some diversity won't be tolerated'. As we elaborate in Chapter 5, this is read as turning LGBT equalities into discrimination against Christians. Here, in seeking to establish and exploit a '"murky" legal landscape', tensions between LGBT legal inclusions and speech that questions these rights are created. These tensions seek to place LGBT rights in opposition to free speech.

Freedom of Speech Prevented by 'Ideology' and 'Indoctrination'

LGBT equalities are presented as a mode of 'indoctrination' that not only cannot tolerate dissent, but that require the creation of ideologies that work against 'science', 'truth' and 'fact' in order to exist. Heteroactivists argue that LGBT equalities require a form of ideological indoctrination in multiple ways to defend the right to question LGBT equalities, including same-sex marriage and trans people's existence. In this way, heteroactivists can frame their arguments as focusing on 'ideology' and as therefore a standpoint or opinion, deflecting accusations that they are attacking the identities of actual people. Heteroactivists argue that through the 'shutting down' of debates, particular ideologies are imposed because there is no room for discussion. Here, we consider how trans and gender rights are contested through discussions of 'ideologies' (see Chapter 3). In particular, we examine how these arguments directly attack universities (and faculty and research in particular that examines LGBT equalities) by arguing that these LGBT 'ideologies' are not 'science', 'fact' or 'truth' and further are not presented to students in a balanced way.

Central to free speech debates regarding trans people's rights are heteroactivist claims that these ideas are being imposed without proper debate which would include a 'range of valid viewpoints'. Multiple viewpoints are important, because, it is argued, 'a conflict exists between transgenderism and sex-based women's rights' in the UK (Christian Institute, Oct. 5, 2019: para. 5). In Canada, for example, women were seen as endangered by trans inclusions in public spaces including women sharing public bathrooms with 'random men' and daughters sharing a washroom with 'a man she has never met' (Perrins, 2018).

Objectors to Bill C-16, Canada's human rights gender identity protection legislation, contended that the Bill would have the effect of 'enshrining the theory of a gender spectrum into law' (Standing Senate Committee on Legal and Constitutional Affairs, 2017). The supposed inherent conflict between women and trans people then is argued to require debate, and any attempt to question the need for this debate is read as 'shutting it down' and imposing 'trans ideologies'. These ideologies were 'astonishing' and gaining strength within the adult lifetimes of commentators, making them unimaginable as well as 'weird':

> Never could I have begun to imagine that the qualification for speaking in a university, or holding down certain types of job, would become whether or not you believed that someone born a man, who mentally preferred to be seen as being a woman, had to be called a woman, or offered made up personal pronouns of their own preference. I couldn't have conceived that even Germaine Greer or Peter Tatchell, paragons of right-on, compassionate liberalism, would fail the test and have their voices silenced. And ultimately, that's what it seems to me to be all about. A strange, creeping movement of emotionally driven but ideological censorship, centred on sex, that is closing down free speech. (Conger, 2018: paras 8–9)

This 'emotional' drive of trans/gender ideologies is 'centred on sex', which could be read both as sex between people and the 'biological sex' that is foundational for heteroactivist arguments. Thus, trans/gender ideologies are, as we saw in Chapter 3, 'ludicrous', alienate 'paragons of right-on compassionate liberalism' and thus are dangerous. Part of this danger is the 'strange creeping movement' that 'closes down free speech'. It also poses dangers to (heteronormative and often religious) people's employment, the right to speak at universities and in the case of Dr Mackereth, to practise medicine, 'even though transgender ideology is contrary to science – which forms the basis of medicine and medical training' (Christian Concern, July 13, 2018).

The blame for the crisis in freedom of speech on campuses was laid squarely at the feet of academics and their universities. Heteroactivists argue that the supposedly 'poor state of free speech' on campus is a result of 'five decades of tenured radicals executing their Gramscian "long march" through the academy' (Kay, Nov. 21, 2017). Thus, heteroactivists, and mainstream media can use incidents such as the case of Lindsey Shepherd (see note 1) as evidence of the 'sorry state' of Canadian universities which no longer 'function as educative undertakings but as commitments to a narrow, predestined ideological viewpoint' (Murphy, 2017). Prominent Canadian media commentator Rex Murphy asserts that universities are riven with what is termed the 'social justice warrior' curriculum that imposes the 'iron bars of political correctness' (Murphy, 2017). Other groups have called for the shutting down of specialised institutions to 'stop tax dollars from funding the indoctrination of students' (Everyday for Life Canada, 2017). This was also called for by commentators in the UK, whose students 'go to lectures, go to the pub, go home' and are apparently influenced by left-leaning lecturers (Harris-Quinney, 2017). Students then become the innocent interlocutors, like primary school children (Chapter 2) who are not given a full range of views, because of ideological impositions by faculty, lecturers and university staff.

Heteroactivists include in their arguments about ideologies, 'the new 'values' of the LGBT movement' in the UK. They argue that you must be ideologically aligned and where 'one wrong word on homosexuality or failing to express sufficient zeal for the political ideology of the LGBTQI ... movement can end your career' (Williams, Apr. 12, 2019). One key topic was the banning of 'conversion therapy'. Heteroactivists contend that arguments against conversion therapies rested on ideologies that refused to understand alternative viewpoints. Those who wanted to access 'conversion therapy' were being 'silenced' in government consultations and associated discussions. Indeed, a film called *Voices of the Silenced* could not be shown in its intended venue due to protests against its content. This demonstrated to heteroactivists a closing down of 'debate about the value of therapeutic support to these people' and 'individual rights to change' (Christian Concern, Feb. 7, 2018). Those who shut down debate were in denial of the 'truth' that there are people who 'have no wish to remain in a gay lifestyle' and in this way were seeking to reinforce their ideological standpoints without considering other people's needs and desires.

Heteroactivists contend that these ideologies are understood as forced, because if a full range of views were presented, LGBT equalities would not be supported. For example, when the Westminster government passed legislation to legalise same-sex marriage in Northern Ireland in October 2019, as the devolved assembly had not sat since January 2017, it was contended that this also shut down debate. This was directly attributed to the weakness of the case for same-sex marriage, which was arguably not compelling and would not win support if there was an open public debate:

> Why is it that supporters of same-sex marriage so often resort to underhand tactics? If redefining marriage is so great, why can't the case be argued? (Coalition for Marriage, July 11, 2019: para. 3)

The contention that LGBT people use 'underhand tactics' rests on the claim that LGBT ideologies are not supportable by open reasonable rationale debate. Instead, as we saw in Chapters 2 and 3, heteroactivists argue they have to be forced because they are 'against reality' and neglect the 'common sense' of the majority.

'A Hill We Have to Fight On': Protecting Free Speech

Free speech is a hill that we have to fight on. If we can't express ourselves freely within the law, none of the other rights we have mean anything. (Harry Miller, quoted in Christian Concern, Feb. 1, 2019: para. 4)

The ideologies promoted through 'shutting down' debate are varied, but are seen as totalitarian, stifling and leading to the end of liberal democratic freedom (see also Chapters 2 and 3). These ideologies and those promoting them are also regarded as part of a broad cultural shift which hetero-activists define as a 'war' within universities and beyond. Thus a 'fight' is needed. Here we briefly consider not only how heteroactivists construct this 'fight' as against LGBT equalities, but also how they broaden this to include 'leftists', 'cultural Marxists' and 'progressives'. A full discussion of this area and specifically claims regarding neoliberalism and Marxist theory is beyond the scope of this book. Here we use these contentions to point to how the 'dangers' of LGBT ideologies are constructed as being imposed through human rights, and are purportedly a form of totalitarianism.

Heteroactivist arguments can go beyond discussions of LGBT equalities to suggest these equalities are only a small part of a much broader set of social and cultural problems. For example, Jordan Peterson positioned his refusal to use trans pronouns within a broader condemnation of what he regarded as progressivism, postmodernism and 'cultural Marxism'. Peterson argued that these approaches were dominating Canadian universities,[10] and that the substantial presence of Marxist and neo-Marxist faculty was promulgating a 'murderous ideology' which included 'vicious, untenable and anti-human ideas' (Peterson, 2016). Separating the human from human rights, Peterson claimed that these ideologies, as well as political correctness, dominated the campus, stifling freedom and society. Murphy (2017) has continued this form of attack by singling out the 'studies' departments (women's, queer and critical race studies) as promoting an ideological viewpoint that fostered 'fixed thought' with 'pre-chosen political goals including social justice'. The effectiveness of these heteroactivist discourses can be seen in mainstream Canadian commentary that reflects Peterson's claim that the university is controlled by Marxists. For example, Lindsey Shepherd was led to an 'interrogation room' to be 're-educated' (Everyday Life Canada, 2017) and she endured a 'Maoist "struggle session"' where her 'interrogators demonstrated that they consider "transphobia" to be an egregious thoughtcrime' (Kay, Nov. 28, 2017; see note 1, this chapter).

In the UK, 'thoughtcrimes' also emerge as a discourse (Christian Concern, Feb. 1, 2019),[11] with free speech challenged by 'a climate of fear and secrecy' (Christian Institute, May 16, 2019) because people are afraid to say what they believe about LGBT rights.[12] Gomes (2018) contended that the end result would be the 'ultimate totalitarian state' with 'human-imposed slavery' arising from 'acquiescing to a regime of political correctness'. Christian Concern (Apr. 12, 2019) quoted Lord Templeman to argue that in British society people were being watched and judged in ways that were 'reminiscent of Nazi Germany', such that 'individuals who believe in freedom are clearly facing a new Dark Age' (Apr. 12, 2019). This 'dark age' is coming about because of the 'ideological totalitarianism' weaponised by 'secularists and LGBTQ activists':

> Like it or not, this nation is caught in an ideological battle, and at stake is freedom of belief and free speech. Using the weapons of rebranded morality, secularists and LBGTQ activists are fighting to impose ideological totalitarianism that will only allow expression of their own views. They must not be allowed to succeed.
>
> In this era of rebranded morality, it is not 'alright' for followers of the libertarian god of sexual licence to attack and intimidate those who, without bigotry or hatred, express Christian belief. Only those who fear they are wrong would go to such lengths to silence and suppress any and all views that express dissent. For the future of our nation, they must not prevail. (Voice for Justice UK, n.d.a: paras 7–8)

This quote neatly encapsulates many of the arguments of this chapter, namely, that those defending free speech are 'without bigotry or hatred'. Heteroactivists contend that (heteronormative) people are experiencing silencing, because LGBT activists and others 'fear that they are wrong'. They, thus, apparently have to suppress dissenting views and this creates an 'ideological battle', which has also been termed the 'cultural wars'. Bringing together the assertions of silencing, suppression and unsupported ideologies creates an imperative to defend the 'future of our nation'.

The 'our' in the call to 'fight' is calling to a specific heteronormative group that are not 'secularists or LGBT activists'. This fight is needed to protect the nation and 'the family' against those who 'have made facts hateful' and have had a 'chilling effect on freedom of expression' (Christian Concern, Jan. 30, 2019). The 'battle' marks the UK at a 'watershed' moment, with 'militant transgender activists' pitted against 'the decent silent majority' who believe in (man/woman) marriage and (fixed sex at birth) science. Deviation from this 'nonsense' requires 'brave people' to 'pushback' and 'call out' to ensure 'all is not lost', 'for the sake of our children' (Kurten, 2017).

For many heteroactivists engaging in these arguments, the good of the nation is not only about the 'our' that is interpellated but also about needing to defend the 'future', of 'all people'. Accusations of totalitarianism, slavery and the return of the 'dark ages' pertain to the understanding that:

> Without free speech, the ideas and ideology of cultural elites – whomever they may be – cannot be challenged and democracy becomes impossible. (Christian Concern, Mar. 10, 2019: para. 9)

Democracy produced through 'free speech' in this reading is more than the need for protection for heteroactivists (and Christians). It is about protection against what they see as the abuse of power, located within, and emerging from, their resistance to the 'slavery' of 'political correctness', 'forced speech' or 'ideologies'. For many heteroactivists in the UK and Canada, if heterosexuality is for the good of society and children, free speech that seeks to put this at the forefront of debate is the pinnacle of a democracy. Democracy is read as under attack because LGBT equalities are unsupported ideologies that cannot support debate and therefore suppress it through totalitarian dictates. This attack is dangerous for everyone, and victories, such as those for Ashers Bakery, are celebrated by heteroactivists as a victory for everyone. Thus, heteroactivists, when arguing for the right to contest LGBT equalities, are simultaneously contending that when their right to challenge trans rights and claim the inferiority of same-sex marriage is secured, 'democracy becomes possible' for everyone.

Conclusion

Free speech claims are used to create spaces to contest LGBT equalities in the social and political realm. As we have shown in this chapter, these claims are complex and multifaceted but are also effective in seeking to change university spaces, and more broadly discourses regarding free speech in the popular press. In Canada, a spate of editorials, articles and online blogs vigorously asserted that freedom of speech was under serious attack on Canadian university campuses. Although a number of voices argued that there was no 'free speech' issue at Canadian universities, the assumption that there was a 'problem' prevailed (e.g. Coren, 2017; Gruneau, 2017; Woolley, 2018; Giovannetti and Hauen, 2018). These moves, alongside Doug Ford's free speech policies and UK government pronouncements on free speech at universities and colleges, illustrate the questionable presumptions that heteroactivism is irrelevant or 'dying out'. Instead it shows a resurgence of possibilities for opposing sexual and gender equalities under the guise of 'freedom of speech'. Therefore, contestations of free speech are critical to understanding heteroactivism, and heteroactivists' deflection and rejection of accusations of harm and bigotry are critical to creating space in UK, Irish and Canadian legislative landscapes.

Seeking space to debate LGBT rights is particularly important where equalities and human rights laws explicitly prohibit discrimination, hate speech and incitement to violence against LGBT people. Freedom of speech counters accusations of bigotry and homophobia, and there is an ongoing resistance around accusations of hate. Heteroactivists seek to deflect accusations of being homophobic by limiting its meaning to a narrow understanding of the term. The reframing of arguments away from vilification of gays and lesbians to alternative arguments renders accusations of homophobia increasingly ineffective if it is understood in the narrow sense. Freedom of speech claims have become a dominant theme in the Canadian and UK debates about gender and trans rights (see Nash and Browne, 2019 for a discussion of Canadian debates in this area). Here we also showed how arguments against trans rights and gender non-conformity have been developed through 'compelled speech', and ideologies to which the 'majority' would object.

While we have focused on those debates that do relate to LGBT equalities, there is much more to be done to explore how sexualities and genders are affected by free speech debates, without necessarily referencing them, or referring specifically to sexual/trans/gender rights in passing as a list of areas where free speech is restricted. Building from the arguments in this chapter we now turn to examine how claims to the restrictions and dangers of LGBT equalities can be further interrogated through how hetero-activists claim their rights to public space.

5

Public Inclusions: Claiming the Place of Heteroactivism

Introduction

With the implementation of LGBT equalities in Canada, the UK and Ireland, as we have seen in the previous chapter, heteroactivists argue that their right to dissent is under threat. We extend this discussion here by focusing on how heteroactivists are increasingly arguing that they are required to cope with the visible public acknowledgement (and often acceptance) of LGBT people. Many argue that in the everyday spaces of public life, not only are heteronormative values no longer considered the dominant (or respected) moral framework for social life, but LGBT

equalities are driving the expression of these heteronormative values (as well as those who hold those views) from
public life. This chapter explores how, for heteroactivists,
LGBT equalities have reconstituted public spaces including
workplaces, state institutions and commercial or corporate
entities, in ways that undermine the dominance of heteronormative values and practices in the public sphere.

In this chapter, we begin with a brief discussion of
several core themes found in the scholarship on geographies of 'the public', including sexualities work in this area,
before outlining key transformations underway in both UK
and Canada related to LGBT equalities and public space.
We then consider how heteroactivist organisations approach these transformations and the arguments they make
about their exclusion from public life, including through
positioning Christianity in opposition to LGBT rights.
Thus, despite demonstrating throughout that secular argumentation is critical for 21st-century heteroactivism in
Canada, the UK and Ireland, we show here that where
rights are put into a binary and constructed as oppositional,
particularly in court rooms, religious freedom discourses
are re-centralised (see also Cooper, 2019). Again, however,
heteroactivists do not make theological claims but instead
frame their arguments as rights claims. Heteroactivist
groups argue that changes in the public sphere that require
acceptance of LGBT equalities challenge their fundamental human rights, and are thus totalitarian, highlighting
the supposed threat of LGBT equalities. This chapter, in

bringing together key themes from across the book, shows how public spaces are constructed as exclusionary to heteroactivists, and how they use this to argue that LGBT equalities pose threats to the wellbeing of the West, 'their' nation, the family and society.

Defining 'Publics': Rights, Exclusions and Spaces

Several decades of sexualities and queer research points out how individuals whose sexual or gendered expression operates outside of accepted heteronormative expectations are often excluded from full participation in public spaces under threat of harassment and violence (e.g. Callaghan and van Leent, 2019; Piekut and Valentine, 2016; Rushbrook, 2002; Smith, 2019; Uhrig, 2015). Sexual and gender minorities have worked to participate in public life as full citizens through inclusion in state institutions such as marriage, the military and access to health and family benefits (Bell and Binnie, 2000; Bell et al., 1994; Binnie, 2007; Stychin, 2003). Scholarship and queer activism have long asserted the importance of queer visibility, recognition and acceptance in public space for promoting tolerance and equality for LGBT people (Gorman-Murray and Nash, 2016; Johnston, 2005; Richardson, 1998; Tucker, 2009). With the advent of LGBT equalities in Canada, the UK and Ireland, heteroactivists find themselves having to grapple with the visible presence of LGBT people in public spaces. LGBT visibility includes annual Pride parades, rainbow flags in businesses and symbols of support that may be visible in one's workplaces. LGBT visibility in local institutions such as places of worship, libraries, community centres and schools arguably challenges the dominance of heteronormative values in public spaces. As we discussed in Chapter 2, heteroactivists have often claimed that institutions such as public schools are value 'neutral' without recognising the historically specific heteronormative values entrenched in those spaces (e.g. Nash and Browne, 2019). Before we explore heteroactivist responses to changes in public life, we pause to locate these changes within the broader literature of 'publics', and particularly how sexual and gender geographers have discussed exclusions from publics, in ways that can be traced through heteroactivist arguments.

What is meant by 'public life', the 'public sphere' or the 'public realm' is the subject of considerable geographical scholarship (e.g. Fraser, 1990; Harvey, 2003b, 2010, 2012; Lefebvre, 1991; Mitchell, 2003; Rose, 1999; Staeheli and Mitchell, 2008; Staeheli et al., 2009). For our purposes here, we use the term 'public life' in several ways in order to understand heteroactivist arguments. First, public life entails access to and participation in those myriad material public spaces of political and social engagement including public parks and streets, entertainment venues, restaurants, cafes, stores and shopping malls where strangers may interact through serendipitous encounters (Staeheli and Mitchell, 2008). As geographers have argued, fair and open access to public spaces is one of the hallmarks of a free and open society although such spaces have never been completely open and access for particular groups, including women and LGBT people, has been historically restricted (Bell and Valentine, 1995b; Valentine, 1989; Wilson, 1992). For this reason, LGBT people have struggled to occupy public spaces not only to affirm their identities but to make a political statement about their existence and inclusion (e.g. Johnston and Waitt, 2015; Kenttamaa Squires, 2019; Murphy and Watson, 1997; Stychin and Herman, 2000). Geographers, planners and urbanists have also long argued about the importance of creating open public spaces to foster harmony, tolerance and shared social and cultural values (Lefebvre, 1991; Mitchell, 2017). Therefore, public spaces, in their idealistic conceptualisation, are understood as critical for social and political engagements which can alter the fabric of everyday life (Harvey, 2003a; Marcuse, 2009). For this reason, the ability to fully participate in public spaces requires visibility, recognition and acceptance as a full citizen who is able to engage in such debates on their merit (Gorman-Murray and Nash, 2016; see also Davis 1990; Mitchell, 1996; Mitchell and Heynen, 2009; Young, 1990). Heteroactivists, as we will show, are arguing that they are being excluded as full citizens from myriad public spaces through what they see as the diminishment of their heteronormative values. As a result, they contend that they no longer have free and open access to public spaces and their identities and values are not affirmed but, in many cases, are in fact denigrated.

In this understanding of public space, we also include certain micro-geographies, including those of the workplace. As geographers argue, such places are also constituted through myriad engagements that cross gendered, racialised and classed social and cultural contexts that reflect uneven hierarchical social relations (e.g. Leitner, 2012; Nayak, 2016; Ray and Preston, 2015). Finally, we include in this understanding of public space the ordinary interactions with the state which now render LGBT lives and families visible and mainstream through those mundane activities such as renewing a driver's license or obtaining a passport. Our focus in this chapter is on those moments when these public interactions become heteroactivist flashpoints in the UK and Canada, such as in court cases, media debates or other forms of engagement.

Contexts: Canada and the UK

In order to explore how heteroactivists are challenging this reordering of public spaces, we explore specific contestations around public life in Canada and the UK. These include flashpoints discussed across the book, drawing together key themes in this final data-based chapter. There is less prominence to these debates in Ireland in our data, thus we focus on Canada and the UK.

In the UK, sexual orientation and gender identities are named as protected characteristics in legislation (Equality Act, 2010). This leads directly to a public sector duty enshrined in law to protect against discrimination in the workplace and in the delivery of goods or services, and to promote 'good relations' between different 'protected' groups (see Browne and Bakshi, 2013; McGlynn, 2014). LGBT visibility has also been noted by heteroactivists in their perceptions of transformations in media representations, and various initiatives such as Pride buses, local council initiatives such as gender equalities and inclusions, and shops/department stores introducing gender-neutral clothing. All of these, it could be argued, have altered the way the state is sexualised and gendered, and in turn how public spaces can be sexualised and gendered. Heteroactivist opposition to these inclusions has been wide ranging. The legalities of gender and sexual inclusions have been tested through workplace disciplinary procedures and dismissals from universities, government organisations and non-profits. Heteroactivist resistances have included opposition to activities by shops and the media that seem to promote gender and sexual inclusivity.

In Canada, same-sex marriage (2005) has altered the social and political landscape over the last decade and a half. In this chapter, we examine several high-profile events to detail how heteroactivists understand the impact of LGBT equalities in terms of their engagement in public life. We closely examine the case of Trinity Western University, a Christian Evangelical University in British Columbia that, in seeking to establish a law school, required students sign a mandatory pledge abstaining from sexual relations outside of man/woman marriage. The proposal was opposed by several provincial law societies who were successful on appeal to the Supreme Court of Canada. For heteroactivist Christians, the loss is portrayed as having profound implications for Christian participation in public life. In addition, many workplaces in Canada are largely supportive of LGBT rights though corporate workplace policies and there is a highly visible corporate presence at Pride parades in major cities across the country. Finally, at all levels of government, official state policies have been revised to reflect LGBT equalities; documents such as driver's licences and passports now reflect LGBT participation in public life.

Religious Freedom or LGBT Rights

Religion, including Christianity, is not necessarily antithetical to LGBT equalities, and Christianity has been shown to include LGBT people, for example, across various factions of the Anglican church (see Andersson et al., 2013; Valentine et al., 2012; Vanderbeck et al., 2010). As Yip and Nynäs (2016) argue, there has been an overemphasis on negative religious precepts against homosexuality while overlooking the agency of those sexual and gender minorities who practise religion/spirituality (see also Browne et al., 2010; Hunt and Yip, 2016; Taylor, 2016; Yip, 2018). Nonetheless, religion, and specifically Christianity, still plays an important role in Canada, the UK and Ireland in animating oppositions to LGBT equalities. These play out as 'public' around public expressions of religion and claims related to religious freedom. Public religious expression is often defined by speech acts and incorporates free speech arguments as well.

While religious heteroactivists raised various free speech arguments which we discussed in the previous chapter, we examine in more detail here what Christian Legal Centre's chief executive, Andrea Minichiello Williams calls: '[t]he face of the new political orthodoxy ... It tries to silence opposing views and if it fails it crushes and punishes the person who holds those views' (Christian Concern, Mar. 10, 2016: para. 16). Despite evidence of disagreements within religious organisations over how to manage the impacts of LGBT equalities, heteroactivist discussions of religion and sexual and gender equalities are often based on binary understandings that pit religious freedom as inherently opposed to sexual and gender rights (Hunt and Yip, 2016; Valentine et al., 2013). In Canada, for example, as we discussed in Chapter 2, Leishman (2018) argued that it is 'evident' that 'the judiciary has obliterated the historic right to the free exercise of religion' in the case of Scott Brockie, who refused to print material for the Lesbian and Gay Archives (a historical society) because of his religious beliefs. The Ontario Human Rights Commission, in 2000, held Brockie was not free 'to practice those beliefs in a manner that discriminates against lesbians and gays by denying them a service available to everyone else' (Leishman, 2018: para. 13). Similarly, Care UK contended:

There are nine protected characteristics under the Equality Act 2010 ... In theory all the protected characteristics should be treated as equally important and all rights protected, but in practice these different rights often push in diametrically opposing directions. This is particularly problematic if one protected characteristic repeatedly clashes with and quashes another protected characteristic. For example, religious discrimination has been given lower priority than discrimination on the grounds of sexual orientation. The rationale for such a reality is that religion is a choice, whereas other protected characteristics are 'objective' ... Such a perception of religion as a hobby or as a choice damages the right of individuals who would wish to manifest their religious belief, including in places like the workplace. (Care UK, 2017)

In feeling 'quashed' by sexual orientation, heteroactivists see religious rights and LGBT equalities as pushing in 'diametrically opposing directions'. According to heteroactivists, religious rights have existed since 'Anglo-Saxon times' and that 'men and women, being made in the image of God, were all alike and worthy of honour and respect' (Voice for Justice UK, 2015). The Anglo-Saxon reference is both racial and religious, claiming both longevity and whiteness as underpinning British society – a point we return to below. What is important to note here is that heteroactivists regard themselves as under threat because they are being 'remade by society' and 'the unfortunate result [is] that we are no longer all equal' (Voice for Justice UK, 2015). For heteroactivists, pursing an equality agenda is important in arguing for Christian/religious rights which have until now been historically enshrined and unassailable biblical precedents. The 'no longer' in this quote illustrates a loss, and a nostalgia for a specific version of the past where 'all' were equal. Instead of seeing the 21st-century inclusions as creating equalities, UK society is perceived by some as stripping rights from (particularly Christian) men and women, who were once 'all alike and worthy of honour and respect' (Voice for Justice UK, 2015).

The perception of the loss of religious freedom to sexual and gender equalities means that in the workplace, Christians are perceived as endangered by the 'new belief system' which is hostile to Christians (Voice for Justice UK, 2015). In Canada, heteroactivist groups argued that the decision of the Supreme Court of Canada regarding Trinity Western University amounted to the exclusion of the religious from the public sphere and reflected 'anti-Christian bigotry' in the court's negative perception of the impact of the community covenant (Campaign Life Coalition, June 15, 2018). In that case, law societies in both Ontario and British Columbia indicated they would not admit Trinity Western University law graduates, effectively preventing them from practising in those provinces despite acknowledgement that the university's proposed programme would graduate qualified candidates. In June 2018, the Supreme Court of Canada upheld the law societies' decision on several grounds, including the argument that the community covenant would deter LGBT students from attending, and that equal access to legal education and protecting LGBT people was important for law societies to uphold in the public interest.[1] This case has implications beyond the legal profession for professions that are also self-governing, including the medical profession, social workers and engineers who might also exclude some from membership for views perceived as discriminatory.

The Supreme Court of Canada decision, in the eyes of those who opposed it, represents a desire to 'push religion from the public square so that it will no longer be an integral part of public dialogue' (Real Women of Canada, 2018). This was seen as marking an infringement of the rights of religious entities to determine their own internal institutional policies matching their beliefs and moral values while participating in the public sphere (Real Women of Canada, 2018). As Margaret Wente, a columnist from the mainstream Canadian newspaper *Globe and Mail* argued, the decision marked 'another giant step in the marginalisation of conservative Christians who are becoming ever more endangered species in public life' (Wente, 2018). Bruce Clemenger, President of the Evangelical Fellowship of Canada argued:

The freedom of all Canadians to express, exercise, and associate on the basis of our faith is under attack. Professional accrediting agencies may not approve of the moral and religious positions of TWU, but our faith *can* not and *should* not be subjected to public validation. They should not have the authority to ban qualifying graduates from working in their profession, impose barriers, or create additional hurdles for them to qualify. (Evangelical Fellowship of Canada, 2016, emphasis in the original)

For heteroactivists, the Trinity Western University decision seemingly made clear that while it was acceptable to be a Christian 'within the four walls of your church', if you wanted to 'apply that faith in a community, outside the institutional church, all bets are off' (Ritchie, 2018). As a result, faith is 'essentially banned from public spaces' (Van Maren, June 18, 2018). It was also contended that people were being forced to act against their conscience and their religion. Heteroactivists pointed out that marriage commissioners in Saskatchewan are forced to perform same-sex marriage and doctors in Ontario were denied the right to refuse to undertake procedures they might object to on religious, faith-based or conscientious grounds (Ross and Kinsinger, 2019; see also Lewis, July 4, 2018).

In the UK, Kurten (2017) details the multiple ways that those opposed to sexual and gender rights might find themselves confronted with new laws and regulations. He contends that people should be allowed to express opposition to same-sex marriage or to same-sex couples adopting children, 'without fear of penalty or punishment' and that 'parents with traditional, conservative viewpoints are being struck off adoption and fostering lists'. In Canada, a similar situation arose in 2018, when a Christian couple sought to foster and indicated that they believed homosexuality was a sin. They were advised that their application to foster had been dismissed based on 'values and beliefs', a decision they are currently challenging (Gryboski, 2019).

These examples highlight heteroactivist concerns that Christians and, by extension, other religious groups, are being deliberately excluded from public life. In Canada, heteroactivists portrayed the Trinity Western University decision as part of an escalation in attacks on Christian communities. They argued that communities in Canada, 'whether it's the Catholic Church, the Salvation Army or Muslim and Jewish charitable organisations' as well as those they termed 'traditionally minded', are increasing understood as under attack through the institutionalisation of LGBT equalities throughout all levels of government as well (Van Maren, June 18, 2018; see also Lewis, Mar. 14, 2018).

For heteroactivists, this marginalisation of Christianity in public life in Canada and the UK was designed to privatise religion within the walls of the church or render it a personal domestic matter. Christianity as a faith has had a significant role in shaping public discourses and policies in the 20th century and indeed 21st century in the UK and Canada (and Ireland) (see Johnson and Vanderbeck, 2015; McAuliffe and Kennedy, 2017). Given its goal is to recruit and convert others, restrictions on public expressions of 'traditional' Christianity and 'biblical' truths are read as extremely problematic to 'what it means to live out your faith in the public sphere' (Christian Legal Centre, June 19, 2019). Living one's faith in the public sphere means that it is more than what one believes, but a willingness 'to talk about it in the public square' (Christian Today, 2019). For Andrea Minichiello Williams, chief executive of Christian Legal Centre, exclusion from the public square has the effect of 'ruling out conscientious, informed Christians' from public life (Christian Legal Centre, June 19, 2019; see also Flyn, 2018). 'Christian views' are being therefore discriminated against in a way that punishes 'individuals … for beliefs which are held in good faith by many sincere and reasonable people' (Christian Concern, May 9b, 2019).

For some, the question is about more than removing Christians from public life. As the Family Education Trust (2018) asserts, 'the UK is a Christian country. Our laws and culture are founded on Christian beliefs'. The focus on Christianity and references to 'Anglo-Saxon' histories point to what heteroactivists see as the significant contributions to, and underpinnings of, Canadian and British society. In Canada, Jordan Peterson, whose religious positioning is unclear, argued that 'society might implode without the Judea-Christian traditions and ethics it is built upon' (Van Maren, June 20, 2018). The assertion of Judeo-Christian values, as well as Anglo-Saxon histories, as central to both Canadian and British society enables heteroactivists to argue that the focus should be on the challenges for the 'majority' rather than 'promoting minority interests' (Family Education Trust, 2018). This then leads to claims for 'Equal rights for Christians! Protect the right of Christians to uphold and practise their faith' (Family Education Trust, 2018). Consequently, in these readings, 'minority' priorities are outside of the public interest and are resulting in the silencing of Christians, whose values and beliefs are pivotal to Canadian and British societies. These 'Judea-Christian societies' implicitly foreground the whiteness (Anglo-Saxon) of these societies through assertions of 'majority' interests that also position heteronormative relationships and lives as superior (Boulila, 2019). Finally, by challenging Christianity, LGBT equalities are understood as detrimental to Canadian and British society more broadly.

Separating the Message and the Messenger: Challenging the Binary?

To this point, we highlight how, in these debates, religious conviction and Christianity more directly, is positioned as distinct from, opposed to and better for society than one that supports LGBT equalities. In Canada and the UK, heteroactivists see religious freedoms as 'losing' to LGBT 'agendas'. Legally, however, in the UK, Christian Concern and the Christian Legal Centre have had success in separating the message from the messenger, blurring the lines between oppositions to LGBT rights based on religious freedom. In particular, in separating the lack of support for 'gay rights' from perceptions that this is discriminating against individual people, they have carved a legal space in the UK that contests the portrayal of opposition to LGBT rights and religious freedom as an either/or proposition.

In 2017, the Christian Legal Centre lost the Richard Page case against the National Health Service (NHS) which prevented Page from being a non-executive director, in part because of the potential impact of his appointment on LGBT patients as he refused to use their preferred pronouns. Christian Concern argued that there was a better way to handle this situation that could accommodate Page's views while reassuring LGBT patients that there would be no effects on services. Christian Concern argued the NHS trust could have:

> issued a public statement to achieve this balance, reiterating that Richard was speaking in a private capacity and that his opinions were not necessarily shared by the trust and more so, that his position in the trust was wholly separate from any decisions made in relation to patient care. (Christian Concern, June 21, 2019)

This tactic of separating the messenger from the message worked on appeal in the Ashers Bakery case, where refusing to bake a cake supporting gay marriage was differentiated from discriminating against a person who asked to be served because of their sexual orientation (see Chapter 4). This creates an entitlement for everyone 'to refuse to promote a message they disagree' with (Christian Concern, Aug. 16, 2019). In England, a bus driver asked passengers to wait while he swapped a bus from one branded with Pride rainbow colours because, as he told passengers 'I am not driving this bus because it promotes homosexuality'. Andrea Williams contended:

> If the driver's objection to the rainbow colours was based on his religious or philosophical beliefs, it is illegal for an employer to discriminate against him because of those beliefs. Employers have to be very careful in handling such situations, because in the eyes of the law, discrimination on the grounds of beliefs is just as bad as discrimination on the grounds of sexual orientation. (Christian Concern, Aug. 16, 2019: para. 9)

In separating the messenger and the message, discrimination is possible when it is not directed at people, rather at the refusal to engage with symbols or material things (such as buses or cakes). This enables Andrea Williams to argue that it is *the bus driver's rights* that are at stake in refusing to 'promote homosexuality', and that this does not contravene laws that prevent discrimination in the delivery of goods or services. Her position also contests the supposed divide between Christianity and LGBT rights, because they recognise the bus driver (as with Ashers bakery) cannot engage with LGBT people in discriminatory ways.

Heteroactivists have also supported the separation of belief from actions, which blurs the line between oppositional readings of religion and supporting LGBT equalities. Peter Tatchell (a UK gay rights activist), who experienced being no platformed (see Nash, Gorman-Murray and Browne, 2019), was quoted by the Christian Institute as saying:

> I think it is perfectly possible that a person can hold a deep religious view that homosexuality is wrong, such as my own mother, but she would never ever discriminate against a gay person. I know that from experience. (Christian Institute, July 9, 2019: para. 11)

Here Tatchell argues it is possible to both hold 'deep religious views that homosexuality is wrong' and not discriminate against 'a gay person'. He argues there can be a separation of the person, and their expressed anti-LGBT views, from the position they hold and their actions. This enables heteroactivists to claim that they can both express a public form of anti-LGBT views and continue to hold leadership positions and/or jobs that require inclusivity around LGBT equalities or at least in the UK non-discrimination on the grounds of sexual orientation and gender identity.

LGBT People Are to Blame for Religious Exclusions from the Public Sphere

In these arguments, the 'blame' for the potential exclusion of the religious or 'traditionally minded' from the public

Heteroactivism

sphere is often placed on LGBT activists, a grouping that heteroactivists both homogenise and vilify. *LifeSite News* claims churches and places of worship were going to be under fire as 'the next strategic move on the part of Canadian LGBT activists' (Van Maren, Nov. 19, 2018). LGBT activists were portrayed as 'unremitting and vicious' (Voice for Justice UK, n.d.c) in their attacks against 'any and all Christians who hold to traditional beliefs' (Voice for Justice UK, n.d.a). Christian Concern (Oct. 3, 2017) focused their arguments on proving:

> just how totalitarian the LGBT movement is. They cannot tolerate any whiff of dissent. They demand not just tolerance, but unanimous approval and celebration. Anything less is met with name-calling, vilification and punishment. This lobby is deeply illiberal and unkind. We can only pray for them. (para. 28)

Such an approach once again pits LGBT in opposition to, and indeed in battle with, 'Christians who hold traditional beliefs', with those 'traditional' Christians being subjected to a totalitarian LGBT movement. *LifeSite News* argued that LGBT activists would now be challenging the charitable tax status of religious institutions and those who objected to 'their ideology of sexuality' would be labelled as 'homophobes' or 'transphobes' (Van Maren, Nov. 19, 2018, see also Chapter 4). Current LGBT activism then for heteroactivists demonstrates the 'ugly face of the LGBT lobby' who 'will not be satisfied until they have eliminated any whiff of dissent in public life. They are the bullies' (Christian Concern, Aug. 1, 2017).

In focusing on 'the LGBT movement', heteroactivists in both Canada and the UK avoid appearing to attack LGBT people individually by blaming contestations on the 'radical' or 'extreme' agendas of LGBT activists and their perceived assault on religious communities. However, there were exceptions to this, for example in the case of social work student Felix Ngole who lost his place on a course at the University of Sheffield, UK, for explaining the 'Bible's position on marriage and homosexuality'. Professor Jacqueline Marsh chaired the committee that determined Ngole's removal and was described as a 'long-standing LGBT campaigner'. Christian Concern argued this was an 'undisclosed conflict of interest' that 'makes the committee's decision unsafe' (Christian Concern, Oct. 3, 2017). There was no indication of her religion – as it was assumed that her LGBT 'campaigning' made her unsuitable. In Canada, individual politicians, particularly those who are out as LGBT or overtly supportive of LGBT equalities, were also targeted, including Ontario Premier Kathleen Wynne, an out lesbian, Prime Minister Justin Trudeau, and his father, Pierre Trudeau, who was instrumental in decriminalising homosexuality in the late 1960s. Justin Trudeau in particular was targeted because of his participation in gay Pride parades and his formal apology on behalf of the Canadian government in November 2017 for the government's past treatment of gays and lesbians (e.g. Real Women of Canada, Dec. 4, 2017).

Heteroactivists understand their opponents not only as made up of radical LGBT activists but as also including 'Leftist radicals', 'progressives' and 'elites' who are engaging in a war on faith (Van Maren, June 18, 2018; see also Chapter 4). This helps deflect accusations that heteroactivists are opposed to just LGBT activists by widening their fight against a broader group. Christian Concern concluded that the case of Felix Ngole demonstrated the nature and consequences of this opposition:

> Some of those he [Felix Ngole] was in communication with were not so polite about Christians. Then came the anonymous complaint. This student need never be identified or required to give an account for her actions of discrimination and hatred of Christians. The student continues her life as normal; presumably now pursuing her career in social work; she eats, sleeps, continues and never has to face the consequences of her actions or be forced to go public with her accusations ... Better not say what you think at school, university, or work. Someone will not like it. Christian – you know what will happen – anonymous complaint; internal 'investigation'; Christian out. Felix's case is important because it illuminates the open hostility

to the teaching of Christ by our elites. (Christian
Concern, Apr. 12, 2019: paras 8–12)

Seeing Christians as under attack by elites who are supportive of LGBT rights, paints a very particular picture of
the place of heteroactivists. They are discriminated against
and hated, according to Christian Concern, and subjected
to 'unparalleled bigotry and intimidation by self-appointed
spokespersons for minority groups' and by those who want
to 'drive Christianity entirely from the public domain'
(Voice for Justice UK, n.d.a). Naming all Christians, rather
than 'Christians who follow traditional beliefs' here, recon-
stitutes a collective (often considered a majority) in need of
protection in order to defend their rights.

Heteroactivists point to the dangers of LGBT inclusions
that are pushed by 'the LGBT agenda'. Both public and
state support of the LGBT agenda 'elites', 'progressives'
and 'feminists' for them highlight the dangers of LGBT
inclusions. These 'agendas' and those 'pushing them' are
powerful enough to pressure for the enactment of legislation, to encourage production of guidelines for state bodies
and to, in effect, remake the state and the nation. For example, bodies such as the Government Equality Office (GEO)
in the UK (and provincial and federal Human Rights
Commissions in Canada) have been critiqued by heteroactivists for neglecting (or indeed persecuting them in the
case of the Equality Commission for Northern Ireland), as
well as ignoring 'public concern and opposition':

[D]espite its name, the GEO only really concerns itself with an 'equal outcomes' feminism and LGBT rights ... [T]he GEO has no serious intention whatsoever of taking into account public concern and opposition to its crazy plans, such as making changing gender easier, pushing for a 'must-stay-gay' law to punish counsellors, therapists and pastors, and nodding towards more abortion rights and appointing more women to public leadership roles – but only as long as they toe the ideological line. (Christian Concern, July 11, 2019: para. 2)

Toeing the 'ideological line' is not just the role of government organisations, but also the media who, in Christian Concern's terms, are 'fomenting a culture war in the UK' by 'pushing LGBT ideology' (Christian Concern, June 7, 2019). Whereas once the 'elites' and those in power were seen as 'neutral' in their support of heteronormative families, they are now promoting an 'ideology' foisted on 'the silent majority' by aggressive, organised and bullying LGBTQ activists, 'the LGBT movement', 'feminists', 'the elite' and 'liberals'.

Dangers of LGBT Public Inclusions

For heteroactivists, a major goal has been to demonstrate that state's support of LGBT equalities, through legislative and policy changes, has had a serious impact on a broad range of groups. These moves are seen to have broad national and worldwide implications and have to be enforced through the supposed 'totalitarianism' of LGBT equalities, in part because these equalities are so 'ludicrous' that they are not justifiable to 'reasonable' people (see Chapter 3). Threats these equalities pose included precipitating the decline of the family, being threatening to children, and undermining Canadian and British society. Thus, the supposed exclusion of Christianity from the public sphere was seen to affect a broad swathe of people, and society itself.

The Law Societies of Ontario and British Columbia were successful in their suit against Trinity Western's required community covenant for those entering their proposed law school. Following closely on the Supreme Court of Canada's decision, the Law Society of Ontario introduced a new policy requiring all members to sign a diversity statement.[2] In effect, all members:

> are required to create and abide by an individual Statement of Principles that acknowledges your obligation to promote equality, diversity and inclusion generally, and in your behaviour towards colleagues, employees, clients and the public. (Law Society of Ontario, n.d.)

Opponents of the Law Society of Ontario's diversity policy painted it as only one of a series of initiatives that might lead to the exclusion of the religious and the 'traditionally minded' from the workplace and public life. Opponents argued that the Law Society's diversity policy demonstrated that the Trinity Western decision could affect a number of professions with accrediting administrative bodies including doctors, nurses, social workers as well as lawyers. Some of those professionals may have personal moral or religious commitments that might impact on their being able to obtain employment or to publicly declare their moral or religious beliefs (Van Maren, June 18, 2018; see also Evangelical Fellowship of Canada, May 1, 2016; Carpay, July 30, 2018). In the UK, in 2017, there was a suggestion that holders of public office might have to 'swear an oath to "British values"' (which were read to be inclusive of LGBT equalities, as well as Islam) which would lead to 'Christians being excluded from public office because of what they believe' and 'barred from serving' their communities (Williams, Jan. 13, 2017). The 'freedom to be a committed Christian while holding a professional role' was threatened as 'magistrates to nurses, teachers to doctors, Christian professionals are increasingly under pressure to hide away their beliefs' (Christian Concern, Mar. 10, 2019).

In Canada, the Trinity Western University case was held out as an example of the narrowing of the freedom of association, that is, the ability to 'gather with like-minded people' (e.g. sports clubs, political groups or cultural associations) who might not support LGBT equalities and which could adversely affect employment opportunities (Evangelical

Fellowship, May 1, 2016). Similarly, in the aftermath of the Felix Ngole case in the UK (in July 2019 the Court of Appeals ruled that the university should reconsider Ngole's case), Christian Concern contended:

> If social workers and social work students must not express such views, then what of art therapists, occupational therapists, paramedics, psychologists, radiographers, speech and language therapists: all professions whose students and practitioners work under the rubric of the same general regulations? What of teachers and student teachers? … As the judges recognised, this would not just be a bar to Christians, but Jews, Muslims, Hindus, Buddhists, and members of other faiths. This is a victory for all of us and for freedom of expression for professionals of all kinds. (Christian Concern, July 10, 2019: paras 6–8)

'Victories' such as these were seen as benefitting people beyond those Christians who seek to oppose LGBT equalities. Here Christian Concern invites other religions to share their victory, assuming that they would also want to oppose LGBT equalities. This invited inclusion (see Ahmed, 2012 for a discussion of invited diversity) is contrasted with LGBT equalities which, heteroactivists assert, result in 'totalitarian' regulations that oppose both the full functioning of democracies and undermine the 'truth' of family and society (see also Chapter 3 and 4). In the UK, a person's social media pages were used as evidence in court cases to support grounds for dismissal. Christian Concern used this to contend that freedom in the UK was under threat, through a 'secret policing' that seeks to keep Christians 'quiet and present themselves in a way that seems reasonable and acceptable' (Christian Concern, Apr. 26b, 2017).

Focusing on the 'truth' of the best place for children within heteronormative marriages or the 'realities' of sex, UK heteroactivists contended that a 'world of totalitarianism' is upon us along with a loss of 'common sense', with the elites serving minority interests, in contrast to the majority (Dieppe, 2018; Kurten, 2017; Voice for Justice UK, 2015). The perception of the loss of common sense has come about through a lack of focus on 'the truth', and is also understood to be contained within UK law:

> [S]ection 149 of the Equalities Act 2010, otherwise known as the 'Public Sector Equalities Duty' ... requires all those working in the public sector to foster good relationships with people with 'protected characteristics'. This is ill-defined, but after the long march through the institutions where Marxian ideologues now have power in the majority of public bodies, it is being implemented in a totalitarian manner. (Kurten, 2017: para. 11)

Similar state moves to affirm rights that seek to limit discrimination in Canada have also been labelled a form of totalitarianism (and Marxism). For example, in December 2017, Prime Minister Trudeau's liberal government required those seeking federal government funding to support student summer employment (including religious organisations, charities, non-profits and small business), to attest that their core mandate and the jobs being funded respected human rights and the 'values underlying' the Charter. This included 'reproductive rights and the right to be free from discrimination on the basis of sex, religion, race, national or ethnic origin, colour, mental or physical disability, sexual orientation, or gender identity or expression' (Geddes, 2018). This attestation was clearly problematic for organisations that did not support LGBT equalities, such as same-sex marriage. Heteroactivists portrayed this attestation as a religious test (although it applied to all applicants) and as limiting access to government funds 'to those who affirm not only the laws of the country, but the ideology of the dominant party' (Laurence, Jan. 11, 2018) and functioned as an 'ideological purity test' (Association for Reformed Political Action, 2017).

Canadian heteroactivists called these actions by the federal government 'totalitarian' actions by 'radical social liberals' who were demonising those dissenting from the left-wing agenda (Boquet, 2017; see also Tuns, 2018). The federal government's position was an example, they argued, of the threat to 'freedom of pro-life and pro-family activists all across the West and throughout the world' (Boquet, 2017). In the UK, Voice for Justice UK claimed that the 'nation is caught in an ideological battle' with 'secularists and LBGTQ activists … fighting to impose ideological totalitarianism' (Voice for Justice UK, n.d.a). By framing LGBT inclusions as a threat to the 'nation', 'the West and the world', heteroactivists sought to reclaim the importance of Christianity and heteronormative family life to contemporary Western societies (which are portrayed as the pinnacle of civilisation).

This presumption of a threat to Western values also has specific and distinctive racial and class overtones. As we noted in Chapter 2, those opposed to the Ontario sexual education curriculum drew together a broad coalition of immigrant groups, claiming that immigrants are inherently conservative and therefore, by implication, unsupportive of LGBT equalities. Taking this racial perspective further, in a 2019 article, Van Maren (Aug. 7, 2019) racialised opposition to LGBT equalities by claiming that Trudeau's support of LGBT people 'largely appeals to white people'. He argued that those who suggest that some people are 'intolerant' are actually speaking against 'Sikhs, Hindus, Muslims, Orthodox Jews, and orthodox Christians, [who] all reject the LGBT redefinition of marriage'. Further, new Canadians, according to a recent poll, are 'profoundly conservative on social issues' and Trudeau is therefore calling non-white Canadians 'intolerant'. This argument is echoed by REAL Women who suggest that 'individuals with these faith-based beliefs refuse to accept the changes demanded by the radical thinkers on the left' (Real Women of Canada, 2019).

The dangers posed to nations and the West are also made evident in heteroactivist reactions to the government's decision to issue non-binary and gender-neutral passports. In June 2019, the Canadian government permitted three gender categories: male, female and 'x' for another gender (Government of Canada, 2019). Heteroactivists argued that this move further entrenched the 'false ideology of "gender fluidity"' in state documents (Laurence, Aug. 30, 2017). Jack Fonseca, of CLC argued that '[t]he government [is] trying to force its citizenry, *en masse*, to deny scientific fact and biological reality' and places children 'at risk for sexual confusion' (Laurence, Aug. 30, 2017). Andrea Williams, from Christian Concern, argued that similar moves to create gender-neutral passports in the UK were 'the authorities pandering to excessive ideologically driven movements that want to obliterate the notion of biological sex' (Knowles, 2017). This initiative was understood as evidence of trans/ gender non-conforming inclusions being 'a global security risk and would undoubtedly make the UK a serious nuisance as it tries to get along with most of the world's countries' (Christian Concern, June 28, 2018).

At the provincial level, in 2017, Ontario adopted new guidelines allowing birth certificates, health cards and driver's licences to display and 'X' or 'U' for those who do not identify as male or female. While many argued the new provisions provided recognition and acceptance, heteroactivists argued that the move was 'indulging transgender ideology' and was 'not only unnecessary but harmful, arguing that the APA regards gender dysphoria as a mental disorder (Freiburger, 2018). For heteroactivists, then, even the more mundane and everyday administrative engagements with the state such as the process of renewing a driver's licence renders LGBT people, and in this case trans individuals, visible. They point to this as examples of how heteronormative understandings are being challenged and, in their terms, undermined.

Heteroactivists claim significant dangers will ensue from LGBT inclusions, including a loss of democracy, free speech and the foundations of nations and Western civilisation built on a form of Christian heteronormativity. These dangers also threaten national security through gender-neutral passports. As Jack Fonseca above illustrates, children are central to how these risks are portrayed. We now turn to explore the implications that LGBT inclusions are supposed to have on children and families.

Children and Changing Families

Heteroactivists argue that there are dangers to these public visibilities of LGBT equalities. These include understanding same-sex relationships as equal to heterosexual marriage or families in ways that might 'coerce' or encourage children into that 'lifestyle'. As we noted in Chapter 3, heteroactivists portray the trans child as a danger to themselves and in need of assistance to enable them to conform to biological imperatives of sex. The notion of 'our children' is evoked to highlight the dangers to 'everyone else' from trans children and the 'global transgender movement'. Bringing these arguments together with the visibilities and oppositions discussed in this chapter, we show how heteroactivists argue that the decline of state-supported heteronormative policies, and the supposed 'removal' of Christianity from the public sphere poses specific and tangible threats to children and families.

In Canada, a series of legislative amendments in various provinces and at the federal level (including Bill C-16 discussed in Chapter 4) have convinced heteroactivists that it is the state's intention to eradicate heteronormative values about family and children from the public sphere (e.g. Westen, 2017) and to '[put] ideology ahead of children's interests' (LifeSite News, June 20, 2019). These include Ontario's Bill 33, Toby's Act (2012) which added gender identity and expression to the Ontario Human Rights Act and Bill 13, Accepting Schools Act (2012) which required public and Catholic schools to allow Gay–Straight Alliances and to institutionalise anti-homophobia and anti-bullying policies. In 2015, Ontario Bill 77, the Transgender Therapy Bill, was passed prohibiting conversion therapy for children who are 'gender confused'. These legislative changes are seen to put children at risk (Baklinski, 2014; Laurence, June 30, 2016).

In the UK, heteroactivists opposed numerous LGBT equalities initiatives including gender-neutral school uniforms; gender-neutral clothing in John Lewis department stores' range; asking parents to recognise that children may not identify as male or female when applying for school places; and an all-girls remake of Lord of the Flies. Enacting gender inclusive policies and practices such as these arguably represented a 'lie about science' with 'clear evidence of transgender indoctrination attempting to normalise a perverted and damaging view of reality'. All this reflected 'child abuse at its worst' (Voice for Justice UK, n.d.b; see also Moseley, Mar. 1, 2018). Consequently, children were read as being under 'assault' through attacks on 'their innocence and reality itself [which has] been relentless' (Anglican Mainstream, 2017). This can supposedly 'only further endanger the nation's young' (Voice for Justice UK, n.d.b). The 'nation's young' is a reference to 'our children' (see Chapter 3) and by implication those who are British, white, Christian and heteronormative. The danger posed and the 'child abuse' then refer directly to engagements with LGBT inclusions which will result in the 'nation's young' being 'damaged' and 'perverted' (Voice for Justice UK, n.d.b).

The damage seemingly wrought by gender and sexual inclusivity that includes all children within spaces such as education, shopping and films is understood as being for the sake of adults and 'driven by the belief that what makes adults happy must make children happy too' (Farmer, 2019). This is perceived as an 'intrusion of adult angst about gender identity into the world of childhood' that will:

unsettle, disturb and even traumatise. It is a cruelty perpetrated on children by adults who believe they are, somehow, doing 'good'. Rather, they are robbing children of their childhood ... Children with issues of gender identity certainly need support but it is unacceptable to provide this support at the cost of damaging the emotional wellbeing of other children. The casualties of the current gender-awareness offensive will be the silent majority of young children. (McGovern, 2016: paras 6 and 10)

There is, in heteroactivists' views, a 'cost' to supporting 'children with issues of gender identity', for others (read: heteronormative children within heteronormative families). This cost rests on the individualisation of a 'problem' with these children that does not implicate or affect 'other children'. The position implies a separation of those children who 'need support' from 'other children'. It suggests these children represent a contagion that could spread to what is often seen as the 'silent majority of young children'.

Adults promoting gender inclusion were not only a threat to children but could also be damaging to 'the family' (read the heteronormative British/Canadian settler/white family). In Ontario, Bill 28 (2016), the All Families Are Equal Act, amended several acts that displaced the heteronormative family as the penultimate institution in society. The main goal of the Act was to ensure that individuals assuming the role of parent were recognised regardless of sexual orientation or their capacity to reproduce (including through assisted reproductive technologies or surrogacy/ adoption). For heteroactivists, the Act is understood as fundamentally altering the way families are understood in Ontario (e.g. Laurence, Nov. 29, 2016). For example, removing the terms 'mother' and 'father' from birth certificates, heteroactivist groups argued, would 'normalise and indoctrinate the rest of the population about the practice of surrogacy' and also '[s]ubjugates the natural family to the transgender agenda' (Everyday for Life Canada, Oct. 26, 2016). According to Charles McVety of Canada Christian College, Premier Kathleen Wynne is 're-engineering the family' in ways that undermine the 'traditional heterosexual family' (cited in Everyday for Life Canada, Oct. 26, 2016). Similarly, REAL Women argue that Bill 28 is 'revolutionary' and designed to 'completely restructure "family relationships solely to please the LGBT community"' (Real Women of Canada, 2016; see also Interim, Nov. 25, 2016).

On 8 December 2016, the Wynne government in Ontario also introduced Bill 89, 'Supporting Children, Youth and Families Act', which overhauled the province's child welfare system as it related to child protection, foster care and adoption services. Of major concern for heteroactivists was the inclusion of gender identity and gender expression in considering the best interests of the child (Evangelical Fellowship of Canada, n.d.). Heteroactivists argued the 'totalitarian' Bill 89 expanded state power to intervene in families and needed to be amended to include specific protections for religious parents to raise children in accordance with their beliefs (LifeSite News, Jan. 25, 2017; Evangelical Fellowship of Canada, n.d.; Real Women of Canada, 2016). Again, opponents argued that Wynne, as the lesbian premier, was imposing 'her ideological views on innocent children' and 'targeting the traditional family and its values' (Real Women of Canada, Jan. 26, 2017; Chapters 3 and 4; see also Laurence, Jan. 25, 2017).

As we have discussed in other chapters, heteroactiv-ists' children and families are perceived as endangered by LGBT inclusions. The public state here is read as interfering with the 'private life of family', but as also perpetuating child abuse through misrepresenting reality and promoting 'LGBT ideologies'. LGBT inclusions through state processes are thus constructed as threatening to 'the family' and 'innocent children' in ways that are targeted and dangerous to all, in order to 'please the LGBT community'.

Conclusion

Public spaces and state institutions are often represented as 'neutral' with respect to gender and sexuality although, as scholars have shown, the nation-state has been invested in enforcing specific heteronormative values (Bell et al., 1994; Bell and Binnie, 2000; Binnie, 2004; Richardson, 1998). Access to public space as well as having a voice in the public square has been a fruitful line of investigation for sexual geographers seeking to engage with and enhance spatial justice, through claims to citizenship and inclusion in public spaces, including workspaces (Bell and Binnie, 2000; Callaghan and van Leent, 2019; Johnston, 2005; Nash, Maguire and Gorman-Murray, 2019; Piekut and Valentine, 2016; Richardson, 1998; Smith, 2019; Stychin, 2003; Tucker, 2009; Uhrig, 2015). This chapter, starting from these premises, has examined how heteroactivist arguments construct public spaces as exclusionary to them, threatening not only their citizenship, but the health and wellbeing of the West, their nation, the family and society. In particular, we have shown how they contend that LGBT equalities are enacted through legislative changes and inclusion agendas across state institutions and public spaces, in ways that are powerful, ideologically driven, repressive and exclusionary. This, they contend, means that they are losing the ability to express views in opposition to LGBT equalities in public spaces, institutions and debates, that is, to be recognised as a 'public' in and of their own right.

In showing how heteroactivists are seeking to reconstitute the public square as under threat, this chapter began by exploring the place of religion, and in particular Christianity, in these debates. It has long been argued that religion, including Christianity, can be inclusive of LGBT people (Andersson et al., 2013; Browne et al., 2010; Taylor, 2016; Valentine et al., 2012; Yip and Nynäs, 2016). This chapter has shown that heteroactivists set a specific form of Christianity, and particularly 'traditional', 'Biblical' beliefs, in contradistinction to sexual and gender equalities.

The latter are seen as threatening the place of heteronormative Christians in public life, through totalitarian forms of activism that are read as detrimental to children, families, nations, the West and the world. This argument rests on an understanding that in the public realm in Canada and the UK, not only are heteronormative values no longer considered the dominant (or respected) moral framework for social life, but that LGBT equalities (and 'the LGBT agenda') work to eliminate expression of these values (as well as those who hold those views) from the public sphere. In this way, we have shown that heteroactivist opposition to sexual and gender equalities seeks to reclaim heteronormativity's 'rightful' place through recuperating the 'rights' of heteronormative Christians and the 'rightful place' of Christianity' (read also whiteness) as central to the British and Canadian nation-state. These rights link directly to the expression of 'Biblical views' that heteroactivists strenuously deny are bigoted, including those related to trans/gender identities, same-sex marriage and public representations of LGBT lives (which are still at times discussed through the 'promotion of homosexuality').

Concluding
Considerations

Introduction

Twenty-first-century legislative and cultural changes around sexualities and genders are both unprecedented and contested. Our aim in this book has been to explore these contestations offering the concept of heteroactivism as an analytical tool to articulate the nature of the resistances to LGBT equalities. More particularly, heteroactivism names the ways that oppositions to these equalities seek to (re)establish heteronormativities in multifaceted ways locally, nationally and transnationally, in ways that are predominantly secular. This analytic may be useful in other historical or geographical contexts and we encourage others to consider, rework or reject the concept as appropriate. We want to avoid the suggestion that theories or conceptualisations produced in specific locations are universally applicable in others (Browne and Bakshi, 2013; Mikdashi and Puar, 2016). Instead, by focusing on flashpoints as spatialised battles that contest meaning in order to resist the implications of sexual and gender rights, this book has explored transnational, national and local challenges to LGBT equalities, including claims about the need to protect society and the nation through the reiteration of the heteronormative family.

In writing this book, it was clear to us that although we could extend discussions of heteroactivism in new directions, and expound upon some features of the resistances to LGBT equalities, there is far more work to be done. The time to publication means that much will have changed by the time this book emerges. Yet in showing how heteroactivism creates systems of meaning that seek to reiterate heteronormativities, we hope to have offered something that moves beyond the specifics of the flashpoints discussed. This includes providing a framework through which these changes can be understood, and developing our conceptual (and practical) engagements with heteroactivism. In this concluding chapter, we draw together some of the key points developed throughout the book to enable, we hope, further discussion, engagements and theoretical/activist advances. We then discuss areas that the book has not addressed, before offering reflections on heteroactivism's potential trajectories that we argue need academic (and potentially activist) attentions.

Key Themes or (Some of) What This Book Has Done

This book progresses understandings of the strident (and increasing) resistances to sexual and gender equalities in Canada, the United Kingdom and Ireland. These are gaining traction, particularly in terms of free speech and political, social and legal challenges against 'compelled speech' (see also Browne and Nash, 2014, 2017; Nash and Browne, 2015, 2019). These contexts are important because equal rights are legislatively enshrined and are increasingly evoked as core national social and cultural values (Browne and Bakshi, 2013; Formby, 2017; Nash and Browne, 2019; Puar, 2007). In contrast, resistances to sexual and gender equalities are often geographically imagined and placed into the Global South (Browne et al., 2015; Rao, 2015). Our focus here is on the beacons of success in this arena, namely Canada, the UK and Ireland. This emphasis calls into question the progress/backwardness narratives of the Global North/Global South which suggest that the Global North is progressive and the Global South is backward (see Browne et al., 2015; Kulpa and Mizielinska, 2011; Mikdashi and Puar, 2016; Rao, 2015). It shows that resistances to LGBT equalities are also apparent in the Global North. This geographical focus works to negate presumptions that resistances to sexual and gender rights will simply 'die out' or should be ignored in the hope that they disappear once certain equalities such as same-sex marriage are obtained. The national values in the places under study arguably include acceptance of (some) sexual and gender minorities, LGBT visibility in schools, the workplace and in national symbols such as the new Canadian two-dollar coin commemorating the decriminalisation of homosexuality in 1969 (Cummings McLean, 2019; Harris, 2017). In assessing the limitations of these equality 'successes', scholars point to various normativities and the shoring up of racial, classed, nationalistic and other power relations through the approval of same-sex marriage and other associated equalities (see e.g. Ahmed, 2012; Bryant, 2008; Conrad, 2014; Duggan, 2002; Puar, 2007; Richardson, 2004, 2005, 2017). This book offers insights into how these successes are resisted and challenged.

This section discusses several key points emerging across the chapters which, we argue, are important to conceptualising contemporary heteroactivism. We firstly outline how heteroactivists perceived the dangers of LGBT equalities including the specific dangers to children. We then offer a discussion of how spatialities are read through multi-scalar engagements and how geography is central to conceptualising heteroactivism. We deliberately put our considerations of the 'traditional' as constituted through race, religion, nationalities and colonialism last in the 'what we have done' section, because we feel this area could be co-located within the 'what we have not done' section.

We do not offer enough depth and engagement with this area here or throughout the book, highlighting that far more research and theorisation is needed.

The Dangers of LGBT Equalities

Heteroactivists see their vision of heteronormativities as central to the nation, the state and 'society' such that, in their terms, silencing and excluding these views is read as inherently damaging. As we have shown throughout the book, heteroactivist groups seek to avoid or deflect accusations of homo- or transphobia (see in particular Chapters 1 and 4, note that bisexuals are invisibilised, alongside intersex people). At the regional, national or international level, heteroactivist resistances can often gain a higher profile through mainstream and social media coverage which focuses on the hype about the 'unintended consequences' of LGBT equalities. Key to the consequences suggested by heteroactivists is the undermining of the 'traditional' family which has the effect of undermining society, and civilisation. As Nicholas (2019) notes with regard to Australia, some of these discourses are viewed as apocalyptic in their challenge to 'normal' heteronormativities, and such a description has resonances here. Below, we outline some of the key lines of argument developed throughout the book, including the dangers of same-sex marriage, the understanding of 'totalitarianism' and heteroactivists seeing their losses as losses for everyone including those with whom they would disagree.

Same-sex marriage undoubtedly has had a significant effect on sexual and gendered lives, politics and scholarship, queer or otherwise. Critics argue that where same-sex marriage is the key focal point for powerful gay rights organisations, other sites of LGBT social struggle are rendered invisible (see e.g. Halberstam, 2005; Warner, 1993). Non-conforming heterosexual affiliations, relationships and intimacies are also rendered problematic (Wilkinson, 2013). Scholars argue that LGBT people are also complicit in narrowing and limiting the range of human connection through their support of an activism that privileges neoliberal consumerist cultures that are experienced as exclusionary for some (but see Brown, 2008, 2012; Gorman-Murray and Nash, 2017; Oswin, 2006, 2008). Thus, while queer and sexuality studies have extensively explored the effects of equalities for LGBT, queer and non-normative sexual and gender communities, lives and politics, particularly in the UK, the USA and to an extent Canada (Against Equality, n.d.; Ball, 2016; Barker and Monk, 2015; DeFilippis et al., 2018; Jones et al., 2018; Yarbrough et al., 2018), this book offers very different insights.

Same-sex marriage can be seen as central in reviving and supporting the development of heteroactivist resistances. In the UK, resistances to same-sex marriage galvanised and united diverse groups to oppose the 2014 legislation (see Browne and Nash, 2014; Nash and Browne, 2015). It was argued that UK Conservative Prime Minister David

Cameron's support of same-sex marriage led to an EU vote to re-establish sovereign control and appease those in his party disaffected by this neo-conservative move.[1] As we have argued elsewhere, heteroactivists' reaction to same-sex marriage illustrates how permission to engage in neoliberal consumerism and institutions such as same-sex marriage does not mean that the world has been won, that oppositions to LGBT rights disappeared or that all are in favour of sexual and gender inclusions (Browne and Nash, 2014, 2015; Browne et al., 2018; Nash and Browne, 2015). However, this book has also gone well beyond considering historical resistances to the passing of marriage equality to show that the incorporation of same-sex marriage by state legislatures into the social and cultural fabric of the nation is seen by heteroactivists as creating serious issues. These include issues with education, which now has to teach about legal relationships as part of state supported relationship and sex education (see Chapter 2); issues about freedoms of speech where hate legislation proscribes against discrimination and exclusion (see Chapter 4); and marginalisation in public spaces such as work where speaking against same-sex marriage might lead to loss of employment (see Chapter 5). Same-sex marriage might be seen as normative and exclusionary to some queer others, but our work suggests that it has also disrupted specific versions of hegemonic normativities in ways that affect more than those who are engaging in these state-sanctioned relationships.

Heteroactivists can take an *apocalyptic* view of these disruptions which are understood as contesting the 'bedrock of society' and of Western civilisation. Further, heteroactivists in the UK, Ireland and Canada argue that LGBT rights such as same-sex marriage and trans rights are 'non-sensical', 'ludicrous' and 'against common sense', leading to another key contention, namely that these changes have to be imposed on society, because they will not be accepted by 'normal' people or 'everybody else'. Heteroactivists contend that there is no rational basis to argue for LGBT equalities, such as same-sex marriage, but this is especially professed in terms of trans rights that seemingly refute 'biological truths'. Support for LGBT equalities are characterised as lacking a coherent argument, and as being outside rationality. Therefore, these equalities have to be imposed on a resistant or unaware populous. As we wrote this chapter, this was a prominent heteroactivist discussion in relation to Northern Ireland when same-sex marriage was introduced by the UK Westminster parliament in October 2019 (see also Chapters 4 and 5).

The supposed requirement for undemocratic control in order to implement LGBT equalities is equated with totalitarian regimes, including references to 'communism', 'Nazis' and fascists, in ways that are believed to silence dissent and shut down debate, including in school spaces (see Chapters 2 and 4). Indeed for many heteroactivist groups across the UK and Canada (this is less so in the case of Ireland, although it is emerging), their argument is that it is now impossible to voice their opposition to lesbian, gay, bisexual and trans rights and therefore that their rights and freedoms are being violated. In this way, a 'global transnational movement' is narrated (and indeed created) as having significant and oppressive state support. The media and the entertainment industry are understood as also being corrupted and 'biased' in favour of LGBT inclusions, which together leads to oppressing those who believe ideas such as gender variance are a 'lie'. This totalitarianism has been read as part of the destruction of Western civilisation through the purported restriction on freedom of speech and accusations of compelled speech. As part of that freedom, heteroactivists are seeking to create room to offend in order to challenge equalities, by distancing, for example, speech acts from physical harm (see Chapter 4). Reducing the meaning of harm to just physical attacks enables them to argue that verbal harm does not exist and that 'debates' are justifiable, particularly in university spaces. Thus, resistances to naming harm/hurt seek to reclaim the right to 'hate' in order to reiterate and recreate specific heteronormative orders.

Heteroactivists can associate LGBT equalities with 'leftists' and 'cultural Marxism' in ways that create a totalitarianism that cannot defend itself, and thus creates practices that ensure no direct challenge can be undertaken (such as 'no platforming'). They work hard to create a narrative where LGBT people, and those who support them, are in control and must be resisted as oppressors.

Heteroactivists can then claim that it is ironic that those advocating for LGBT equalities are themselves intolerant of 'alternative viewpoints' and seek to render them unheard (through shutting down debate), and/or unhearable because of accusations of bigotry, homophobia and transphobia (Chapters 1, 3, 4 and 5). Indeed, these accusations can be challenged, by claiming that they are the ones being oppressed. Heteroactivists can read LGBT activism as wanting to impose 'absolute acceptance' and as 'forcing everybody else to accept this on pain of legal punishment and social ostracism' (Moseley, Nov. 16, 2017). They contend that this 'forcing' of everybody else represents a loss of freedom and is something that should concern everyone, not only those who oppose LGBT equalities. In the case of Ashers Bakery, the victory against compelled support of same-sex marriage, was seen as a victory for all, including 'lesbians' and 'feminists' (see Chapter 4). This seeks to allow unfettered resistances to LGBT rights.

In schools and universities, accusations of totalitarianism on the part of LGBT activists are not only linked to communist 'forced education', but also support claims that the presence and support of trans children is *dangerous for all children*, and thus 'our children' who are implicitly cis-gender (and heterosexual) (see Chapters 2, 3, 4 and 5). As we noted in Chapter 2, children and the figure of the child have been explored in queer thinking, including critiques of the figure of the heteronormative child as engendering a focus on particular forms of heteronormative futures

(Edelman, 2004; Stockton, 2016). The centrality of the dangers posed by LGBT equalities thus remains critical in resistances to the loss of this heteronormative future. These dangers relate both to 'our children', and in particular 'transgender' children who are exploited and used by the 'global transgender movement' (see Chapter 3). This seeks to present some children as requiring help from the 'suffering' of 'gender dysphoria'. Thus, those who deviate from heteronormative, and particularly normative gendered orders, are both improperly influenced, and in need of help (but not medical intervention in terms of hormones, puberty blockers or indeed access to medical services, see Chapter 3). 'Our' children, then, need protection, not only from trans children (Chapter 3), but also within public schools from sexual education and LGBT inclusions that challenge parental values with implications for their home lives (Chapter 2), as well as within universities from 'leftist' and 'Marxist' faculty (Chapter 4). Protecting 'our children' alongside the 'threats to freedom' is purported as requiring urgent action to work against LGBT equalities that sexualise, corrupt and confuse 'our children'.

Overall then, heteroactivists argue that the transformations resulting from LGBT equalities are of serious concern and began with same-sex marriage. The consequences are, in part, the undermining of the very foundations of society, that is, heterosexual marriage, gender complementarity, gender roles and the place of the traditional heterosexual family (e.g. Browne and Nash, 2014; Nash and Browne, 2015).

However, they have now expanded their arguments to also claim that free speech and the right to public expressions of anti-LGBT animus in public spaces (such as work, school and street spaces, see Chapters 2 and 5) are fundamental to Western civilisation. Restriction on such 'freedoms' is read as oppression and, when related to children, is understood as posing dangerous threats to 'our children', via 'indoctrination'. The focus on the dangers of LGBT equalities is not only about what is best for society but is also about arguing for individuals to 'choose' heterosexual and cisgender ways of being as 'better'. Therefore, while they are not attacking LGBT people directly on the grounds of the moral reprehensibility of alternative genders and sexualities, they are still arguing that LGBT people are inferior and LGBT equalities are dangerous. Heteroactivists are then suggesting that it is a duty to make sure children are not influenced by 'the LGBT agenda'. More than this, Western society and individual nations require 'freedom to dissent'. Thus, they contend that people are being 'forced' and 'compelled' into acceptance of LGBT equalities or are potentially facing social ostracism and loss of employment. The dangers are thus multi-scalar, moving from schools, streets and workplaces to nations and throughout 'Western civilisation'.

Transnational Movements, National Politics and Local Uprisings: The Importance of Multiple Spatialities

The emergence of opposition to globalised gender ideology and the rise of anti-gender movements is often linked to the far right or is rooted in Catholicism but such opposition is not necessarily wedded to this religious heritage (Corrêa et al., 2018; Kováts, 2018; Nicholas, 2019; Paternotte and Kuhar, 2018). These important investigations offer understandings of these resistances, particularly within social movement scholarship. Heteroactivism, as an analytical tool augments this work, demonstrating that heteroactivism does not necessarily cleave left or right, although it might, and does not rely on religion per se, although again this can become important and utilised to resist LGBT equalities as we saw in Chapter 5. In contrast to understandings of gender ideologies as globalised (Corrêa et al., 2018), heteroactivism as an analytic tool incorporates understandings of the spatialised and transnational creation of resistances to LGBT equalities. We created the book, and indeed the research that underpins it, with a specific geographic foundation in mind. As geographers, we centralise how place matters to understanding how contemporary sexual and gender politics are manifest. We thus are interested in how heteroactivism is formed within as well as across spaces.

In this geographical conceptualisation, we are not doing comparative work, nor do we see ideas 'diffusing' (e.g. Weiss and Bosia, 2013), rather we utilised the fluidity and flexibility of transnational theorisations which recognise that discourses (composed of ideas, people, concepts, politics and objects) circulate and touch down in ways that cannot be predicted or assumed. Therefore, in bringing the spatial as a defining feature of heteroactivism, we incorporated various spatial scales. A transnational approach helps us to understand how heteroactivism operates across Canada, the UK and Ireland and we explored them as places in their own right, as well as how various ideas and discourses moved and translated across different places. In Chapter 1 we also looked at how these contexts directly speak to each other (e.g. writing a letter from Canada to oppose same-sex marriage, see Chapter 1). We argued that at times national identities and imaginings were critical (e.g. British values and Canadian multiculturalism, Chapter 2 or Irishness in Chapters 1 and 2) while the regional can be a site of contestation in ways that then could be used to create national and transnational debates (e.g. Birmingham, or Ontario, Chapter 2). Finally, in interrogating public spaces (Chapter 5), spaces of school and home (Chapter 2) and campuses (Chapter 4), we offered insights into how these distinctive locations are presented as under threat and as requiring heteronormative underpinnings.

These scales cannot be seen as distinct national movements that might clearly display heteroactivist positions. As we have argued, resistances to sexual and gender equalities can arise at the grassroots level when LGBT equalities are perceived as affecting 'our children' at school, operative in health decisions and in relation to support offered to trans kids (Chapters 2 and 3, see also below). As we saw in Chapter 2, in the Canadian and UK context for example, resistances to school curricula that include references to LGBT people or their families erupted around claims about parental rights, and the education of children or the age appropriateness of certain material. This was both informed by and informed national debates regarding these LGBT inclusions in schools and the overlaps in the discourses indicate a travelling that is not uniform. Moving between multiple scales in this way allows insights into how supposed 'personal' issues regarding sexual and gender politics can be rendered central and defining features of contemporary societal (UK, Ireland and Canada) failings. These transnational perspectives were augmented with an understanding of space as socially produced, which enabled us to offer insights into, for example, who is perceived to be allowed to speak in the public sphere (campus/schools, Chapters 2 and 4). Therefore, as an analytic that incorporates certain understandings of the spatial, heteroactivism requires acknowledgement of both the differentiation and overlaps between places, as well as within spaces through how they are created. Our use of flashpoints as defining key battles then enabled us to examine spatialised contestations around the meanings embedded in certain spaces.

Whiteness, Christianity and Tradition

The heteroactivism that we have examined focused on whiteness and, at times, Christianity. This somewhat overlaps with discussions of the US Christian Right (Burack, 2014a, 2014b; Stein, 2001), but religion, race and racial relations are geographically specific, and cannot be generalised

(McKittrick and Woods, 2007; Neely and Samura, 2011; Price, 2010). Moreover, as we have shown, the secularity of the argumentation is critical in these arenas. In focusing on the unnamed, yet central place of whiteness, we have not produced an explicit critique of privilege (Bhopal, 2013; Flagg, 2005; McIntosh, 1998). Instead, we have centralised whiteness as developing systems of meaning that normalise and centralise heterosexualities around terms such as 'tradition' and claims to British/Canadian/Irish national identities. We have also noted the co-option of immigrants and the incorporation of racialised discourses in Canada. Here we pause to articulate some key points in the construction of the heteronormative white heteroactivism considered in this book. We do so while acknowledging that this discussion is partial and has not formed the main focus of the book. We would invite others to continue this important analysis into whiteness and resistances to LGBT equalities in places where 'we have won' (see also Boulila, 2019; Nicholas, 2019).

A key aspect of the whiteness and Christianity that defines 'traditional', as well as particular heteroactivisms, is through the ways in which these bodies and religiosities are considered benign, and thus not dangerous (Boulila, 2016). How these groups are understood is very different to how Muslim groups who protested, for example, the inclusion of sexual education in schools (in the UK), are represented and these understandings form part of the discursive creation of the Muslim homophobe (Haritaworn, 2015). In Chapter 2, we saw that in Britain, 'Muslim parents' had to work hard to present themselves as falling in line with British values (and of course claims to 'traditional' British values would be out of reach). This is not the case for Christian groups who can contend that they are defending 'traditional values', without naming Britishness or seeking to claim a place in these new values. Instead, in Britain, their Christianity and predominant whiteness means that they are often given extensive press coverage both for issues that they raise and also to find the 'opposing' voice for LGBT laws or court cases. Evoking the traditional then is about evoking white Christianity in ways that assume benign-ness, in contrast to the threat of 'others', particularly brown, Muslim bodies. This benign-ness means that not only can Christian groups work against accusations of hate, as well as extremism for their views on LGBT equalities, but this racial and religious position means that these views are not explicitly understood as related to race/religion.

Christianity, in places such as Ireland, the UK and Canada cannot be separated from whiteness. Moreover, the ongoing influence of the Anglican church in British politics and its social and cultural life and values (see Johnson and Vanderbeck, 2014; Vanderbeck and Johnson, 2016), and Catholicism in Ireland across institutions such as schools (see Neary, 2016; McAuliffe and Kennedy, 2017) cannot be overlooked. These religions must be afforded a complexity when it comes to issues of sexual and gender equalities and LGBT rights, given for example, there are divisions in the Anglican church regarding these issues (Valentine et al., 2012; Valentine et al., 2013; Vanderbeck et al., 2015), and there is far more to explore in terms of how heteroactivism is created in different religious institutions and denominations. This stands in stark contrast to the Muslim homophobe (Haritaworn, 2015) who in the Birmingham case is represented as the other and inherently dangerous. Islam is presented as a monolith in its approach to sexual and gender equalities, ignoring exclusions, disagreements and divisions within Islam (Browne et al., 2010; Yip, 2008). Seeing religion as a site of racialisation also helps us to understand what is meant by the 'traditional' in terms of religion in specific ways when manifest in white-majority and -ruled contexts that are under investigation here.

Heteroactivists often seek to reiterate a specific form of 'traditional marriage' based on British/colonial conceptualisations of privatised couples and family formations in post-industrial eras. In addition, claims about the longevity of particular forms of gender binaries, in places like Canada (and to an extent Ireland) ignores and overlooks other forms of gendered indigeneity, such as two-spirited people who contest the very sexual/gender constructs of LGBT, as well as colonial heteronormativities (see e.g. Morgensen, 2013; Robinson, 2010). Thus, presumptions of historical longevity are key to 'tradition', in ways that overlook, for example, disruptions to gender binaries during the Second World War (Valentine, 2002). The past is evoked as a specific moral compass, privileging specific hegemonic versions of sexual and gender practices, lives and norms. In doing so, it is reiterating a nativism that presumes specific gendered and sexualised difference as inherent and unchanging and in Canada and Ireland, evoking a specific form of (settler) colonialism (see also Morgensen, 2013; Nash, 1993; Nicholas, 2019). 'Tradition' is paramount here, because the danger comes from the 'non-traditional', which is not only not 'normal' but disrupts the 'foundations of society' and 'Western civilisation' itself, based on a presumption of historical coherence and lineage. Thus, societies, nations and civilisation itself are evoked as being, and as always being, white, and specifically Anglo-Saxon and heteronormative in modern conceptualisations. The supposed newness, and disruption of LGBT equalities to historical claims on 'civilisation' not only involves the past, it also impacts the future possibilities of the nation through the threat to the child (Edelman, 2004). Children are implicated in ensuring longevity and tradition from primary school to university. The figure of the trans child is co-opted (see Chapter 3), as threatening to 'our children' who are not protected by parents in school spaces (see Chapter 2) or by the state in universities (see Chapter 4). The heteronormative reproductive future that is under threat is gender normative, based on biological essentialisms and does not include alternative family forms. This future is imagined through whiteness, unless otherwise stated. Where heteroactivism is not white, then the claim to the nation has to be made, showing a different side to the racialised discussions of LGBT inclusions, which see them as under threat from 'homophobic others' (Boulila, 2019; Haritaworn, 2015). Here, we showed how the threat to 'inclusive' British values around LGBT equalities had to be addressed by Muslim parents. In making heteroactivist claims, they had to align themselves to these British values, in ways that heteroactivist groups which are predominantly white did not. Indeed, the latter, could claim to be working *for* the good of the British nation by directly opposing inclusive values around sexual and gendered equalities.

The final point that we note about whiteness, Christianity and the benign-ness of much of the visible heteroactivism is that white heteronormativities have been central to states and citizenship for decades (see Bell and Binnie, 2000). LGBT inclusions have been shown to adhere to whiteness, as well as reiterating geopolitical power relations (see e.g. Boulila, 2019; Duggan, 2003; Haritaworn, 2015; Puar, 2007). Thus, even in the queer disruptions to heteronormativities, whiteness, settler colonialism and hegemonic international power relations have been reinforced rather than contested. In the 21st century, the contentions and positions of heteroactivists as seemingly 'losing' in relation to LGBT equalities are very different to discussions of LGBT marginalisations. As we develop further in the next section, there is a need to move beyond understanding these contestations within a binary framework of marginalisations/privilege, where the forms of heteronormativities espoused by heteroactivists are no longer supported by the state and are not centralised in popular culture.

We put this section at the end of our discussion of 'what we have done' and argue that we see this area as underdeveloped and in need of further research. In this book, we have foregrounded resistances to LGBT equalities in our discussions and as many have noted before us, these equalities are racialised (Boulila, 2019). In what comes next, we want to argue for further work on resistances to LGBT equalities, and more broadly, on resistances to sexual and gender equalities.

Areas to Develop or What the Book Has Not Done

This book has focused in depth on heteroactivist discourses and their manifestations in the UK, Canada and, to a lesser extent, Ireland. This has meant that other explorations, methodologies and foci have not been addressed, including an outline of specific groups, their aims, activities and/ or interconnections. We see a pressing need for more studies and investigations if we are to expand our understanding of resistances to sexual and gender equalities within, and beyond, heteroactivism. We begin with a brief summary of some key areas that have not been addressed, before naming the need to examine the effects of heteroactivism on LGBT people and LGBT equalities and on those who are opposed to them. Finally, we discuss the lack of any discussion of counter-arguments to heteroactivism in this book, and the ways these might develop. We finish by noting the geographical specificity of the book, and the need for further explorations beyond English-speaking, and Global North contexts.

Sexual and Gender Rights, Neoliberalism and Class

In this book, we have not investigated resistances to 'feminisms', abortion and broader sexual and gender rights, including women's rights which also might be understood through the concept of heteroactivism. Elsewhere, we have considered how anti-abortion campaigning might be considered heteroactivist in creating specific forms of 'pro-woman' and equality-based stances that seek to reiterate specific forms of gendered and sexual normativities (see Browne and Nash, 2019; Saurette and Gordon, 2013). Pushing against feminism and women's rights is also a feature of heteroactivism and can be captured within the term 'anti-gender'. Further, we have not examined how trans rights can be contested by those who argue that they are 'feminists', identify as lesbians and occupy progressive positions with regards to LGBT rights. Heteroactivism offers useful conceptual possibilities in this area, but these require further consideration and development.

We have not explored links to the far right, or relations between heteroactivism and homonationalism (Corrêa et al.,

2018; Paternotte and Kuhar, 2018). For example, Wellner and Marienfeld (2019) persuasively argue that homonationalism and heteroactivism co-exist in the German far right AFD party. We have also not investigated interactions with neoliberalism or class-based politics that emerge in various ways, including accusations of 'cultural Marxism' and 'communism'. We would note that these are complex areas that refute simplistic assertions and require in-depth analysis and theorisation. For instance, our work suggests that heteroactivism does not naturally or inherently cleave left or right, and heteroactivists might well be characterised as middle class in terms of the organisations that we examined. There can be no presumed link between the 'far right' and heteroactivism, and it should be noted the use of arguments regarding civil partnerships (Chapter 1) and freedom of speech (Chapter 4) draw heavily on arguments usually associated with 'the left'. These political distinctions are of course geographic (and in Ireland, politics does not currently cleave left–right), and thus engagements between heteroactivism and political ideals and parties will also vary geographically.

Each of these areas (and there will be many more that we have not identified) requires explorations that recognise these complexities and take various lenses to explore the intersectionalities that are reconstituting social issues in the 21st century. What this book has shown is that sexuality and gender, including LGBT equalities, must be a central point in these conversations.

Effects of Heteroactivism on Everyday Lives

There is a need for more research into the everyday spatialities of those whose rights or values are resisted by heteroactivists. Using a methodological focus on exploring resistances to LGBT equalities in depth, it was not possible to adequately assess how heteroactivism is felt, encountered and dealt with. These encounters are important because of power imbalances or the less valued social identities of those who exist outside of heteronorms, and who will find their mere presence challenged or their views and experiences denigrated or dismissed. This challenges narratives that harm only refers to physical abuse (Chapter 4). Instead, it recognises the harm resulting from the cumulative effects that denigration can cause. It is important to note that it is these same people (marginalised minorities) who have, historically and culturally, experienced difficulties gaining access to universities for example. However, there is also some evidence that some LGBT people agree with certain heteroactivist arguments, for example around trans rights, free speech or the 'sexualisation' of children, and thus a uniform response to heteroactivist discourses cannot be presumed (Nash, Gorman-Murray and Browne, 2019). There can be little doubt, however, that for many LGBT people and those supportive of sexual and gender rights, heteroactivist activities and speech acts can be demeaning and offensive and seek to roll back protections introduced to support LGBT people. This can cause harm for marginalised individuals and groups. The effects of heteroactivism will not be uniform and attention to multiple and overlapping marginalisations is needed to examine these effects.

Conversely, we can perhaps summarise from our data that heteroactivists are finding difficulties sharing space with LGBT people as equal and legitimate citizens within the nation-state, in their schools and workplaces. Heteroactivists argue that they are marginalised or side-lined, and out of step with nationalist values that support LGBT equalities, as well as in conflict with local enactments of legislation and cultural changes. Our research suggests, but cannot show, that these encounters are affecting them, their engagement in politics and the media as well as in their everyday lives. However, we have not explored the effects of LGBT legislation on heteroactivists or those who hold to the import of heteronormativities as central to their values. How they encounter LGBT equalities in their everyday lives remains unknown, and yet critical to how heteroactivism is emerging from local, and at times individual encounters with LGBT equalities that can become regional and national flashpoints.

There is also no engagement with those who do not support LGBT equalities or broader sexual and gender rights and who do not enter the limelight. It could be argued that the ways heteroactivist viewpoints are being treated is similar to those that supported citizenship for LGBT people in the late 20th century. Whereas once heteronormative orders silenced LGBT people and denigrated inclusive and accepting values as 'dangerous' to national projects, heteroactivists are now arguing that they are 'no platformed' and ignored or vilified in the press. However, this is a very different context to the one that LGBT people and activists faced in the 20th century. Heteronormative values were once powerful and still retain a claim on society, government and popular consciousness even in places such as Canada, the UK and Ireland. The loss of a particular form of privileged status has resonances and effects that have not disappeared. For example, as Vanderbeck and Johnson (2015) highlight the ongoing position of the Anglican church in UK governance and similarly over 90% of primary schools in Ireland remain under the patronage of the Catholic church, which stills influences governance. Thus, the adjustment of heteronormative orders cannot be theorised in the same way as citizenships and exclusions for LGBT people were discussed at the end of the 20th century. More is needed to understand these moves between marginalisation and privilege.

This research has focused on textual and public representations. It has not spoken to people. This approach puts the motivations and underpinning purposes of heteroactivist groups beyond the scope of the systematic analysis. While these might be surmised from their public arguments, we have avoided this form of guesswork. This would lead to easy and overly simplistic conclusions that we want to avoid. The presumption of uniformity and coherence within heteroactivism and those working against LGBT equalities is important to challenge. To undertake this, our work seeks to afford similar nuance and complexity to heteroactivism to that given to LGBT/queer politics, motivations and activisms in scholarship (Formby, 2017; Sears, 2005; Warner, T., 2002). Thus, more is needed to fully assess the purposes and complexities of the motivations of heteroactivisms.

Finally, it is difficult to know the effects of heteroactivism in terms of its reach and importance or in terms of the broader societal and public perceptions in the places that we have studied. While we have seen a growth in heteroactivist activities and groups and the rise of politicians who are sympathetic to heteroactivist arguments, it is difficult to assess how far this reaches and how (or even if) this support is growing. We do not have insights into how many people are seeing and engaging in heteroactivist discussions, how these arguments are being received and read, how they affect things like voting practices or engagements with workplaces and schools. Therefore, it is clear that the effects of heteroactivism need multi-disciplinary investigations that offer insight across areas such as political science, sociologies, religious studies, sexual and gender studies, critical race studies, media and cultural studies.

The 'Other Side'

We wanted to explore heteroactivism in depth and on its own terms, rather than presenting 'both sides' of the arguments or their relationship to each other. There has been a significant amount of research in social movement studies and within discussions of same-sex marriage that seeks to engage 'both sides' of debates, for example around same-sex marriage. These studies often find that arguments and tactics are mutually formative and interdependent (e.g. Dorf and Tarrow, 2014; Paternotte and Kuhar, 2018; Zivi, 2014). We chose not to look at 'both sides', which means that the book has not looked at the effects of heteroactivism nor examined the counter-arguments put forward in opposition to heteroactivist claims. These have been seen in the Irish referenda (see e.g. Neary, 2016), as well as against free speech claims and in court rooms around workplace and employment rights. However, there is, we believe, a pressing need to explore the counter-arguments in relation to the heteroactivist discourses that we have shown here. In examining their effectiveness in engaging with the underpinning systems of meaning identified in this book, it will be important to assess where heteroactivist arguments are granted merit and where they are seen as flawed or inadequate. In this section, we outline some key areas in developing counter-discourses that we have identified, but far more is needed.

Part of our rationale for producing this book was to highlight how heteroactivist arguments are being made and to consider the potential damage of dismissing these arguments under labels such as homophobia, biphobia and transphobia. There is no denying that these terms can be useful, but they are also increasingly limited in their effectiveness. Although we have not looked in depth, counter-discussions can fail to adequately address the key terms of the debate that heteroactivists are making, meaning that they are not being adequately refuted. This might be deliberate in refusing to allow heteroactivists to create the agenda. However, we would also note that this in part may lead to assertions that the answers/counter-arguments are not there. In turn, such assertions regarding an absence of 'rational' or 'logical' arguments, as we have seen above, links to claims that LGBT equalities have to be forced because they are supposedly not on a sound rational footing. Similarly, arguments and successes around 'no platforming' can have unexpected consequences and effects, such as government interventions into freedom of speech that are not based in the prevalence of 'banning speakers in universities' but instead based on perceptions that this is an endemic issue – as we saw in Chapter 4 in the UK and Canada.

Another issue that requires investigating is how counter-arguments can reinforce particular structures of power. For example, in relation to free speech debates in universities, feminists have created arguments in terms of the creation of 'proper' academic knowledge (see e.g. Butler, 2017, Ferguson, 2018; Sultana, 2018). Or to counter the Parkfield school protests arguments, the media suggested that 'national values' and state enforcement should be used to support LGBT teachings in schools. These reiterate forms of power relations that critical scholars have been contesting for several decades. Indeed, claims to free speech are only possible because of some 40 years of feminist and critical race scholarship and activism that forced the university to include previously excluded groups such as women and people of colour and to support spaces that generated and disseminated knowledge on marginal lives and experiences. Heteroactivists have successfully deployed these arguments to claim their place at the table. Conversely, those who have sought to stop homophobic/transphobic speakers have encountered the very arguments that made feminist, queer and critical race scholarship possible. Thus, careful and appropriate counter-arguments that do not reiterate relations of power that were once used against LGBT people (as well as feminists and those seeking to counter racism) are required.

Geographical Focus

This book has a very specific and deliberate geographical focus which we have argued throughout is central to the manifestations of heteroactivism that we identify. Such a geographical focus both limits the book in terms of not claiming generalisability and avoids the 'god trick' of academic/research (see Haraway, 1988), by advancing a concept that is geographically sensitive and offers significant potentials for the development of the concept beyond Canada, the UK and Ireland.

Across Europe, explorations of 'anti-gender' and 'gender ideologies' have highlighted the relevance of heteroactivism in the non-English-speaking contexts such as Germany, France, Spain and Eastern Europe (Kováts, 2017; Kuhar and Paternotte, 2017a). Heteroactivism might also be useful in exploring resistances to sexual and gender equalities in Latin America (Corrêa et al., 2018) and South Africa as both are regions/nations with same-sex marriage and legislative support for LGBT people. Scholars and activists might find heteroactivism useful to explore how resistances to LGBT equalities, and more generally, reiterations of heteronormativity, are manifest locally, regionally, nationally and transnationally. These manifestations may well differ significantly from our explorations and the geographic element of this research provides the tools to explore such distinctions by not enforcing particular framings or assuming comparative models that can be uniformly applied.

This book has deliberately avoided analysis and engagement with the US Christian Right, although its financial and cultural import is (or perhaps was?) undeniable in a global context and particularly in international institutions such as the UN (Butler, 2006; Rao, 2015). However, turning the lens away from the US enabled us to explore different manifestations of resistances to sexual and gender rights on their own terms rather than transposing these models. Moreover, the legal context of the US does not prohibit anti-gay rhetoric, same-sex marriage is not seen as guaranteed, and the focus on both Christianity, theology and the right-wing may be imperative in this context.

In many ways the US is not an example of the 'world we have won' in terms of sexual and gender rights. We welcome others to interrogate the usefulness of heteroactivism in the US context and in developing the concept in relation to the scholarship that details the tactics, politics, theology and influence of the US Christian Right. We would encourage complexity in the analysis of the US and beyond, acknowledging not only that Christianity and right-wing movements can be LGBT inclusive, but also engaging with the differences that institutional religion and denomination make to heteroactivist movements, and the political and public contexts in which they operate. Finally, we would follow Rao (2015) in challenging the presumption of US influence as deterministic in African nations and beyond. Instead seeing this as a complex interplay of local agencies, regional and national governance, historical contexts and transnational engagements. Thus, the transnational geographic viewpoint that we espouse does not presume the movement of ideas, policies and activisms is unfettered. Instead it argues that in studying social phenomena contexts are created through interconnected networks that are multi-scalar.

Where Next?

Alongside the areas of academic research that we have noted in the section regarding what this book has not done, we invite your indulgence as we consider what might happen as we move into the third decade of the 21st century. Overall our work suggests that heteroactivist resistances will continue to grow, develop and emerge across various places. The ways in which gender and sexual struggles are manifest in politics shows that presumptions of unfettered progress are misplaced, and perhaps misleading and complacent. In Canada, Ontario's Doug Ford linked provincially approved 'free speech' policies to university funding, demonstrating that these arguments have traction and can develop. Thus, in contrast to the presumptions of LGBT trajectories of progress that will lead to ever more queer futures, we believe that heteroactivist resistances may well develop support that enables the shoring up of heteronormativities. These cannot be predicted and will vary across different national, regional and local contexts; they will also vary in relation to microspaces of work/school/high streets/social spaces.

Some heteroactivists are keen to reassert long-standing claims about the LGBT community, the roles of women and the centrality of biology in the structuring of society (e.g. Peterson, 2019; Fieldnotes Lumen Fidei conference, 2018). If certain free speech claims are realised and all viewpoints are permissible, then arguably, debunked or discredited ideas about people based on biology or other traits would be permitted without censure. Seeking to resist LGBT equalities opens up the possibilities for speech that has been considered homo- or transphobic, as any speech, no matter how 'uncivil, hurtful or rude' would be permissible speech (and would not be considered 'hate speech'). Claims about homosexual men as paedophiles or women as biologically unsuited for certain intellectual work might resurface and be given credence in locations, such as universities, where such views have long been debated and are rejected. Moreover, these free speech claims and resistances to discourses of harm, homophobia, biphobia and transphobia could have effects on LGBT groups and communities who rely on the salience of these discourses and nomenclature to provide for those affected by prejudice and discrimination.

We might expect the emergence of further workplace issues, including employees refusing to take diversity training or employees refusing to 'promote' LGBT rights. As we have seen, fields that are dealing with vulnerable people and seeking LGBT inclusions, including in universities and workplaces, are encountering resistances (see Chapters 4 and 5). These are likely to develop further coming from those who find their personal views under attack, even if they are do not espouse these views at work or in university classes. However, where they do, it is likely to cause problems for their employment/degree attainment, leading to court cases, and media coverage of their rights to express their views, regardless of, or indeed denying, the offence and harm they may cause. Employees, when refusing to display an 'ally' or safe space symbol might not be fired but may be shamed or shunned. Those with heteroactivist values could be implicitly labelled a 'danger' to colleagues or as creating a hostile work environment under harassment policies. They might be labelled as working against 'company values', or in educational contexts, refusing to teach national curricula could see them losing their ability to teach or indeed to gain employment. They might also be refused places in university courses or denied their qualification on the basis of not achieving learning outcomes. In turn they might use these policies to protest their own treatment. This could include accusations of 'bullying', or issues with promotion and other forms of recourse that would enable their views to be legitimated. These can be manifest as flashpoints that gain attention and support from heteroactivist groups.

There may also be implications for people's everyday lives that might not gain prominence, at least initially. These might affect LGBT people and allies, heteroactivists and those who support heteroactivist values differently. Their spatialities may be affected in unanticipated ways that may or may not emerge, at least initially, through heteroactivist groups and flashpoints that generate local, national and international attention. Research is needed into these everyday spatialities in order to understand the potential effects of sexual and gender equalities. We need to consider and perhaps address the effects of heteroactivist values in places where LGBT equalities are enshrined but never guaranteed.

The effects of sexual and gender equalities on people's lives, we believe, will require new ways of engaging with their everyday experiences. If we understand sexual and gender equalities as insecure, the question of how to treat those who encounter LGBT equalities unexpectedly and in ways that challenge their values, needs careful consideration. It cannot be presumed that they will simply 'get on board' and require 'education' or training. Instead, it poses more fundamental questions regarding the maintenance of LGBT equalities in the face of heteroactivist resistances that draw on experiences of the 'negative' effects on their lives. Exclusion, marginalisation and shunning is not only ineffective, it potentially works against LGBT equalities. It does this by creating an 'other' that marginalises 'us'/'normal people' creating support for heteronormativities and communities who could once again vilify LGBT people. This time LGBT people and allies could be perceived as becoming the oppressors (or at least utilised by the state to create oppressive policies and practices), as well as a represented as a danger to children and 'normal' people (as we have seen in some of the arguments across these chapters). Thus, consideration needs to be paid to what else might be done to engage with those who resist LGBT equalities differently. This is particularly pertinent, if it cannot be assumed that everyone's mind can be changed by education, training and proximity to LGBT people. Yet, we recognise that there are dangers in validating these viewpoints for minorities who rely on rights and protections. There are not simplistic solutions, but complex problems to be grappled with in interdisciplinary and multifaceted ways.

Conclusion

Academic work dealing in social inequalities, exclusions and marginalisations, including activism, needs to better conceptualise and explore resistances to equalities beyond noting their limitations and normalisations. In 2012, we started this research when many heteroactivist groups were seen as 'fringe' or marginal and their views easily dismissed. Then, as now, we understood these positions to be more powerful than many thought. We are concerned by the compliancy that we have witnessed. We would now suggest that in the next decade we will see further resistances to LGBT equalities, and more broadly, resistances to sexual and gender equalities, including women's rights and abortion rights. We finish this book with a challenge to those who work within the fields of equalities and human rights (some of which have never been seen as 'won', in the way sexual and gender rights are understood). The resistances to LGBT equalities are only one piece in the ongoing need for analytical considerations of the resistances to social (including sexual/gender) progress in the 21st century. There is much to be done.

Notes

Introduction

1 This conference was organised by Lumen Fidei Institute, a Catholic organisation made up of lay people 'engaged in cultural and educational matters' and who advocate for 'traditional' Catholic teachings including that marriage is only between a man and a woman (www.lumenfidei.ie/the-lumen-fidei-institute). It was organised to coincide with the Catholic World Meeting of Families, a Vatican-sponsored event that Lumen Fidei thought to be too supportive of LGBT rights and without a proper focus on Catholic teaching on marriage and family life (Bourne, 2018).

2 In this book, we use the term LGBT recognising that it is limited. The term is problematic for those who might be included under its umbrella, because it can force definitions and identities (see Browne and Nash, 2010). It can also be exclusionary for sexual and gender others who do not fit within these terms, for example in Canada of Two-Spirited indigenous gender/sexualities. It is also problematic in its use for heteroactivist groups, because of its inclusion of bisexuals who are rarely mentioned. Intersex individuals, issues or groups were not named or recognised in the discussions that we explored. We use LGBT here both

because it allows us to engage with resistances to sexual and gender equalities that use the term, alongside gay and trans, and because it enables us to discuss challenges to sexualities and gender interpellated by it (e.g. same-sex marriage rights and trans rights).

3 We use 'equalities' rather than rights because equalities reflects the broader social, cultural and political transformations for LGBT people and trains attention on LGBT lives including what is being taught in schools about LGBT people or how sexualities and genders that are outside of heteronormative orders are being made visible in state documents.

4 It also sought to challenge abortion and women's rights, including equalities at work and home, but these are not addressed in this book (see Browne and Calkin, 2020).

5 These more anti-gay/bi/trans activities might also be considered heteroactivism, in that they seek to assert the superiority of heteronormativities, but they may not be 'activism' in the same way. However, this is not the focus of the book and requires more detailed attention.

6 As mentioned in the section on context, we do not discuss Northern Ireland in depth. However, we do draw on Northern Irish examples where warranted.

7 Canadian Charter of Rights and Freedoms, s. 8, Part 1 of the Constitution Act, 1982, being Schedule B to the Canada Act 1982 (UK), 1982, c 11.

8 *Egan v. Canada* (1995) 2 S.R.C, 513. See also *Vriend v. Alberta* (1998) 1 S.C.R 493, where the court held that provincial human rights legislation that failed to include sexual orientation violated s. 15 of the Charter.

9 Ontario included sexual orientation in 1986, with Manitoba and the Yukon passing legislation in 1987, Nova Scotia in 1991, British Columbia, New Brunswick and North West

Territories in 1992, Saskatchewan in 1993, Newfoundland and Labrador in 1995 and Prince Edward Island in 1998.

10   Bill C-16, an Act to amend the Canadian Human Rights Act and the Criminal Code enacted 19 June 2017.

11   Our focus is on English Canada and not on Quebec largely because we do not work in French and because most of these major issues have been fought in English Canada.

12   Heteroactivist motivations underlie more than anti-gender and sexual equalities and are also reflected in opposition to reproductive rights (including abortion surrogacy and fertility treatments, which we do not address in this book but see Browne and Nash, 2019) and LGBT foster care and adoption (discussed in Browne and Nash, 2018).

Chapter 1

1   This is not to say that there was no opposition. Several issues have arisen over the past 20 years in the Canadian context. For example, in 2011 the Saskatchewan Court of Appeal ruled that religious beliefs cannot be used as a reason to refuse to perform same-sex marriages, after some marriage commissioners attempted to refuse to perform same-sex marriages in the province (Graham, 2011). In another example dating back to 2000, Toronto printer, Scott Brockie, was found to have discriminated on the basis of sexual orientation for refusing to print letterhead for the Canadian Lesbian and Gay Archives (Gunter, 2011).

2   Margaret Somerville, a well-known and widely respected academic, was a professor at McGill University during the same-sex marriage debates in Canada. Although the recipient of numerous honours and awards, she is perceived as a controversial figure because of her opposition to same-sex marriage, among other things, in Canada.

Chapter 2

1   In this section, we are predominantly examining state-funded schools in all three countries.

2   A prominent example is that of Steve Tourloukis, who lost his parental rights case against the Hamilton-Wentworth District School Board in 2017. Tourloukis had requested advanced notice about lessons in his children's elementary school on topics including homosexuality, abortion and gender identity so that he could remove his children from the classroom. The Ontario Court of Appeal rejected his claim on several grounds but most notably, for present purposes, cited lack of evidence that the school board 'interfered with his ability to bring up his son and daughter in his Greek Orthodox faith' (Laurence, Jan. 26, 2018).

3   *Chamberlain v. Surrey School District No. 36* (2002), see also *Board of School Trustees of School District No. 44 North Vancouver v. Jubran et al.* (2005). *Chamberlain* (2002) was recently cited with approval in *E.T. v Hamilton-Wentworth District School Board* (2016), denying a claim by a father, S. Tourloukis, to withdraw his children from class when they might be present for 'false teachings' that conflicted with his religion.

4   The Wynne government in Ontario was defeated in June 2018 by the provincial Conservative Party under the leadership of Doug Ford.

5   British values here can be read in Hobsbawm's (1983) terms as invented traditions that are created through repetition, with a presumed continuity to the past. This continuity in values of tolerance and inclusion is tenuous at best, given the extensive colonial histories, as well as historical and more recent state repressions of LGBT people, including through section 28.

Chapter 3

1   While the chapter deals with heteroactivist opposition to trans equalities, there have also been increasing contestations between feminist and trans people in Canada and the UK which are beyond the scope of this chapter. In Canada, this is evidenced in the ongoing battle between Vancouver Rape Crisis centre and trans activists (Kearns, 2019), as well as the Twitter banning of Canadian feminist Meghan Murphy (e.g. Christiansen, 2019). In the UK, certain self-described feminists are currently opposing rights for trans people using very similar arguments to those we discuss here. While we include some articles from these groups that appear on heteroactivist websites, we do not analyse the broader work by UK or Canadian feminist groups opposed to trans rights. As Christian Concern (2019, June 14) argues, 'The lesbian feminist argument is, of course, largely mistaken'. This form of anti-trans feminism is not apparent in Ireland, at the time of writing.

2   We use heteronormative to refer to normative heterosexuality, and also to indicate the normalisation of gender/sex within binary modes of male/female, man/woman.

3   There are significant limits both to trans and gender non-conforming legislative and societal acceptances. These have been detailed elsewhere (see e.g. Johnston, 2018; Stryker, 2009). The focus here is on how these changes are perceived and resisted by those who seek to recuperate a specific heteronormative order that is seen as dissipating.

4   Saad is a Professor of Marketing and a Research Chair in Evolutionary Behavioral Sciences and Darwinian Consumption at the John Molson School of Business at Concordia University, Montreal, Canada and is a public

commentator whose views often sit comfortably alongside those of Jordan Peterson and others on the political and social right.

5   Stella O'Malley presented a programme on Channel 4 called 'Trans Kids: It's Time to Talk' and in this article is presented as: 'convinced that she was a boy and strongly defended her identity as a boy to those around her. Now, however, she is happily married with children and says she loves being a mother' (Christian Concern, Nov. 29, 2018, para. 2).

6   Mermaids is an organisation in the UK that supports gender-non-conforming children, young people and their parents (Mermaids, 2019). They have been targeted by heteroactivist and anti-trans feminist groups, with their funding brought into question, secret filming and regular negative coverage of their work by these groups.

7   A similar Canadian example is a recent case where parents are taking the Ottawa-Carleton District School Board, the school, and its principal and the Grade 1 teacher to the Ontario Human Rights Tribunal for what they call an 'issue of moral conscience' because they claim a lesson called 'He, She and They?!? – Gender: Queer Kid Stuff #2' 'traumatised [their] child with gender ideology' (Laurence, June 28, 2019).

8   Trans men are rarely mentioned in these conversations, beyond their potential return to appropriate womanhood.

Chapter 4

1   Lindsey Shepherd, a teaching assistant at Wilfred Laurier University (WLU) screened in her classroom a 3–4 minute clip of Jordan Peterson discussing trans pronouns on a CBC show *The Agenda*. Shepherd's supervisor met with Shepherd, another professor and a person from the Gender Violence Prevention and Support Centre. Shepherd secretly recorded

the meeting and released it to the press several days later. In the subsequent uproar, Shepherd claimed using the clip in class was a freedom of speech issue and that she was unfairly 'reprimanded' by her supervisor (see Shepherd, Dec. 4, 2017).

2   Groups have been trying to make free speech an issue on Canadian university campuses with little real success until recently. While not gaining much of a profile, the Justice Centre for Constitutional Freedoms, for example, has published a 'Campus Freedom Index' since 2011, ranking Canadian universities based on issues of freedom of speech which includes treatment of unpopular speakers including conservative and anti-abortion student activists, the use of security fees and student union policies.

3   Although not a focus here, it is important to note that these claims have also been located within arguments about protests against abortion rights, specifically contestations around exclusion zones that prevent protests outside clinics. In this book we do not address anti-abortion politics, suffice it to note their place within broader discussions of freedom of speech.

4   There were some critical commentaries that objected to Google, which banned any advertising on its platform during the Campaign to Repeal the 8th Amendment, which severely restricted abortion in Ireland. Similarly, there were social media restrictions on advertising paid for outside of Ireland during this 2018 referendum. These are beyond the scope of the discussion here but see Browne and Calkin (2020) for further discussions of this.

5   Despite these claims, several media reports highlighted that some protestors did, in fact 'brandish signs with more extreme messages' that could be interpreted as homophobic even in the narrower sense (e.g. National Post, 2015).

6 Panti Bliss's subsequent Noble Call speech in the iconic Abbey theatre, made a similar argument about who can label actions as homophobic (www.youtube.com/watch?v=WXayh UzWnl0).

7 As we argue in Chapter 5, religion can be set in opposition to LGBT equalities, which are often read in and through a form of dogmatic and oppressive secularisation and/or a liberalisation of various churches.

8 UKIP is the UK Independence Party, a political party which was prominent during the same-sex marriage debates. At the time, it had both a heteroactivist wing and an LGBT group, illustrating the complexity of right-wing parties on LGBT equalities.

9 At the time of writing, Northern Ireland has passed legislation to legalise same-sex marriage, and the first weddings are set to take place in February 2020.

10 This is despite there being some research indicating that Canadian university faculty are more centrist than left-leaning (Nakhaie and Brym, 2011).

11 This is related to believing that LGBT rights should not be granted and stating this in a personal capacity (over social media for example), but insisting that this would not affect your work position or dealing with LGBT people (see also Chapter 5).

12 This was seen as having significant implications for employment as well as participation in what they term 'the public square', which we discuss in detail in Chapter 5.

Chapter 5

1 *Law Society of British Columbia v. Trinity Western University,* 2018, Supreme Court of Canada, 32. Note that on 4 August 2018, Trinity Western University announced that the

community covenant was no longer mandatory, a decision critiqued by some as an abdication of Christian principles in the face of public pressure (e.g. Risdon, 2018).

2 In September 2019, the Law Society of Ontario withdrew the policy, replacing it with what heteroactivists understood as an equally controversial requirement that lawyers and paralegals acknowledge on their annual report their 'awareness of their existing obligation to abide by human rights legislation' (Humphreys, 2019).

Concluding Considerations

1 This illustrates that resistance to LGBT rights may not be 'conservative' given Cameron's government offered support for same-sex marriage, alongside a 'hostile' environment with regard to immigration and significant welfare cuts.

References

5 Pillars (2019). Muslim parents protest against Birmingham school's LGBT promotion. *5 Pillars*. Retrieved from https://5pillarsuk.com/2019/02/07/muslim-parents-protest-against-birmingham-schools-lgbt-promotion/ (Accessed Nov. 13, 2019).

Adam, B., Duyvendak, J.M. and Krouwal, A. eds. (1992). *The Global Emergence of Gay and Lesbian Politics: National Imprints of a Worldwide Movement*. Philadelphia, PA: Temple University Press.

Adey, P. (2006). If mobility is everything then it is nothing: towards a relational politics of (im) mobilities. *Mobilities*, 1(1), 75–94.

Against Equality (n.d.). *Against Equality*. Retrieved from www.againstequality.org/ (Accessed Nov. 13, 2019).

Aggleton, P., Boyce, P., Moore, H.L. and Parker, R. eds. (2012). *Understanding Global Sexualities*. London and New York: Routledge.

Ahmed, S. (2012). *On Being Included: Racism and Diversity in Institutional Life*. Durham, NC: Duke University Press.

Ahmed, S. (2013). *The Cultural Politics of Emotion*. London and New York: Routledge.

Altman, D. (1997a, July 3). On global queering. *Australian Humanities Review*. Retrieved from www.australianhum anitiesreview.org/archive/Issue-July-1996/home.html.

Altman, D. (1997b). Global gaze/global gays. *Gay and Lesbian Quarterly: A Journal of Gay and Lesbian Studies*, 3, 417–436.

Altman, D. and Symonds, J. (2016). *Queer Wars*. Cambridge: Polity Press.

Andersen, R. and Fetner, T. (2008a). Economic inequality and intolerance: attitudes toward homosexuality in 35 democracies. *American Journal of Political Science*, 52(4), 942–958.

Andersen, R. and Fetner, T. (2008b). Cohort differences in tolerance of homosexuality: attitudinal change in Canada and the United States, 1981–2000. *Public Opinion Quarterly*, 72(2), 311–330.

Andersson, J., Vanderbeck, R., Sadgrove, J., Valentine, G. and Ward, K. (2013). Same sex marriage, civil rights rhetoric, and the ambivalent politics of Christian evangelicalism in New York City. *Sexualities*, 16(3–4), 245–260.

Anglican Mainstream (2017, Apr. 19). Songs of innocence, and harmful experience. *Anglican Mainstream*. Retrieved from https://anglicanmainstream.org/120371-2/ (Accessed Nov. 12, 2019).

Anyon, J. (2005). *Radical Possibilities: Public Policy, Urban Education, and a New Social Movement*. New York: Routledge.

Association for Reformed Political Action (ARPA) (2016, Nov. 9). On Bill C-16: gender ideology, freedom, and our neighbours' good. *ARPA*. Retrieved from https://arpacanada.ca/news/2016/11/09/bill-c-16-gender-ideology-freedom-neighbours-good/.

Association for Reformed Political Action (ARPA) (2016, Dec. 16). Policy report for parliamentarians. Retrieved from https://arpacanada.ca/wp-content/uploads/2016/07/Respectfully-Submitted-Gender-ID-updated-1216.pdf.

Association for Reformed Political Action (ARPA) (2017, Apr. 25). Summer student job funding pulled from pro-life group. *Lighthouse News.* Retrieved from https://arpacanada.ca/lighthouse-news/prolife-education-appropriate/#lhn-article-7160 (Accessed Nov. 11, 2019).

Auchmuty, R. (2004). Same-sex marriage revived: feminist critique and legal strategy. *Feminism & Psychology*, 14(1), 101–126.

Badgett L. (2014). *The Economic Cost of Homophobia and the Exclusion of LGBT People: A Case Study of India.* Washington, DC: The World Bank.

Baklinski, P. (2014, Sept. 23). First grade girls at Toronto Catholic school forced to share bathroom with boy. *LifeSite News.* Retrieved from www.lifesitenews.com/news/first-grade-girls-at-toronto-catholic-school-forced-to-share-bathroom-with (Accessed Nov. 12, 2019).

Baklinski, P. (2015, Mar. 12). Parental uproar against sex-ed explodes as call for a referendum emerges: Liberal MPP flees from program. *LifeSiteNews.* Retrieved from www.lifesitenews.com/opinion/parental-uproar-against-sex-ed-explodes-as-call-for-a-referendum-emerges-li (Accessed Apr. 19, 2018).

Baklinski, P. (2016, Nov. 30). 'Pro-death storm' looms over France as gvmt gears up to criminalize pro-life websites. *LifeSite News.* Retrieved from www.lifesitenews.com/news/pro-death-storm-looms-over-france-as-gvmt-gears-up-to-criminalize-pro-life (Accessed Nov. 9, 2019).

Ball, C.A. (2016). *After Marriage Equality: The Future of LGBT Rights.* New York: New York University Press.

Banerjea, N. and Browne, K. (2018). Liveable lives: a transnational queer-feminist reflection on sexuality, development and governance. In C.L. Mason (ed.) *Routledge Handbook of*

Queer Development Studies (pp. 169–179). London and New York: Routledge.

Barker, J., Alldred, P., Watts, M. and Dodman, H. (2010). Pupils or prisoners? Institutional geographies and internal exclusion in UK secondary schools. *Area*, 42(3), 378–386.

Barker, M.-J. (2017, Dec. 27). A trans review of 2017: the year of transgender moral panic. *The Conversation*. Retrieved from http://theconversation.com/a-trans-review-of-2017-the-year-of-transgender-moral-panic-89272.

Barker, N. and Monk, D. eds. (2015). *From Civil Partnership to Same-Sex Marriage: Interdisciplinary Reflections*. London and New York: Routledge.

Bell, D. and Binnie, J. (2000). *The Sexual Citizen: Queer Politics and Beyond*. Cambridge: Polity Press.

Bell, D., Binnie, J., Cream, J. and Valentine, G. (1994). All hyped up and no place to go. *Gender, Place and Culture: A Journal of Feminist Geography*, 1(1), 31–47.

Bell, D. and Valentine, G. (1995a). The sexed self: strategies of performance, sites of resistance. In S. Pile and N.J. Thrift (eds.) *Mapping the Subject: Geographies of Cultural Transformation* (pp. 143–157). London: Routledge.

Bell, D. and Valentine, G. (1995b). *Mapping Desire: Geographies of Sexualities*. London: Routledge.

Bennett, R. (2018, May 3). Crackdown on university students silencing free speech. *The Times*. Retrieved from www.thetimes.co.uk/article/65556204-4e56-11e8-9812-5f003d09c84c (Accessed Nov. 8, 2019).

Bhattacharyya, G. (2013). *Dangerous Brown Men: Exploiting Sex, Violence and Feminism in the 'War on Terror'*. London: Zed Books.

Bhopal, R.S. (2013). *Migration, Ethnicity, Race, and Health in Multicultural Societies*. Oxford: Oxford University Press.

References

Binnie, J. (1997). Coming out of geography: towards a queer epistemology? *Environment and Planning D: Society and Space*, 15(2), 223–237.

Binnie, J. (2004). *The Globalization of Sexuality*. London: Sage.

Binnie, J. (2006). *Cosmopolitan Urbanism*. London: Routledge.

Binnie, J. (2007). Globalization of sexuality. *The Blackwell Encyclopedia of Sociology*. Malden, MA: Blackwell.

Binnie, J. and Klesse, C. (2013a). The politics of age, temporality and intergenerationality in transnational lesbian, gay, bisexual, transgender and queer activist networks. *Sociology*, 47(3), 580–595.

Binnie, J. and Klesse, C. (2013b). 'Like a bomb in the gasoline station': East–West migration and transnational activism around lesbian, gay, bisexual, transgender and queer politics in Poland. *Journal of Ethnic and Migration Studies*, 39(7), 1107–1124.

Bird, S. (2018, July 8). Government drops doctor who says gender given at birth. *The Telegraph*. Retrieved from www. telegraph.co.uk/news/2018/07/08/government-drops-doctor-says-gender-given-birth/ (Accessed Nov. 13, 2019).

Blizzard, C. (2015, Feb. 18). Ben Levin case casts shadow over new sex ed curriculum. *Toronto Sun*. Retrieved from https://torontosun.com/2015/02/18/ben-levin-casts-a-shadow-over-new-sex-ed-curriculum/wcm/6b62518e-65a3-4a53-83e2-7cc4ac8aab9a (Accessed Nov. 8, 2019).

Board of School Trustees of School District No. 44 (North Vancouver) v. Azmi Jubran, et al. (British Columbia) (30964) (2005). Retrieved from www.scc-csc.ca/case-dossier/info/ sum-som-eng.aspx?cas=30964 (Accessed Nov. 13, 2019).

Boellstorff, T. (2004). The emergence of political homophobia in Indonesia: masculinity and national belonging. *Ethnos*, 69(4), 465–486.

Boquet, S. (2017, Dec. 18). In the name of tolerance the Canadian government promotes discrimination against pro-lifers. *LifeSite News*. Retrieved from www.lifesitenews. com/opinion/in-name-of-tolerance-canadian-govt-promotes-discrimination-against-pro-life (Accessed Nov. 14, 2019).

Boulila, S.C. (2015). What makes a lesbian salsa space comfortable? Reconceptualising safety and homophobia. In K. Browne and E. Ferreira (eds.) *Lesbian Geographies: Gender, Place and Power* (pp. 133–152). Farnham: Ashgate.

Boulila, S.C. (2016). What makes Europe 'post-homophobic'? Conference Paper. Royal Geographical Society/Institute of British Geographers (RGS-IBG) Annual International Conference. Stream: Resisting equalities and civil rights: Gender and sexuality (1), Royal Geographical Society, London.

Boulila, S.C. (2019). *Race in Post-Racial Europe: An Intersectional Analysis*. London: Rowman & Littlefield.

Bourne, L. (2018, Feb. 26). Irish Catholics protest LGBT agenda at World Meeting of Families, host separate conference. *LifeSite News*. Retrieved from www.lifesitenews. com/news/irish-catholics-protest-lgbt-agenda-at-world-meeting-of-families-host-separ.

Braun, J.G. (2017). Whose law? Queer Mennonites and same-sex marriage. *Journal of Mennonite Studies*, 32, 97–113.

Brooks, R. and Waters, J. (2015). The hidden internationalism of elite English schools. *Sociology*, 49(2), 212–228.

Brown, G. (2008). Urban (homo)sexualities: ordinary cities and ordinary sexualities. *Geography Compass*, 2(4), 1215–1231.

Brown, G. (2012). Homonormativity: a metropolitan concept that denigrates 'ordinary' gay lives. *Journal of Homosexuality*, 59(7), 1065–1072.

Brown, G. and Browne, K. eds. (2016). *The Routledge Research Companion to Geographies of Sex and Sexualities.* London: Routledge.

Brown, G., Browne, K., Elmhirst, R. and Hutta, S. (2010). Sexualities in/of the Global South. *Geography Compass,* 4(10), 1567–1579.

Brown, M.P. (2005). *Closet Space: Geographies of Metaphor from the Body to the Globe.* London: Routledge.

Brown, M.P. (2012). Gender and sexuality I: intersectional anxieties. *Progress in Human Geography,* 36(4), 541–550.

Browne, K. (2005). Snowball sampling: using social networks to research non-heterosexual women. *International Journal of Social Research Methodology,* 8(1), 47–60.

Browne, K. (2006). Challenging queer geographies. *Antipode,* 38(5), 885–893.

Browne, K. and Bakshi, L. (2013). *Ordinary in Brighton?: LGBT, Activisms and the City.* London: Routledge.

Browne, K., Banerjea, N., Bakshi, L. and McGlynn, N. (2015, May 11). Intervention: gay-friendly or homophobic? The absence and problems of global standards. *Antipode.* Retrieved from: https://antipodeonline.org/2015/05/11/gay-friendly-or-homophobic/.

Browne, K., Banerjea, N., McGlynn, N., Bakshi, L., Beethi, S. and Biswas, R. (2019). The limits of legislative change: Moving beyond inclusion/exclusion to create 'a life worth living'. *Environment and Planning C: Politics and Space.*

Browne, K., Banerjea, N., McGlynn, N., Sumita, B., Bakshi, L., Banerjee, R. and Biswas, R. (2017). Towards transnational feminist queer methodologies. *Gender, Place & Culture,* 24(10), 1376–1397.

Browne, K. and Calkin, S. (2020). *After Repeal: Rethinking Abortion Politics.* London: Zed Books.

References

Browne, K., Lim, J. and Brown, G. eds. (2007). *Geographies of Sexualities: Theory, Practices and Politics.* Burlington, VT: Ashgate.

Browne, K., Munt, S.R. and Yip, A.K.T. eds. (2010). *Queer Spiritual Spaces: Sexuality and Sacred Spaces.* Aldershot: Ashgate.

Browne, K. and Nash, C.J. eds. (2010). *Queer Methods and Methodologies: Intersecting Queer Theories and Social Science Research.* London: Ashgate.

Browne, K. and Nash, C.J. (2014). Resisting LGBT rights where 'we have won': Canada and Great Britain. *Journal of Human Rights,* 13(3), 322–336.

Browne, K.A. and Nash, C.J. (2015). Opposing same-sex marriage, by supporting civil partnerships: resistances to LGBT equalities. In N. Barker and D. Monk (eds.) *From Civil Partnership to Same-Sex Marriage 2004–2014: Interdisciplinary Reflections* (pp. 61–78). London: Routledge.

Browne, K. and Nash, C.J. (2017). Heteroactivism: beyond anti-gay. *ACME: An International Journal for Critical Geographies,* 16(4), 643–652.

Browne, K. and Nash, C.J. (2018). Resisting marriage equalities: the complexities of religion. In N. Bartolini, S. MacKian and S. Pile (eds.) *Spaces of Spirituality* (pp. 37–53). London: Routledge.

Browne, K. and Nash, C.J. (2019). Losing Ireland: heteroactivist responses to the result of the 8th amendment. In K. Browne and S. Calkin (eds.) *Post Repeal: Reflections and Futures.* London: ZED Books.

Browne, K., Nash, C.J. and Gorman-Murray, A. (2018). Geographies of heteroactivism: resisting sexual rights in the reconstitution of Irish nationhood. *Transactions of the Institute of British Geographers,* 43(4), 526–539.

Bruhm, S. and Hurley, N. (2004). *Curiouser: On the Queerness of Children*. Minneapolis, MN: University of Minnesota Press.

Bryant, K. (2008). In defense of gay children? 'Progay' homophobia and the production of homonormativity. *Sexualities*, 11(4), 455–475.

Bryant, K. and Vidal-Ortiz, S. (2008). Introduction to retheorizing homophobias. *Sexualities*, 11(4), 387–396.

Burack, C. (2014a). The politics of a praying nation: the presidential prayer team and Christian Right sexual morality. *Journal of Religion and Popular Culture*, 26(2), 215–229.

Burack, C. (2014b). *Tough Love: Sexuality, Compassion, and the Christian Right*. Albany, NY: State University of New York Press.

Burack, C. and Josephson, J. (2005). Origin stories: same-sex sexuality and Christian Right politics. *Culture and Religion*, 6(3), 369–392.

Burack, C. and Wilson, A. (2012). Where liberty reigns and God is supreme: the Christian Right and the Tea Party movement. *New Political Science*, 34(2), 172–190.

Buss, D. and Herman, D. (2003). *Globalizing Family Values: The Christian Right in International Politics*. Minneapolis, MN: University of Minnesota Press.

Butler, J. (1990). *Gender Trouble*. New York: Routledge.

Butler, J. (2006). *Born Again: The Christian Right Globalized*. London: Pluto Press.

Butler, J. (2017). Limits on free speech? *Verso blog*. Retrieved from www.versobooks.com/blogs/3529-limits-on-free-speech.

Calhoun, C. (2000). *Feminism, the Family, and the Politics of the Closet: Lesbian and Gay Displacement*. Oxford: Oxford University Press.

Callaghan, T. and van Leent, L. (2019). Homophobia in Catholic schools: an exploration of teachers' rights and experiences in Canada and Australia. *Journal of Catholic Education*, 22(3), article 3.

Campaign Life Coalition (2015a). Hundreds of parents protest liberal sex-ed. *Campaign Life Coalition News & Analysis*. Retrieved from www.campaignlifecoalition.com/hot-news/id/243 (Accessed Nov. 13, 2019).

Campaign Life Coalition (2015b). New Ontario sex-ed pamphlets by CLC. Retrieved from www. campaignlifecoalition.com/hot-news&id=253 (Accessed Nov. 13, 2019).

Campaign Life Coalition (2017, May 3). Q&A with Dr. Scott Masson. *The Interim*. Retrieved from www.theinterim.com/issues/abortion/qa-with-dr-scott-masson/.

Campaign Life Coalition (2018, June 15). This Supreme Court decision is an attack on religious rights in Canada. *Campaign Life Coalition*. Retrieved from www.campaignlifecoalition.com/press-room&id=204 (Accessed Nov. 13, 2019).

Campaign Life Coalition (n.d.a). Ontario's radical sex ed curriculum. *Campaign Life Coalition*. Retrieved from www.campaignlifecoalition.com/sex-ed-curriculum.

Campaign Life Coalition (n.d.b). School board. *Campaign Life Coalition*. Retrieved from www.campaignlifecoalition.com/school-board (Accessed Nov. 13, 2019).

Campbell-Jack, C. (2018, Aug. 18). How to deal with SJWs: a conservative's guide. *The Conservative Woman*. Retrieved from www.conservativewoman.co.uk/how-to-deal-with-sjws-a-conservatives-guide/ (Accessed Nov. 8, 2019).

Canadian Press (2015, Feb. 26). Wynne says some sex-ed protesters motivated by homophobia. *MacLean's*. Retrieved from www.macleans.ca/politics/wynne-says-some-sex-education-protesters-motivated-by-homophobia/ (Accessed Nov. 8, 2019).

Care UK (2017). Religious liberty. *Care UK*. Retrieved from www.care.org.uk/our-causes/more/religious-liberty (Accessed Nov. 10, 2019).

Carpay, J. (2017, Apr. 24). 'Phobias' kill our freedom of expression. *The Interim*. Retrieved from www.theinterim.com/issues/society-culture/phobias-kill-our-freedom-of-expression (Accessed Nov. 9, 2019).

Carpay, J. (2017, Oct. 17). Freedom of speech for all Canadians. *Everyday for Life Canada*. Retrieved from https://everydayforlifecanada.blogspot.com/2017/10/freedom-of-speech-for-all-canadians.html (Accessed Nov. 8, 2019).

Carpay, J. (2017, Oct. 24). Safety and security. *The Interim*. Retrieved from www.theinterim.com/issues/society-culture/safety-and-security/ (Accessed Nov. 8, 2019).

Carpay, J. (2018, July 30). Canadian Supreme Court evicerates [sic] religious rights. *The Interim*, Retrieved from www.theinterim.com/issues/religion/canadian-supreme-court-evicerates-religious-rights/ (Accessed Nov. 11, 2019).

Cavanagh, S.L. (2010). *Queering Bathrooms: Gender, Sexuality and Hygienic Imagination*, e-book. Toronto: University of Toronto Press.

CBC (2018, Apr. 10). Tanya Granic Allen under fire for online comments against gay marriage, Muslim dress. *CBC News*. Retrieved from www.cbc.ca/news/canada/toronto/tanya-granic-allen-under-fire-for-online-comments-against-gay-marriage-muslim-dress-1.4613483 (Accessed May 7, 2018).

Chamberlain v. Surrey School District No. 36 (2002). 4 SCR 710, 2002 SCC 86.

Charter of Rights and Freedoms (1982). Retrieved from https://laws-lois.justice.gc.ca/eng/const/page-15.html (Accessed Nov. 13, 2019).

Chin, M. (2019). Reconfiguring time, love, and money: adjusting chronotopic realities among queer and trans of color community organizers in Toronto, Canada. *Time & Society*, 28(4), 1577–1595.

Christian Concern (2016, Mar. 10). Christian magistrate removed from office for belief about family. *Christian Concern*. Retrieved from https://archive.christianconcern.com/our-concerns/family/christian-magistrate-removed-from-office-for-belief-about-family (Accessed Nov. 13, 2019).

Christian Concern (2017, Apr. 26a). Christian student granted judicial review after being expelled for views on sexuality. *Christian Concern*. Retrieved from https://christianconcern.com/ccpressreleases/christian-student-granted-judicial-review-after-being-expelled-for-views-on-sexuality/ (Accessed Nov. 13, 2019).

Christian Concern (2017, Apr. 26b). University 'thought police' remove student from social work course. *Christian Concern*. Retrieved from https://archive.christianconcern.com/our-concerns/freedom-of-speech/andrea-williams-university-thought-police-remove-student-from-social- (Accessed Nov. 14, 2019).

Christian Concern (2017, Aug. 1). Christian Magistrate taking legal action against NHS for dismissal over family views. *Christian Concern*. Retrieved from https://christianconcern.com/ccpressreleases/christian-magistrate-taking-legal-action-against-nhs-for-dismissal-over-family-views/ (Accessed Nov. 11, 2019).

Christian Concern (2017, Oct. 3). University accused of 'appalling double standards' over LGBT, Islam and Christian beliefs. *Christian Concern*. Retrieved from https://christianconcern.com/ccpressreleases/university-accused-of-appalling-double-standards-over-lgbt-islam-and-christian-beliefs/ (Accessed Nov. 11, 2019).

Christian Concern (2017, Nov. 2). A personal message from Nigel and Sally Rowe. Email correspondence.

Christian Concern (2018, Feb. 7). Tragically, they can't tolerate the truth that there are significant numbers of men and women who have no wish to remain in a gay lifestyle. *Christian Concern*. Retrieved from https://christianconcern.com/ccpressreleases/vue-cinema-bans-ex-gay-film-response/ (Accessed Nov. 9, 2019).

Christian Concern (2018, June 28). Why the UK government's mixed signals on gender-neutral passports are so dangerous. *Christian Concern*. Retrieved from https://archive.christianconcern.com/our-issues/sexual-orientation/why-the-uk-governments-mixed-signals-on-gender-neutral-passports (Accessed Nov. 14, 2019).

Christian Concern (2018, July 13). Christian doctor fired for saying gender is biological. *Christian Concern*. Retrieved from https://archive.christianconcern.com/our-issues/freedom/christian-doctor-fired-for-saying-gender-is-biological (Accessed Nov. 13, 2019).

Christian Concern (2018, Sept. 27). Guides leaders expelled for questioning transgender ideology. *Christian Concern*. Retrieved from https://archive.christianconcern.com/our-issues/freedom/guides-leaders-expelled-for-questioning-transgender-ideology.

Christian Concern (2018, Oct. 10). Victory for freedom of expression as bakers win Supreme Court case. *Christian Concern*. Retrieved from https://archive.christianconcern.com/our-issues/equality/victory-for-freedom-of-expression-bakers-win-supreme-court-case (Accessed Nov. 13, 2019).

Christian Concern (2018, Oct. 19). Action alert: tell your MP to oppose plans to make changing gender easier. *Christian Concern*. Retrieved from https://archive.christianconcern.com/our-issues/sexual-orientation/action-alert-tell-mp-to-oppose-plans-make-changing-gender-easier (Accessed Nov. 11, 2019).

Christian Concern (2018, Nov. 29). How do we help 'trans kids'? *Christian Concern*. Retrieved from https://archive.christianconcern.com/our-issues/sexual-orientation/how-do-we-help-trans-kids (Accessed Nov. 11, 2019).

Christian Concern (2019, Jan. 30). If we want to know the truth, we must tolerate 'political incorrectness'. *Christian Concern*. Retrieved from https://archive.christianconcern.com/our-issues/freedom/if-we-want-to-know-the-truth-we-must-tolerate-political-incorrectness (Accessed Nov. 13, 2019).

Christian Concern (2019, Feb. 1). Its time to stop policing the truth about sex in the name of transgender ideology. *Christian Concern*. Retrieved from https://archive.christianconcern.com/our-issues/freedom/its-time-to-stop-policing-the-truth-about-sex-in-the-name-of-transgender-ideology (Accessed Nov. 13, 2019).

Christian Concern (2019, Mar. 10). Court of Appeal to decide if professionals have free speech. *Christian Concern*. Retrieved from https://christianconcern.com/ccpressreleases/court-of-appeal-to-decide-if-professionals-have-free-speech/ (Accessed Nov. 10, 2019).

Christian Concern (2019, Apr. 12). The new terror: we are watching you; one false move and we'll remove you from your job. *Christian Concern*. Retrieved from https://archive.christianconcern.com/our-issues/freedom/the-new-terror-we-are-watching-you-one-wrong-word-and-we-will-remove-you-from-your-job (Accessed Nov. 9, 2019).

Christian Concern (2019, May 9a). Christian magistrate case is 'watershed moment'. *Christian Concern*. Retrieved from https://christianconcern.com/comment/christian-magistrates-case-is-watershed-moment-for-uk/ (Accessed Nov. 13, 2019).

Christian Concern (2019, May 9b). Richard Page: a watershed moment for Christians. *Christian Concern*. Retrieved from : https://archive.christianconcern.com/our-issues/freedom/richard-page-a-watershed-moment-for-christians (Accessed Nov. 14, 2019).

Christian Concern (2019, May 28). Transgender indoctrination at CofE primary school. *Christian Concern*. Retrieved from https://christianconcern.com/general/transgender-indoctrination-at-cofe-primary-school/ (Accessed Nov. 9, 2019).

Christian Concern (2019, June 7). Believing sexuality can change is now a conscience issue. *Christian Concern*. Retrieved from https://christianconcern.com/comment/believing-sexuality-can-change-is-now-a-conscience-issue/ (Accessed Nov. 11, 2019).

Christian Concern (2019, June 14). Education sector damaged by 'conversion therapy' research. *Christian Concern*. Retrieved from https://archive.christianconcern.com/our-issues/education/education-sector-damaged-by-conversion-therapy-research.

Christian Concern (2019, June 21). Standing in the firing line for us all. *Christian Concern*. Retrieved from https://christianconcern.com/comment/magistrate-dismissed-for-trying-to-protect-children/ (Accessed Nov. 10, 2019).

Christian Concern (2019, July 10). Christian Concern Communications Officer Rebekah Moffett comments on Peter Tatchell's defence of Felix Ngole. *Christian Concern*. Retrieved from https://christianconcern.com/comment/

lgbt-campaigner-defends-right-to-criticise-lgbt/ (Accessed Nov. 14, 2019).

Christian Concern (2019, July 11). Time to abolish the Government Equalities Office. *Christian Concern*. Retrieved fromhttps://christianconcern.com/comment/time-to-abolish-the-government-equalities-office/ (Accessed Nov. 11, 2019).

Christian Concern (2019, Aug. 16). Bus driver suspended for personal beliefs. *Christian Concern*. Retrieved from https://christianconcern.com/comment/bus-driver-suspended-for-personal-beliefs/ (Accessed Nov. 10, 2019).

Christian Concern (n.d.). About. Retrieved from https://christianconcern.com/about/ (Accessed Nov. 13, 2019).

Christian Institute (2017, May 5). Parents: UK media are cheerleaders for harmful idea that kids can be trans. *Christian Institute*. Retrieved from www.christian.org.uk/news/parents-uk-media-cheerleaders-harmful-idea-kids-can-trans/ (Accessed Nov. 11, 2019).

Christian Institute (2018, Feb. 6). Transgender staff plans put women in refuges at risk. *Christian Institute*. Retrieved from www.christian.org.uk/news/transgender-staff-plans-put-women-refuges-risk/ (Accessed Nov. 13, 2019).

Christian Institute (2018, Oct. 10). Gay cake case: landmark free speech victory for Ashers Bakery at UK Supreme Court. *Christian Institute*. Retrieved from www.christian.org.uk/press_release/gay-cake-case-landmark-free-speech-victory-ashers-bakery-uk-supreme-court/ (Accessed Nov. 8, 2019).

Christian Institute. (2018, Oct. 18). MPs say trans consultation is 'fundamentally flawed'. *Christian Institute*. Retrieved from www.christian.org.uk/news/mps-say-trans-consultation-fundamentally-flawed/.

Christian Institute (2019, Mar. 15). Ofsted-backed LGBT course suspended by primary school after parent protest. *Christian*

Institute. Retrieved from www.christian.org.uk/news/ ofsted-backed-lgbt-course-suspended-by-primary-school-after-parents-protest/ (Accessed Nov. 13, 2019).

Christian Institute (2019, May 16). Fair cop campaign pushes to overhaul trans guidelines. *Christian Institute*. Retrieved from www.christian.org.uk/news/fair-cop-campaign-pushes-to-overhaul-trans-guidelines/ (Accessed Nov. 9, 2019).

Christian Institute (2019, July 9). Peter Tatchell supports Christians' right to free speech. *Christian Institute*. Retrieved from www.christian.org.uk/news/peter-tatchell-supports-christians-right-to-free-speech/ (Accessed Nov. 14, 2019).

Christian Institute (2019, Oct. 5). LGBT campaigners confront Stonewall 'bullies' over trans policy. *Christian Institute*. Retrieved from www.christian.org.uk/news/lgbt-campaig ners-confront-stonewall-bullies-trans-policy/ (Accessed Nov. 9, 2019).

Christian Institute (2019, July 30). Almost 1000 signatures against drag queen events for kids. *Christian Institute*. Retrieved from www.christian.org.uk/news/almost-100000-signatures-against-drag-queen-events-for-kids/ (Accessed Mar. 23, 2019).

Christian Institute (n.d.).Transgender ideology. *Christian Institute*. Retrieved from www.christian.org.uk/issue/ transsexualism/.

Christian Legal Centre (2019, June 19). Judgment in magistrate Richard Page's case shows 'deep intolerance' of Christians. *Christian Concern*. Retrieved from https://christianconcern. com/ccpressreleases/judgment-in-magistrate-richard-pages-case-shows-deep-intolerance-of-christians/ (Accessed Nov. 10, 2019).

Christian Medical Fellowship (2012). Why not legalize same-sex marriage? *CMF Resources*. Retrieved from www.cmf.org.uk/

resources/publications/content/?context=article&id=25800 (Accessed Nov. 13, 2019).

Christian Today (2019, Feb. 2). Scotland's school transgender guidance 'may have negative impact' on other children. *Christian Today*. Retrieved from www.christiantoday.com/ article/scotlands-school-transgender-guidance-may-have-negative-impact-on-other-children/131638.htm.

Christiansen, R. (2019). The wrong kind of feminism: Meghan Murphy speaks in Vancouver. *The Post Millennial*. Retrieved from www.thepostmillennial.com/the-wrong-kind-of-femi nism-meghan-murphy-speaks-in-vancouver/.

Coalition for Marriage (2018, May 1). Compelled speech can never be free. *Coalition for Marriage*. Retrieved from www. c4m.org.uk/compelled-speech-can-never-free/ (Accessed Nov. 8, 2019).

Coalition for Marriage (2019, July 11). Grubby Westminster politics to legalize same-sex marriage in NI. *Coalition for Marriage*. Retrieved from www.c4m.org.uk/grubby-westminster-politics-to-legalise-same-sex-marriage-in-ni/ (Accessed Nov. 9, 2019).

Coalition for Marriage (2019, Aug. 20). Update on the Ashers case. *Coalition for Marriage*. Retrieved from www.c4m.org. uk/update-on-the-ashers-case/ (Accessed Nov. 8, 2019).

Coalition for Marriage (2019, Aug. 29). Piers Morgan blasts 'illiberal' liberals who won't tolerate dissent. *Coalition for Marriage*. Retrieved from www.c4m.org.uk/piers-morgan-blasts-illiberal-liberals-who-wont-tolerate-dissent/ (Accessed Nov. 9, 2019).

Coleman, P. (2016, July 14). Europe's free speech problem: a cautionary tale. *LifeSite News*. Retrieved from www. lifesitenews.com/opinion/europes-free-speech-problem-a-cautionary-tale (Accessed Nov. 8, 2019).

Conger, G. (2018, Feb. 16). The astonishing change in our social conversation. *Anglican Ink*. Retrieved from http://anglican.ink/2018/02/16/the-astonishing-change-in-our-social-conversation/ (Accessed Mar. 23, 2020).

Conrad, K. (2001). Queer treasons: homosexuality and Irish national identity. *Cultural Studies*, 15(1), 124–137.

Conrad, K. (2004). *Locked in the Family Cell: Gender, Sexuality, and Political Agency in Irish National Discourse*. Madison, WI: University of Wisconsin Press.

Conrad, R. ed. (2014). *Against Equality: Queer Revolution, Not Mere Inclusion*. Edinburgh: AK Press.

Cooper, D. (2019). *Feeling Like a State: Desire, Denial, and the Recasting of Authority*. Durham, NC: Duke University Press.

Cooper, D. and Herman, D. (2013). Up against the property logic of equality law: conservative Christian accommodation claims and gay rights. *Feminist Legal Studies*, 21(1), 61–80.

Coren, M. (2017, Nov. 28). The academic sky is not falling and free speech is far from dead. *The Star*. Retrieved from www.thestar.com/opinion/contributors/2017/11/28/the-academic-sky-is-not-falling-and-free-speech-is-far-from-dead.html (Accessed Nov. 10, 2019).

Corrêa, S., Paternotte, D. and Kuhar, R. (2018). The globalization of anti-gender campaigns. *International Politics and Society*. Retrieved from www.ips-journal.eu/topics/human-rights/article/show/the-globalisation-of-anti-gender-campaigns-2761/.

Cossman, B. (2018). Gender identity, gender pronouns, and freedom of expression: Bill C-16 and the traction of specious legal claims. *University of Toronto Law Journal*, 68(1), 37–79.

Craine, P. (2010, Sept. 23). Hamilton trustee candidate: Ontario equity policy is sexual abuse in 1st degree. *LifeSite News*.

Retrieved from www.lifesitenews.com/news/hamilton-
trustee-candidate-ontario-equity-policy-is-sexual-abuse-in-
1st-deg (Accessed Nov. 13, 2019).

Crang, P., Dwyer, C. and Jackson, P. (2003). Transnationalism
and the spaces of commodity culture. *Progress in Human
Geography*, 27(4), 438–456.

Crenshaw, K., Gotanda, N., Peller, G. and Kendall, T. (1995).
*Critical Race Theory: The Key Writings that Formed the
Movement.* New York: The New Press.

Cummings McLean, D. (2019, Jan. 4). Trudeau to issue a new
coin commemorating decriminalization of gay sex. *LifeSite
News.* Retrieved from www.lifesitenews.com/news/
justin-trudeaus-new-dollar-coin-to-commemorate-
decriminalization-of-gay-sex.

Davis, M. (1990). *City of Quartz: Excavating the Future in Los
Angeles.* New York: Vintage.

DeFilippis, J.N., Yarbrough, M.W. and Jones, A. eds. (2018).
Queer Activism after Marriage Equality. London and New
York: Routledge.

DePalma, R. and Atkinson, E. eds. (2009). *Interrogating
Heteronormativity in Primary Schools: The No Outsiders
Project.* Stoke on Trent: Trentham Books.

Diaz, R. (2016). Queer unsettlements: diasporic Filipinos in
Canada's world pride. *Journal of Asian American Studies,*
19(3), 327–350.

Dieppe, T. (2018, Dec. 14). The heresy of claiming a child wants
a mother and a father. *Christian Concern.* Retrieved from
https://archive.christianconcern.com/our-issues/adoption/
the-heresy-of-claiming-a-child-wants-a-mother-and-a-father
(Accessed Nov. 11, 2019).

Ditchburn, J. (2015). Conservatives dump candidate who called
homosexuals 'unnatural' and supported conversion therapy.

National Post. https://nationalpost.com/news/politics/conservative-candidate-refers-to-homosexuality-as-unnatural-and-says-conversion-therapies-work.

Doan, P.L. (2010). The tyranny of gendered spaces: living beyond the gender dichotomy. *Gender, Place and Culture,* 17, 635–654.

Dorf, M.C. and Tarrow, S. (2014). Strange bedfellows: how an anticipatory countermovement brought same-sex marriage into the public arena. *Law & Social Inquiry,* 39(2), 449–473.

Duggan, B. (2014). Top RTE executive defends 85K payout over homophobia claims. *The Herald.* Retrieved from www.herald.ie/news/top-rte-executive-defends-85k-payout-over-homophobia-claims-29982909.html (Accessed Nov. 13, 2019).

Duggan, L. (1994). Queering the state. *Social Text,* (39), 1–14.

Duggan, L. (2002). The new homonormativity: the sexual politics of neoliberalism. In R. Castronovo and D.D. Nelson (eds.) *Materializing Democracy: Towards a Revitalized Cultural Politics* (pp. 175–194). Durham, NC: Duke University Press.

Duggan, L. (2003). *The Twilight of Equality? Neoliberalism, Cultural Politics, and the Attack on Democracy.* Boston, MA: Beacon Press.

Edelman, L. (2004). *No Future: Queer Theory and the Death Drive.* Durham, NC and London: Duke University Press.

Edenborg, E. (2018). Homophobia as geopolitics: 'traditional values' and the negotiation of Russia's place in the world. In J. Mulholland, N. Montagna and E. Sanders-McDonagh (eds.) *Gendering Nationalism* (pp. 67–87). Cham: Palgrave Macmillan.

Eli, B. (2017, Sept. 12). Parents withdraw 6 year old son accused of misgendering classmate. *Church Militant.* Retrieved from www.churchmilitant.com/news/article/parents-withdraw-

6-year-old-accused-of-misgendering-classmate (Accessed Nov. 13, 2019).

Epstein, D. and Johnson, R. (1998). *Schooling Sexualities.* Buckingham: Open University Press.

Equality Act (2010). Retrieved from www.legislation.gov.uk/ukpga/2010/15/contents (Accessed Nov. 13, 2019).

Evangelical Alliance (2018, Oct. 18). The Gender Recognition Act 2004: consultation on reform. *Evangelical Alliance.* Retrieved from www.eauk.org/news-and-views/the-gender-recognition-act-2004-consultation-on-reform.

Evangelical Alliance (n.d.). What is extremism and how best can we protect ourselves, our freedom and our society from it? *Evangelical Alliance.* Retrieved from www.eauk.org/what-we-do/public-policy/could-you-respond-to-government-consultations/respond-to-a-consultation-on-defining-extremism (Accessed Nov. 13, 2019).

Evangelical Fellowship of Canada (2016, May 1). Trinity Western Law School. Retrieved from www.evangelicalfellowship.ca/Get-involved/Support-the-EFC/Appeal-letters/2016/Religious-Freedom-Trinity-Western-University-Law.aspx (Accessed Nov. 10, 2019).

Evangelical Fellowship of Canada (n.d.). Ontario Child Welfare: fact sheet on Bill 89. Retrieved from www.evangelicalfellowship.ca/Resources/Documents/Ontario-Child-Welfare-Fact-Sheet-on-Bill-89 (Accessed Nov. 12, 2019).

Evans, M. (2016). Comparative insights on civics and citizenship education and the curriculum: a view from Canada. In A. Peterson and L. Tudall (eds.) *Civics and Citizenship Education in Australia* (pp. 189–206). London: Bloomsbury.

Everyday for Life Canada (2016, Oct. 26). No government has the right to remove 'mother' and 'father' from birth certificates. *Everyday for Life Canada Blog*. Retrieved from https://everydayforlifecanada.blogspot.com/2016/10/no-government-has-right-to-remove.html (Accessed Nov. 12, 2019).

Everyday for Life Canada (2017). University higher learning or state mandated indoctrination. *Everyday for Life Canada Blog*. Retrieved from https://everydayforlifecanada.blogspot.com/2017/11/universitys-higher-learning-or-state.html?q=political+correctness+gone+mad (Accessed Nov. 13, 2019).

Everyday for Life Canada (2018). Sexual diversity studies: what a waste of taxpayer money. *Everyday for Life Canada Blog*. Retrieved from https://everydayforlifecanada.blogspot.com/2018/12/sexual-diversity-studies-what-waste-of.html?q=%E2%80%98stop+tax+dollars+from+funding+the+indoctrination+of+students%E2%80%99 (Accessed Nov. 13, 2019).

Family Education Trust (2018, July 6). Fundamental British values. Retrieved from https://familyeducationtrust.org.uk/bulletin-171-july-2018/#fundamental (Accessed Nov. 10, 2019).

Farley, H. (2017, Sept. 11). Christian couple sues Church of England primary over transgender boy. *Christian Today*. Retrieved from www.christiantoday.com/article/christian-couple-sues-church-of-england-primary-over-transgender-boy/113440.htm (Accessed Nov. 13, 2019).

Farmer, A. (2019, July 7). Is this the start of a free speech fightback on campus? *Conservative Woman*. Retrieved from www.conservativewoman.co.uk/is-this-the-start-of-a-free-speech-fightback-on-campus/ (Accessed Nov. 8, 2019).

Faust, K. (n.d.). Them before us: children's rights before adult's desires. Retrieved from https://thembeforeus.com (Accessed Nov. 13, 2019).

Ferguson, E. (2018). Queen's defends choice of speaker. *Kingston Whig Standard*. Retrieved from www.thewhig.com/2018/02/28/queens-defends-choice-of-speaker/wcm/ca546f0f-3cc8-95c7-0212-9caa6ff36015.

Ferguson, R. (2003). *Aberrations in Black: Toward a Queer of Color Critique*. Minneapolis, MN: University of Minnesota Press.

Ferguson, R. (2019). *One-Dimensional Queer*. London: Polity Press.

Fetner, T. (2008). *How the Religious Right Shaped Lesbian and Gay Activism*. Minneapolis, MN: University of Minnesota Press.

Flagg, B.J. (2005). Whiteness: some critical perspectives. *Journal of Law and Policy*, 18(1), 1–11.

Flyn, R. (2018, June 21). Supreme Court's decision on TWU law school reveals flawed view of religion. *Church for Vancouver*. Retrieved from https://churchforvancouver.ca/supreme-courts-decision-on-twu-law-school-reveals-flawed-view-of-religion/ (Accessed Nov. 12, 2019).

Formby, E. (2017). *Exploring LGBT Spaces and Communities*. New York: Routledge.

Fraser, N. (1990). Rethinking the public sphere: a contribution to the critique of actually existing democracy. *Social Text*, (25/26), 56–80.

Freiburger, C. (2018, May 9). Ontario issues first genderless birth certificate to 'non-binary' trans activist. *LifeSite News*. Retrieved from www.lifesitenews.com/news/ontario-issues-first-genderless-birth-certificate-to-non-binary-trans-activ (Accessed Nov. 12, 2019).

Freiburger, C. (2019, Mar. 15). 'Broken promise': Ontario sex ed. will teach kids 'gender identity', gov't says. *LifeSite News*. Retrieved from www.lifesitenews.com/news/broken-promise-ontario-sex-ed-will-teach-kids-gender-identity (Accessed Dec. 12, 2019).

Geddes, J. (2018, Dec. 6). Liberals move to defuse Canada Summer Jobs controversy. *Maclean's*. Retrieved from www. macleans.ca/politics/ottawa/liberals-move-to-defuse-canada-summer-jobs-controversy/ (Accessed Nov. 14, 2019).

Giovannetti, J. and Hauen, J. (2018, Aug. 30). Doug Ford says Ontario postsecondary schools will require free-speech policies. *The Globe and Mail*. Retrieved from www.theglo beandmail.com/canada/article-doug-ford-says-ontario-postsecondary-schools-will-require-free-speech/ (Accessed Nov. 8, 2019).

Gomes, J. (2018, May 20). Deprive us of free speech and you turn us into animals. *Anglican Mainstream*. Retrieved from www.anglican-mainstream.org.za/2018/05/ (Accessed Nov. 10, 2019).

Gomes, J. (2019, Mar. 12). Teaching Muslim kids gay sex is like forcing their forefathers to chew pig fat. Retrieved from www.julesgomes.com/single-post/Teaching-Muslim-kids-gay-sex-is-like-force-feeding-their-fathers-pork-fat (Accessed Nov. 8, 2019).

Gomes, J. (2019, Sept. 12). Free speech is dying in Britain: here's why the US has kept it. *Daily Signal*. Retrieved from www.dailysignal.com/2019/09/12/free-speech-is-dying-in-britain-heres-why-the-us-has-kept-it/ (Accessed Nov. 8, 2019).

Gorman-Murray, A. and Nash, C.J. (2014). Mobile places, relational spaces: conceptualizing change in Sydney's LGBTQ neighborhoods. *Environment and Planning D: Society and Space*, 32(4), 622–641.

Gorman-Murray, A. and Nash, C.J. (2016). LGBT communities, identities, and the politics of mobility: moving from visibility to recognition in contemporary urban landscapes. In K. Browne and G. Brown (eds.) *The Routledge Research Companion to Geographies of Sex and Sexualities* (pp. 247–253). London: Routledge.

Gorman-Murray, A. and Nash, C.J. (2017). Changing geographies of LGBT consumption and leisure space in the neoliberal city. *Urban Studies*, 54(3), 786–805.

Government of Canada (2019). Choose or update the gender identified on your passport or travel document. *Government of Canada*. Retrieved from www.canada.ca/en/immigration-refugees-citizenship/services/canadian-passports/change-sex.html (Accessed Nov. 14, 2019).

Graham, J. (2011, Jan. 20). Same-sex nuptials can't be refused on religious grounds, Saskatchewan court rules. *The Globe and Mail*. Retrieved from www.theglobeandmail.com/news/national/same-sex-nuptials-cant-be-refused-on-religious-grounds-saskatchewan-court-rules/article561234/ (Accessed Nov. 13, 2019).

Granic Allen, T. (2019, July 4). Doug Ford promised to 'repeal and replace' Ontario's sex ed: we are still waiting. *LifeSite News*. www.lifesitenews.com/opinion/doug-ford-promised-to-repeal-and-replace-ontarios-sex-ed-were-still-waiting (Accessed Dec. 12, 2019).

Greene, S.M. (1994). Growing up Irish: development in context. *The Irish Journal of Psychology*, 15(2–3), 354–371.

Gregson, N. and Rose, G. (2000). Taking Butler elsewhere: performativities, spatialities and subjectivities. *Environment and Planning D: Society and Space*, 18(4), 433–452.

Griffith, R.M. (2017). *Moral Combat: How Sex Divided American Christians and Fractured American Politics*. New York: Basic Books.

Gruneau, R. (2017, Dec. 8). The idea of the radical, leftist university is a misleading caricature. *The Globe and Mail*. Retrieved from www.theglobeandmail.com/opinion/ the-idea-of-the-radical-leftist-university-is-a-misleading-caricature/article37244803/ (Accessed Nov. 10, 2019).

Gryboski, M. (2019, Feb. 5). Christians, asked if they believe 'outdated parts of the Bible', denied foster application. *Christian Post*. Retrieved from www.christianpost.com/ news/christians-told-cant-foster-kids-after-asked-if-they-believe-more-outdated-parts-of-the-bible.html (Accessed Nov. 10, 2019).

Gunnarsson Payne, J. (2019). Challenging 'gender ideology': (anti-)gender politics in Europe's populist movement. Retrieved from http://new-pretender.com/2019/02/10/ challenging-gender-ideology-anti-gender-politics-in-europes-populist-moment-jenny-gunnarsson-payne/ (Accessed Dec. 11, 2019).

Gunter, L. (2011, Jan. 12). Protecting gay rights and religious freedoms. *The National Post*. Retrieved from https:// nationalpost.com/full-comment/lorne-gunter-protecting-gay-rights-and-religious-freedoms (Accessed Nov. 13, 2019).

Halberstam, J. (2005). *In a Queer Time and Place: Transgender Bodies, Subcultural Lives*. New York: New York University Press.

Haraway, D. (1988). Situated knowledges: the science question in feminism and the privilege of partial perspective. *Feminist Studies*, 14(3), 575–599.

Harding, R. and Peel, E. (2006). 'We do'? International perspectives on equality, legality and same sex relationships. *Lesbian & Gay Psychology Review*, 7(2), 123–140.

Haritaworn, J. (2015). *Queer Lovers and Hateful Others*. London: Pluto Press.

References

Haritaworn, J., Moussa, G. and Ware, S.M. eds. (2018). *Queering Urban Justice: Queer of Colour Formations in Toronto*. Toronto: University of Toronto Press.

Harris, K. (2017, Nov. 28). 'Our collective shame': Trudeau delivers historic apology to LGBT Canadians. *CBC News*. Retrieved from www.cbc.ca/news/politics/homosexual-offences-exunge-records-1.4422546.

Harris-Quinney, B. (2017, Feb. 28). Why we MUST fight the Leftist thought police banning free speech from our universities. *Daily Express*. Retrieved from www.express.co.uk/comment/expresscomment/773181/university-political-free-speech-campus (Accessed Nov. 8, 2019).

Harvey, D. (2003a). *Paris, Capital of Modernity*. London: Psychology Press.

Harvey, D. (2003b). The right to the city. *International Journal of Urban and Regional Research*, 27(4), 939–941.

Harvey, D. (2010). *Social Justice and the City* (Vol. 1). Athens, GA: University of Georgia Press.

Harvey, D. (2012). *Rebel Cities: From the Right to the City to the Urban Revolution*. London: Verso.

Healy, G., Sheehan, B. and Whelan, N. (2016). *Ireland Says Yes: The Inside Story of How the Vote for Marriage Equality Was Won*. Sallins, Ireland: Merrion Press.

Henry, F. (2006, Nov. 24). Ask the people, Stephen. *The Catholic Register*. Retrieved from www.catholicregister.org/opinion/guest-columnists/item/10256-ask-the-people-stephen.

Herman, D. (1994). *Rights of Passage: Struggles for Lesbian and Gay Legal Equality*. Toronto: University of Toronto Press.

Herman, D. (1997). *The Antigay Agenda*. Chicago, IL: University of Chicago Press.

Herriot, L., Burns, D.P. and Yeung, B. (2017). Contested spaces: trans-inclusive school policies and parental sovereignty in

Canada. *Gender and Education*. DOI: 10.1080/09540253. 2017.1396291.

Hobsbawm, E. (1983). Introduction: inventing traditions. In E. Hobsbawm and T. Ranger (eds.) *The Inventions of Tradition* (pp. 1–14). Cambridge: Cambridge University Press.

Holloway, S.L. and Jöns, H. (2012). Geographies of education and learning. *Transactions of the Institute of British Geographers*, 37(4), 482–488.

House of Commons, House of Lords (2018). Freedom of speech in universities. Retrieved from https://publications. parliament.uk/pa/jt201719/jtselect/jtrights/589/589.pdf (Accessed Nov. 13, 2019).

Humphreys, A. (2019, Sep. 11). Ontario's law society ditches controversial statement on diversity but loses none of the acrimony. *National Post*. Retrieved from https://nationalpost. com/news/ontarios-law-society-ditches-controversial-statement-on-diversity-but-loses-none-of-its-acrimony/ (Accessed Mar. 20, 2020).

Hunt, S. and Holmes, C. (2015). Everyday decolonization: living a decolonizing queer politics. *Journal of Lesbian Studies*, 19(2), 154–172.

Hunt, S.J. and Yip, A.K.T. (2016). *The Ashgate Research Companion to Contemporary Religion and Sexuality*. Farnham: Ashgate.

Interim (2011, Oct. 28). Catholic parents vow to continue fight against Toronto schools. *The Interim*. Retrieved from www. theinterim.com/issues/marriage-family/catholic-parents-vow-to-continue-fight-against-toronto-schools/ (Accessed Nov. 13, 2019).

Interim (2016, Nov. 25). Ontario redefining family. *The Interim*. Retrieved from www.theinterim.com/issues/marriage-family/ontario-redefining-family/ (Accessed Nov. 12, 2019).

Isai, V. (2018, May 5). Tanya Granic Allen will no longer be a candidate for PC Party, Doug Ford says. *The Star*. Retrieved from www.thestar.com/news/queenspark/2018/05/05/tanya-granic-allen-will-no-longer-be-a-candidate-for-ontario-pc-party-doug-ford-says.html.

Jensen, A. (2011). Mobility, space and power: on the multiplicities of seeing mobility. *Mobilities*, 6(2), 255–271.

Johnson, D.W. and Johnson, R. (2016). Cooperative learning and teaching citizenship in democracies. *International Journal of Educational Research*, 76, 162–177.

Johnson, P. and Vanderbeck, R. (2014). *Law, Religion and Homosexuality*. London: Routledge.

Johnston, L. (2005). *Queering Tourism: Paradoxical Performances at Gay Pride Parades*. London: Routledge.

Johnston, L. (2018). *Transforming Gender, Sex, and Place: Gender Variant Geographies*. London: Routledge.

Johnston, L. and Waitt, G. (2015). The spatial politics of gay pride parades and festivals: emotional activism. In D. Paternotte and M. Tremblay (eds.) *Ashgate Research Companion to Lesbian and Gay Activism* (pp. 105–119). Aldershot: Ashgate.

Jones, A. (2016, Sept. 21). Brad Trost compares Ontario sex ed to residential schools. *Maclean's*. Retrieved from www.macleans.ca/politics/brad-trost-compares-ontario-sex-ed-to-residential-schools/ (Accessed Nov. 13, 2019).

Jones, A., DeFilippis, J.N. and Yarbrough, M.W. eds. (2018). *The Unfinished Queer Agenda after Marriage Equality*. London and New York: Routledge.

Jones, M. (2009). Phase space: geography, relational thinking, and beyond. *Progress in Human Geography*, 33, 487–506.

Jordan, M.D. (2011). *Recruiting Young Love: How Christians Talk about Homosexuality*. Chicago, IL: University of Chicago Press.

Joshee, R., Peck, C., Thompson, L.A., Chareka, O. and Sears, A. (2016). Multicultural education, diversity, and citizenship in Canada. In J. Lo Bianco and A. Bal (eds.) *Learning from Difference: Comparative Accounts of Multicultural Education* (pp. 35–50). Cham: Springer.

Kay, B. (2017, Nov. 21). WLU's contemptible conduct proof of intellectual assault underway on campuses. *National Post*. Retrieved from https://nationalpost.com/opinion/ barbara-kay-wlus-contemptible-conduct-proof-of-intellectual-assault-underway-on-campuses (Accessed Nov. 9, 2019).

Kay, B. (2017, Nov. 28). Campus free speech advocates owe pro-life students their help. *National Post*. Retrieved from https://nationalpost.com/opinion/barbara-kay-campus-free-speech-advocates-owe-pro-life-students-their-help (Accessed Nov. 10, 2019).

Kearns, M. (2019, Aug. 28). Women-only rape-relief shelter defunded, then vandalized. *National Review*. Retrieved from www.nationalreview.com/2019/08/women-only-rape-relief-shelter-defunded-then-vandalized/.

Kenttamaa Squires, K. (2019). Rethinking the homonormative? Lesbian and Hispanic Pride events and the uneven geographies of commoditized identities. *Social & Cultural Geography*, 20(3), 367–386.

Kinsman, G. (2018). Policing borders and sexual/gender identities: queer refugees in the years of Canadian neoliberalism and homonationalism. In N. Nicol, A. Jjuuko, R. Lusimbo, N.J. Mulé, S. Ursel, A. Wahab and P. Waugh (eds.) *Envisioning Global LGBT Human Rights* (pp. 97–130). London: School of Advanced Study.

Kinsman, G.W. (1987). *The Regulation of Desire: Sexuality in Canada*. Montreal: Black Rose Books.

Kitzinger, C. and Wilkinson, S. (2004). The rebranding of marriage: why we got married instead of registering a civil partnership. *Feminism & Psychology*, 14(1), 127–150.

Klett, L.M. (2019, Apr. 23). Christian beliefs are 'pro-Nazi'? Teacher fired for opposing pro-transgender lessons recalls ordeal. *The Christian Post*. Retrieved from www. christianpost.com/news/christian-beliefs-are-pro-nazi-teacher-fired-for-opposing-pro-transgender-lessons-recalls-ordeal.html (Accessed Nov. 13, 2019).

Knopp, L. (1995). Sexuality and urban space: a framework for analysis. In D.J. Bell and G. Valentine (eds.) *Mapping Desire: Geographies of Sexualities* (pp. 149–160). New York: Routledge.

Knowles, M. (2017, Oct. 11). Victory in court fight over gender neutral passport. *Daily Express*. Retrieved from www.express. co.uk/news/uk/865307/Gender-neutral-passport-court-fight (Accessed Nov. 12, 2019).

Kojima, D., Catungal, J.P. and Diaz, R. (2017). Introduction: feeling queer, feeling Asian, feeling Canadian. *TOPIA*, 38: 69–80.

Kollman, K. and Waites, M. (2009). The global politics of lesbian, gay, bisexual and transgender human rights: an introduction. *Contemporary Politics*, 15(1), 1–17.

Kováts, E. (2017). The emergence of powerful anti-gender movements in Europe and the crisis of liberal democracy. In M. Köttig, R. Bitzan and A. Petö (eds.) *Gender and Far Right Politics in Europe* (pp. 175–189). Cham: Palgrave Macmillan.

Kováts, E. (2018). Questioning consensuses: right-wing populism, anti-populism, and the threat of 'gender ideology'. *Sociological Research Online*, 23(2), 528–538.

Kriska, R. (2019, May 28). Gender confusion 'spreading in our schools'. *Christian Concern*. Retrieved from https://christianconcern.com/comment/gender-confusion-spreading-in-our-schools/.

Kuhar, R. and Paternotte, D. (2017a). *Anti-Gender Campaigns in Europe: Mobilising against Equality*. London: Rowman & Littlefield.

Kuhar, R. and Paternotte, D. (2017b). 'Gender ideology' in movement: introduction. In R. Kuhar and D. Paternotte (eds.) *Anti-Gender Campaigns in Europe: Mobilizing against Equality* (pp. 1–22). London: Rowman & Littlefield.

Kuhar, R. and Zobec, A. (2017). The anti-gender movement in Europe and the educational process in public schools. *CEPS Journal*, 7(2), 29–46.

Kulpa, R. and Mizielinska, J. (2011). *De-Centring Western Sexualities: Central and Eastern European Perspectives*. Farnham: Ashgate.

Kulpa, R. and Silva, J.M. (2016). Decolonizing queer epistemologies: section introduction. In G. Brown and K. Browne (eds.) *Routledge Research Companion to Geographies of Sex and Sexualities* (pp. 139–142). London: Routledge.

Kuntsman, A. and Miyake, E. eds. (2008). *Out of Place: Interrogating Silences in Queerness/Raciality*. New York: Raw Nerve Books.

Kurten, D. (2017, Dec. 19). Transgenderism and this insane ban on free speech. *The Conservative Woman*. Retrieved from www.conservativewoman.co.uk/david-kurten-transgenderism-insane-ban-free-speech/ (Accessed Nov. 8, 2019).

Kwak, L.J. (2019). New Canadians are new conservatives: race, incorporation and achieving electoral success in multicultural Canada. *Ethnic and Racial Studies*, 42(10), 1708–1726.

Lacken, J. (2018). Fieldnotes from Lumen Fidei Conference, Dublin, Ireland.

Lalor, K. and Browne, K. (2018). Here versus there: creating British sexual politics elsewhere. *Feminist Legal Studies*, 26(2), 205–213.

Lamontagne, E., d'Elbée, M., Ross, M.W., Carroll, A., Plessis, A.D. and Loures, L. (2018). A socioecological measurement of homophobia for all countries and its public health impact. *European Journal of Public Health*, 28(5), 967–972.

Landolt, G. (2016, Nov. 2). Letter to MPs: Trudeau blindsides democracy. *REAL Women of Canada*. Retrieved from www.realwomenofcanada.ca/trudeau-blindsides-democracy-transgender-bill/.

Langstaff, A. (2011). A twenty year survey of Canadian attitudes towards homosexuality and gay rights. In D. Rayside and C. Wilcox (eds.) *Faith, Politics and Sexual Diversity in Canada and the United States* (pp. 49–66). Vancouver: UBC Press.

Laurence, L. (2016, June 30). Ontario gov't tells court: no opt-outs for LGBT lessons, it's embedded in all subjects and grades. *LifeSite News*. Retrieved from www.lifesitenews.com/news/wynne-govt-tells-court-parents-cant-pull-kids-out-of-lgbtq-classes (Accessed Nov. 13, 2019).

Laurence, L. (2016, Nov. 29). Ontario unanimously passes radical LGBT bill redefining parent–child relationship. *LifeSite News*. Retrieved from www.lifesitenews.com/news/breaking-ontario-unanimously-passes-radical-lgbt-bill-redefining-parent-chi (Accessed Nov. 13, 2019).

Laurence, L. (2017, Jan. 25). 'Totalitarian': Ontario gov't bill makes it easier to seize children from Christian homes, say critics. *LifeSite News*. Retrieved from www.lifesitenews.com/news/totalitarian-ontario-govt-bill-makes-it-easier-to-seize-children-from-chris (Accessed Nov. 12, 2019).

Laurence, L. (2017, Aug. 30). LGBT victory in Canada, government allows third gender option on passports. *LifeSite News*. Retrieved from www.lifesitenews.com/news/trudeau-liberals-allow-third-gender-on-passports (Accessed Nov. 12, 2019).

Laurence, L. (2018, Jan. 11). Canadian Christians rise up against Trudeau's pro-abortion pledge for summer job grants. *LifeSite News*. Retrieved from www.lifesitenews.com/news/canadian-christians-rise-up-against-trudeaus-pro-abortion-pledge-for-summer (Accessed Nov. 11, 2019).

Laurence, L. (2018, Jan. 26). Tourloukis loses parental rights case. *The Interim*. Retrieved from www.theinterim.com/issues/marriage-family/tourloukis-loses-parental-rights-case/.

Laurence, L. (2019, June 28). Mom takes school to Human Rights Tribunal for traumatizing child with gender ideology. *LifeSite News*. Retrieved from www.lifesitenews.com/news/mom-takes-school-to-human-rights-tribunal-for-traumatizing-her-child-with-gender-ideology.

Law Society of Ontario (n.d.). Statement of Principles. *Law Society of Ontario*. Retrieved from https://lso.ca/about-lso/initiatives/edi/statement-of-principles) (Accessed Nov. 14, 2019).

Lefebvre, H. (1991). *Critique of Everyday Life: Foundations for a Sociology of the Everyday* (Vol. 2). London: Verso.

Leishman, R. (2013). Tolerance and same-sex 'marriage' threaten freedom. *The Interim*. Retrieved from www.theinterim.com/issues/marriage-family/tolerance-and-same-sex-marriage-threaten-freedom/ (Accessed Nov. 7, 2019).

Leishman, R. (2018). U.S. Supreme Court upholds religious freedom, whereas Canadian Court does not. Retrieved from www.theinterim.com/soconvivium/u-s-supreme-court-upholds-religious-freedom-whereas-canadian-court-does-not/ (Accessed Nov. 10, 2019).

Leitner, H. (2012). Spaces of encounters: immigration, race, class, and the politics of belonging in small-town America. *Annals of the Association of American Geographers*, 102(4), 828–846.

Lewis, C. (2018, Mar. 14). Restriction on summer jobs funding not the first time religious rights in Canada have been trampled on. *National Post*. Retrieved from https://nationalpost.com/news/religion/federal-restriction-on-summer-jobs-funding-is-not-the-first-time-religious-rights-in-canada-have-been-trampled-on (Accessed Nov. 10, 2019).

Lewis, C. (2018, July 4). The Ontario court decision over Trinity Western law school is a travesty of discrimination. *National Post*. Retrieved from https://nationalpost.com/opinion/charles-lewis-the-ontario-court-decision-over-trinity-western-law-school-is-a-travesty-of-discrimination (Accessed Nov. 13, 2019).

Ley, D. (2010). Multiculturalism: a Canadian defence. In S. Vertovec and S. Wessendorf (eds.) *The Multiculturalism Backlash* (pp. 200–216). London: Routledge.

LifeSite News (2010, June 29). Analysis: false gospel of 'equity' lures Ontario Catholic School Board. *LifeSite News*. Retrieved from www.lifesitenews.com/news/analysis-false-gospel-of-equity-lures-ontario-catholic-school-boards (Accessed Nov. 13, 2019).

LifeSite News (2015, Apr. 21). Campaign Life's detailed analysis of Wynne's radical sex-ed np in 6 languages, more to come. *LifeSite News*. Retrieved from www.lifesitenews.com/news/campaign-lifes-detailed-analysis-of-wynnes-radical-sex-ed-now-in-6-language (Accessed Mar. 21, 2020).

LifeSite News (2017, Jan. 25). U.S. Supreme Court refuses to hear Sister Wives case to legalize polygamy. *LifeSite News*.

Retrieved from www.lifesitenews.com/news/scotus-refuses-to-hear-case-by-sisters-wives-star-seeking-to-legalize-polyg.

LifeSite News (2019, June 20). Ontario foster child service rejects couple for professing Christianity. *LifeSite News.* Retrieved from www.lifesitenews.com/news/ontario-foster-child-service-rejects-couple-for-professing-christianity (Accessed Nov. 12, 2019).

Lilley, B. (2015, Apr. 13). Kathleen Wynne calls parents 'homophobic', blames Federal Conservatives over opposition to her radical sex-ed curriculum. *The Rebel.* Retrieved from www.therebel.media/kathleen_wynne_call_parents_homophobic_blames_federal_conservatives_over_opposition_to_her_radical_sex_ed (Accessed Nov. 8, 2019).

Luetke, J. (2017, June 9). Senate holds hearings on C-16. *The Interim.* Retrieved from www.theinterim.com/issues/society-culture/senate-holds-hearings-on-c-16/.

Lumen Fidei Institute (2018). A Conference for Catholic Families. *Lumen Fidei Institute.* Retrieved from www.lumenfidei.ie/a-conference-of-catholic-families/ (Accessed Nov. 13, 2019).

Lynskey, D. (2018, Feb. 7). How dangerous is Jordan B Peterson, the rightwing professor who 'hit a hornets' nest'? *The Guardian.* Retrieved from www.theguardian.com/science/2018/feb/07/how-dangerous-is-jordan-b-peterson-the-rightwing-professor-who-hit-a-hornets-nest (Accessed Nov. 13, 2019).

Maguire, H., McCartan, A., Nash, C.J. and Browne, K. (2019). The enduring field: exploring researcher emotions in covert research with antagonistic organisations. *Area*, 51(2), 299–306.

Mann, A. (2016, Sept. 8). What do we make of Patrick Browne? *Xtra.* Retrieved from www.dailyxtra.com/what-do-we-make-of-patrick-brown-71898.

Marantha Community (2012). Equal civil marriage: a consultation. A response by the Maranatha Community. *Marantha Community*. Retrieved from www.maranathacommunity.org.uk/pdf/june12-equal-civil-marriage-consultation.pdf (Accessed Nov. 8, 2019).

Marcuse, P. (2009). From critical urban theory to the right to the city. *City*, 13(2–3), 185–197.

Massey, D. (1994). *Space, Place and Gender*. Cambridge: Polity Press.

Massey, D. (2002). Globalisation: what does it mean for geography? *Geography*, 87(4), 293–296.

Massey, D. (2005). *For Space*. London: Sage.

Matthews, A. (2019, July 9). 'Gay is not okay': Muslim dad slams school for teaching children 'gay is ok' in fresh protests against LGBT lessons. *The Sun*. Retrieved from www.thesun.co.uk/news/9467598/muslim-dad-slams-school-teaching-gay-is-ok/ (Accessed Nov. 13, 2019).

McAuliffe, M. and Kennedy, S. (2017). Defending catholic Ireland. In R. Kuhar and D. Paternotte (eds.) *Anti-Gender Campaigns in Europe: Mobilizing against Equality* (pp. 133–150). London: Rowman & Littlefield.

McDonald, M. (2010). *The Armageddon Factor: The Rise of Christian Nationalism in Canada*. Toronto: Random House.

McGarry, P. (2014). Waters challenges RTÉ statement on Panti row. *Irish Times*. Retrieved from www.irishtimes.com/news/social-affairs/waters-challenges-rté-statement-on-panti-row-1.1683645 (Accessed Nov. 13, 2019).

McGlynn, N. (2014). *In the Shadow of the Gay Capital: Lesbian, Gay, Bisexual and Trans Equalities in 'Rural' and 'Non-Urban' East Sussex*. Doctoral Thesis. Brighton: University of Brighton.

McGovern, C. (2016, Apr. 24). Brighton's transgender lunacy is a cruelty robbing children of their innocence. *Conservative Woman*. Retrieved from www.conservativewoman.co.uk/chris-mcgovern-brightons-transgender-lunacy-is-a-cruelty-robbing-children-of-their-innocence/ (Accessed Nov. 12, 2019).

McIntosh, P. (1998). White privilege. In M.L. Andersen and P. Hill Collins (eds.) *Race, Class and Gender: An Anthology* (pp. 94–105). Scarborough, Ontario: Nelson Education.

McKittrick, K. and Woods, C.A. eds. (2007). *Black Geographies and the Politics of Place*. Cambridge, MA: South End Press.

Mermaids (2019). Homepage. Retrieved from www.mermaidsuk. org.uk/ (Accessed Nov. 13, 2019).

Mikdashi, M. and Puar, J.K. (2016). Queer theory and permanent war. *GLQ: A Journal of Lesbian and Gay Studies*, 22(2), 215–222.

Mitchell, D. (1996). Introduction: public space and the city. *Urban Geography*, 17(2), 127–131.

Mitchell, D. (2003). *The Right to the City: Social Justice and the Fight for Public Space*. New York: Guilford Press.

Mitchell, D. (2017). People's Park again: on the end and ends of public space. *Environment and Planning A: Economy and Space*, 49(3), 503–518.

Mitchell, D. and Heynen, N. (2009). The geography of survival and the right to the city: speculations on surveillance, legal innovation, and the criminalization of intervention. *Urban Geography*, 30(6), 611–632.

Mitchell, K. (2003). Educating the national citizen in neoliberal times: from the multicultural self to the strategic cosmopolitan. *Transactions of the Institute of British Geographers*, 28: 387–403.

Morgensen, S.L. (2013). The representability and responsibility of cisgender queer men in Women's Studies. *Women's Studies*, 42(5), 534–558.

Morrow, A. (2015, Feb. 24). Wynne suggests Tory MPP homophobic after sex-ed comments. *The Globe and Mail*. Retrieved from www.theglobeandmail.com/news/politics/ wynne-accuses-tory-mpp-of-homophobia-over-sex-ed-opposition/article23189536/ (Accessed Nov. 8, 2019).

Moseley, C. (2017, Nov. 16). Why the transgender issue is not a single issue. *Christian Concern*. Retrieved from https:// archive.christianconcern.com/our-issues/education/ why-the-transgender-issue-is-not-a-single-issue (Accessed Nov. 9, 2019).

Moseley, C. (2017, Dec. 15). Should primary school children learn about gender identity? *Christian Concern*. Retrieved from https://archive.christianconcern.com/our-issues/ education/should-primary-school-children-learn-about-gender-identity (Accessed Nov. 9, 2019).

Moseley, C. (2018, Mar. 1). The abusers behind the idea that children have a 'gender identity'. *Christian Concern*. Retrieved from https://archive.christianconcern.com/our-issues/ family-and-sexual-ethics/the-abusers-behind-the-idea-that-children-have-a-gender-identity (Accessed Nov. 12, 2019).

Moseley, C. (2018, Sept. 12). Counselling and psychotherapy have become transgender propaganda mouthpieces. *Christian Concern*. Retrieved from https://archive. christianconcern.com/our-issues/sexual-orientation/ counselling-and-psychotherapy-have-become-transgender-propaganda-mouth (Accessed Nov. 9, 2019).

Mostov, J. (2000). Sexing the nation/desexing the body: politics of national identity in the former Yugoslavia. In T. Mayer (ed.) *Gender Ironies of Nationalism* (pp. 89–110). London and New York: Routledge.

Mothers and Fathers Matter (2015). mothersandfathersmatter. org (Accessed 2014 for Browne and Nash (2014)). Site now offline but extracts of Mothers and Fathers Matter commentary available at: https://sligonewsfile.com/ category/news-item/page/87/ (Accessed Nov. 7, 2019).

Mulhall, A. (2015, June 20). The Republic of Love: on the complex achievement of the same-sex marriage referendum in Ireland. *Bully Bloggers*. https://bullybloggers.wordpress.com/2015/ 06/20/the-republic-of-love/ (Accessed Nov. 6, 2019).

Murphy, P. and Watson, S. (1997). *Surface City: Sydney at the Millennium*. Annandale, NSW: Pluto Press.

Murphy, R. (2017, Dec. 28). Time to move on from the Shepherd affair? Hardly. *National Post*. Retrieved from https:// nationalpost.com/opinion/rex-murphy-time-to-move-on-from-the-shepherd-affair-hardly (Accessed Nov. 9, 2019).

Murray, D. (2009). *Homophobias*. London: Duke University Press.

Nakhaie, M.R. and Brym, R.J. (2011). The ideological orientations of Canadian university professors. *Canadian Journal of Higher Education*, 41, 18–33.

Nash, C.J. (1993). Remapping and renaming: new cartographies of identity, gender and landscape in Ireland. *Feminist Review*, 44(1), 39–57.

Nash, C.J. (2005). Contesting identity: the struggle for gay identity in Toronto in the late 1970s. *Gender, Place and Culture*, 12(1), 113–135.

Nash, C.J. (2006). Toronto's gay village (1969 to 1982): plotting the politics of gay identity. *Canadian Geographer/Le géographe canadien*, 50(1), 1–16.

Nash, C.J. (2011). Trans experiences in lesbian and queer space. *Canadian Geographer/Le géographe canadien*, 56(1), 192–207.

Nash, C.J. and Browne, K.A. (2015). Best for society? Transnational opposition to sexual and gender equalities in Canada and Great Britain. *Gender Place and Culture*, 22(4), 561–577.

Nash, C.J. and Browne, K.A. (2018). Freedom of speech or hate speech: heteroactivist contestation of no-platforming. Conference Paper. Royal Geographical Society/Institute of British Geographers (RGS-IBG) Annual Conference, Cardiff Aug. 29–31.

Nash, C.J. and Browne, K.A. (2019). Resisting the mainstreaming of LGBT equalities in Canadian and British schools: sex education and trans school friends. *Environment and Planning C: Politics and Space.*

Nash, C.J., Browne, K. and Gorman-Murray, A. (2019). LGBT families and 'motherless' children: tracking heteronormative resistances in Great Britain, Canada and Australia. In L. Johnson and K. Johnston (eds.) *Mothers/Mothering: Space and Place.* Bradford, Ontario: Demeter Press (revised June 2017).

Nash, C.J. and Gorman-Murray, A. (2014). LGBT neighbourhoods and 'new mobilities': towards understanding transformations in sexual and gendered urban landscapes. *International Journal of Urban and Regional Research,* 38(3), 756–772.

Nash, C.J. and Gorman-Murray, A. eds. (2019). *The Geographies of Digital Sexuality.* Singapore: Palgrave Macmillan.

Nash, C.J., Gorman-Murray, A. and Browne, K. (2019). Geographies of intransigence: freedom of speech and heteroactivist resistances in Canada, Great Britain and Australia. *Social & Cultural Geography,* 1–21.

Nash, C.J., Maguire, H. and Gorman-Murray, A. (2019). LGBTQ communities, public space and urban movement: towards mobility justice in the contemporary city. In N. Cook and D. Butz (eds.) *Mobilities, Mobility Justice and Social Justice* (pp.188–200). London and New York: Routledge.

Nast, H.J. (2002). Queer patriarchies, queer racisms. *Antipode*, 34(5), 874–909.

National Post (2015, Feb. 26). Homophobia motivates some anti-sex protesters. *National Post*. Retrieved from https://nationalpost.com/news/politics/homophobia-motivates-some-anti-sex-ed-protestors-ontario-premier-kathleen-wynne (Accessed May 7, 2019).

Nayak, A. (2016). *Race, Place and Globalization: Youth Cultures in a Changing World*. London: Bloomsbury.

Neary, A. (2016). Civil partnership and marriage: LGBT-Q political pragmatism and the normalization imperative. *Sexualities*, 19(7), 757–779.

Neary, A., Irwin-Gowran, S. and McEvoy, E. (2017). Exploring homophobia and transphobia in primary schools in Ireland. Report, University of Limerick & Gay and Lesbian Equality Network, Ireland.

Neely, B. and Samura, M. (2011). Social geographies of race: connecting race and space. *Ethnic and Racial Studies*, 34(11), 1933–1952.

Nicholas, L. (2019). Whiteness, heteropaternalism, and the gendered politics of settler colonial populist backlash culture in Australia. *Social Politics*.

Nicol, N. and Smith, M. (2008). Legal struggles and political resistance: same-sex marriage in Canada and the USA. *Sexualities*, 11(6), 667–687.

O'Brien, B. (2015, Feb. 28). Democratic disaster as government pushes through family bill. *Irish Times*. Retrieved from www.irishtimes.com/opinion/breda-o-brien-democratic-disaster-as-government-pushes-through-family-bill-1.2120526 (Accessed Nov. 7, 2019) (and see series of B. O'Brien articles on *Irish Times* website).

References

O'Brien, J. (2008). Afterword: complicating homophobia. *Sexualities*, 11(4), 496–512.

O'Carroll, Í. and Collins, E. (1995). *Lesbian and Gay Visions of Ireland: Towards the Twenty-first Century*. Tunbridge Wells: Burns & Oates.

Office of the Premier (2018). Ontario protects free speech on campuses. *Ontario*. Retrieved from https://news.ontario.ca/opo/en/2018/08/ontario-protects-free-speech-on-campuses.html (Accessed Nov. 13, 2019).

Olsen, E. and Silvey, R. (2006). Transnational geographies: rescaling development, migration and religion (Guest Editorial). *Environment and Planning A*, 38, 805–808.

Oswin, N. (2006). Decentering queer globalization: diffusion and the 'global gay'. *Environment and Planning D: Society and Space*, 24: 777–790.

Oswin, N. (2008). Critical geographies and the uses of sexuality. *Progress in Human Geography*, 32(1), 89–103.

Paternotte, D. and Kuhar, R. (2017). The anti-gender movement in comparative perspective. In R. Kuhar and D. Paternotte (eds.) *Anti-Gender Campaigns in Europe: Mobilizing against Equality* (pp. 253–276). London: Rowman & Littlefield.

Paternotte, D. and Kuhar, R. (2018). Disentangling and locating the 'global right': Anti-gender campaigns in Europe. *Politics and Governance*, 6(3), 6–19.

Perrins, L. (2018, July 11). Free speech week: Sarah Champion tells the truth about grooming gangs. *Conservative Woman*. Retrieved from www.conservativewoman.co.uk/free-speech-week-sarah-champion-tells-the-truth-about-grooming-gangs/ (Accessed Nov. 9, 2019).

Peterson, J. (2016, Nov. 8). The right to be politically incorrect. *National Post*. Retrieved from https://nationalpost.com/

opinion/jordan-peterson-the-right-to-be-politically-incorrect (Accessed Nov. 10, 2019).

Peterson, J. (2019). Gender politics has no place in the classroom. *National Post*. Retrieved from https://nationalpost.com/opinion/jordan-peterson-gender-politics-has-no-place-in-the-classroom (Accessed Nov. 9, 2019).

Piekut, A. and Valentine, G. (2016). Unpacking prejudice: narratives of homophobia in cross-national context. In U.M. Vieten and G. Valentine (eds.) *Cartographies of Difference: Interdisciplinary Perspectives on Living with Difference* (pp. 15–40). Oxford: Peter Lang.

Plett, D.N. (2017, Mar. 2). Senators' Statements. Senate of Canada. Retrieved from https://sencanada.ca/en/content/sen/chamber/421/debates/101db_2017-03-02-e.

Podmore, J. (2013). Critical commentary: sexualities landscapes beyond homonormativity. *Geoforum*, 49, 263–267.

Preece, A. (2019, Apr. 10). Muslim mums protest outside school for 'promoting homosexuality' to their kids. *BirminghamLive*. Retrieved from www.birminghammail.co.uk/news/midlands-news/muslim-mums-protest-outside-school-15729135 (Accessed Nov. 13, 2019).

Price, P.L. (2010). At the crossroads: critical race theory and critical geographies of race. *Progress in Human Geography*, 34(2), 147–174.

Puar, J.K. (2006). Mapping U.S. homonormativities. *Gender, Place, Culture: A Journal of Feminist Geography*, 13(1), 67–88.

Puar, J. (2007). *Terrorist Assemblages: Homonationalism in Queer Times*. Durham, NC: Duke University Press.

Puar, J. (2011). Citation and censorship: the politics of talking about the sexual politics of Israel. *Feminist Legal Studies*, 19(2), 133–142.

References

Rao, R. (2015). Global homocapitalism. *Radical Philosophy*, 194, 38–49.

Rassmusan, M.L., Cover, R., Aggleton, P. and Marshall, D. (2016). Sexuality, gender, citizenship and social justice: education's queer relations. In A. Peterson, R. Hattam, M. Zembylas and J. Arthur (eds.) *The Palgrave International Handbook of Education for Citizenship and Social Justice* (pp. 73–96). London: Palgrave Macmillan.

Ray, B. and Preston, V. (2015). Working with diversity: a geographical analysis of ethno-racial discrimination in Toronto. *Urban Studies*, 52(8), 1505–1522.

Rayside, D. (2014). The inadequate recognition of sexual diversity by Canadian schools: LGBT advocacy and its impact. *Journal of Canadian Studies*, 48(1), 190–225.

Rayside, D. and Wilcox, C. eds. (2012). *Faith, Politics, and Sexual Diversity in Canada and the United States*. Vancouver: UBC Press.

Real Women of Canada (2013). We all are born from a man and a woman!: 1.3 million demonstrate against same-sex 'marriage' and adoption in Paris. *Real Women of Canada*. Retrieved from www.realwomenofcanada.ca/we-all-are-born-from-a-man-and-a-woman-1-3-million-demonstrate-against-same-sex-marriage-and-adoption-in-paris-2/ (Accessed Nov. 7, 2019).

Real Women of Canada (2016, Oct. 16). Ontario government rams through revolutionary bill. *Real Women of Canada*. Retrieved from www.realwomenofcanada.ca/ontario-government-rams-revolutionary-bill-resturing-families/ (Accessed Nov. 12, 2019).

Real Women of Canada (2017, Jan. 26). Bill 89: another attack on the family by the Province of Ontario. *Real Women of Canada*. Retrieved from www.realwomenofcanada.ca/bill-28/ (Accessed Nov. 12, 2019).

Real Women of Canada (2017, Dec. 4). PM Justin Trudeau's apology to homosexuals deceives the majority of Canadians. *Real Women of Canada*. Retrieved from www.realwomen ofcanada.ca/pm-justin-trudeaus-apology-homosexuals-deceives-majority-canadians/ (Accessed Nov. 11, 2019).

Real Women of Canada (2018, July 18). Religious freedom: Trinity Western University and the Supreme Court of Canada. *Real Women of Canada*. Retrieved from www. realwomenofcanada.ca/trinity-western-university-and-the-supreme-court-of-canada-2/ (Accessed Nov. 10, 2019).

Real Women of Canada (2019, June 7). Storm clouds gathering over religion. *REALity*. Retrieved from www. realwomenofcanada.ca/storm-clouds-gathering-over-religion/ (Accessed Nov. 14, 2019).

Referendum Results (2015). Referendum 2015. Retrieved from www.referendum.ie/results-summary.php?ref=10) (Accessed Nov. 9, 2019).

Reimer, S. (2003). *Evangelicals and the Continental Divide: The Conservative Protestant Subculture in Canada and the United States.* Montreal: McGill-Queen's Press.

Richardson, D. (1998). Sexuality and citizenship. *Sociology*, 32(1), 83–100.

Richardson, D. (2004). Locating sexualities: from here to normality. *Sexualities*, 7(4), 391–411.

Richardson, D. (2005). Desiring sameness? The rise of a neoliberal politics of normalization. *Antipode*, 37(3), 515–535.

Richardson, D. (2017). Rethinking sexual citizenship. *Sociology*, 51(2), 208–224.

Richardson, D. and Monro, S. (2012). *Sexuality, Equality and Diversity.* Basingstoke: Palgrave.

Risdon, J. (2018, Aug. 17). Christian university drops morality pledge after top court said it violated LGBT 'rights'. *LifeSite*

News. Retrieved from www.lifesitenews.com/news/christian-university-drops-sexual-ethics-pledge-after-top-court-ruled-it-vi (Accessed Nov. 13, 2019).

Ritchie, F. (2018). Supreme Court's decision on TWU law school reveals flawed view of religion. *Church for Vancouver.* Retrieved from https://churchforvancouver.ca/supreme-courts-decision-on-twu-law-school-reveals-flawed-view-of-religion/ (Accessed Nov. 13, 2019).

Robertson, D. (2019, Mar. 21). Jordan Peterson, Caroline Farrow and the death of free speech, *Premier Christianity.* Retrieved from www.premierchristianity.com/Blog/Jordan-Peterson-Caroline-Farrow-and-the-death-of-free-speech (Accessed Nov. 8, 2019).

Robinson, M. (2010). Reading Althaus-Reid: as a bi feminist theo/methodological resource. *Journal of Bisexuality,* 10(1–2), 108–120.

Rose, G. (1999). Performing space. In D. Massey, J. Allen and P. Sarre (eds.) *Human Geography Today* (pp. 247–259). Cambridge: Polity Press.

Rosky, C.J. (2012). Fear of the queer child. *Buffalo Law Review,* 61(3), 607–697.

Ross, D. and Kinsinger, K. (2019, July 11). Religious expression is under attack in Canada – and not just in Quebec. *The Globe and Mail.* Retrieved from www.theglobeandmail.com/opinion/article-religious-expression-is-under-attack-in-canada-and-not-just-in/ (Accessed Nov. 10, 2019).

RTÉ (2014, Feb. 6). RTÉ MD of Television defends Iona Institute apology and payout as 'most prudent course of action'. *RTÉ.* Retrieved from www.rte.ie/news/2014/0205/502379-rte-iona/ (Accessed Nov. 13, 2019).

Rushbrook, D. (2002). Cities, queer space, and the cosmopolitan tourist. *Gay and Lesbian Quarterly: A Journal of Lesbian and Gay Studies,* 8: 183–206.

References

Russell, G. (2018, July 31). Controversial academic Jordan Peterson to come to Scotland. *The National*. Retrieved from www.thenational.scot/news/16387283.controversial-academic-jordan-b-peterson-to-come-to-scotland/ (Accessed Nov. 13, 2019).

Ryan, F.W. (2015). Same-sex couples and the Marriage Act 2015: implications for practice. Retrieved from https://ssrn.com/abstract=2700626 (Accessed Nov. 27, 2017).

Ryan-Flood, R. (2005). Contested heteronormativities: discourses of fatherhood among lesbian parents in Sweden and Ireland. *Sexualities*, 8(2), 189–204.

Ryan-Flood, R. (2015). Sexuality, citizenship and migration: the Irish queer diaspora in London. In F. Stella, Y. Taylor, T. Reynolds and A. Rogers (eds.) *Sexuality, Citizenship and Belonging* (pp. 45–62). New York: Routledge.

Sabsay, L. (2012). The emergence of the other sexual citizen: orientalism and the modernisation of sexuality. *Citizenship Studies*, 16(5–6), 605–623.

Saurette, P. and Gordon, K. (2013). Arguing abortion: the new anti-abortion discourse in Canada. *Canadian Journal of Political Science/Revue canadienne de science politique*, 46(1), 157–185.

Sears, A. (2005). Queer anti-capitalism: what's left of lesbian and gay liberation? *Science & Society*, 69(1), Special issue, 92–112.

Seljak, D. (2016). Post-secularism, multiculturalism, human rights, and religion in Ontario. *Studies in Religion/Sciences religieuses*, 45(4), 542–565.

Shepherd, L. (2017, Dec. 4). My Laurier interrogation shows universities have lost sight of their purpose. *National Post*. Retrieved from https://nationalpost.com/opinion/lindsay-shepherd-wlus-interrogation-revealed-how-university-has-lost-sight-of-its-key-purpose (Accessed Nov. 10, 2019).

References

Sherwood, H. (2017, June 23). Gay activist claims she was spiritually abused by evangelical churches. *The Guardian.* Retrieved from www.theguardian.com/world/2017/jun/23/gay-activist-claims-spiritually-abused-church (Accessed Nov. 9, 2019).

Siegel, S. (2017). Marriage equality and rightwing populism in the EU: an intimate conversation. Jean Monnet Center of Excellence Faculty Research Workshop, Marriage Equality in Advanced Industrialized Democracies, University of Pittsburgh, Mar. 31.

Smith, M. (2007). Identity and opportunity: the lesbian and gay rights movement. In M. Smith (ed.) *Group Politics and Social Movements in Canada* (pp. 159–180). Peterborough, Ontario: Broadview Press.

Smith, M. (2008). *Political Institutions and Lesbian and Gay Rights in the United States and Canada.* New York: Routledge.

Smith, M. (2019). Homophobia and homonationalism: LGBTQ law reform in Canada. *Social & Legal Studies.*

Smyth, A. (1995). States of change: reflections on Ireland in several uncertain parts. *Feminist Review,* (50), 24–43.

Society for the Protection of Unborn Children (SPUC) (2012, Jan.). SPUC position paper on same-sex marriage. Retrieved from www.spuc.org.uk/publications-library/718-ssm201201-pdf/file.

Society for the Protection of Unborn Children (SPUC) (2019). Ofsted acting like Big Brother over compulsory same sex school lessons for children. SPUC Press Release.

Somerville, M. (2010). Children's human rights to natural biological origins and family structure. *International Journal of the Jurisprudence of the Family,* 1, 35–53.

Somerville, M. (2010, July 9). Life's essence, bought and sold. *The Globe and Mail.* Retrieved from www.theglobeandmail.com/

opinion/lifes-essence-bought-and-sold/article1386923/ (Accessed Nov. 13, 2019).

Spencer, N. (2012). Green politics, gay marriage and freedom of conscience. *Theos Think Tank*. Retrieved from www. theosthinktank.co.uk/comment/2012/09/17/green-politics-gay-marriage-and-freedom-of-consience (Accessed Nov. 13, 2019).

Staeheli, L.A. and Mitchell, D. (2008). 'Don't talk with strangers': regulating property, purifying the public. *Griffith Law Review*, 17(2), 531–545.

Staeheli, L.A., Mitchell, D. and Nagel, C.R. (2009). Making publics: immigrants, regimes of publicity and entry to 'the public'. *Environment and Planning D: Society and Space*, 27(4), 633–648.

Standing Senate Committee on Legal and Constitutional Affairs (2017, May 17). Minutes of Proceedings and Evidence. 42nd Parliament, 1st Session. (Online). Retrieved from: https://sencanada.ca/en/Content/SEN/Committee/421/lcjc/53339-e.

Stein, A. (2001). *The Stranger Next Door: The Story of a Small Community's Battle over Sex, Faith, and Civil Rights*. Boston, MA: Beacon Press.

Stella, F. and Nartova, N. (2015). Sexual citizenship, nationalism and biopolitics in Putin's Russia. In F. Stella, Y. Taylor, T. Reynolds, and A. Rogers (eds.) *Sexuality, Citizenship and Belonging: Trans-National and Intersectional Perspectives* (pp. 17–36). London: Routledge.

Stewart, C. (2019). The future is queer kids: queering the homonormative temporalities of same-sex marriage. *Politics*.

Stockton, K.B. (2009). *The Queer Child, or Growing Sideways in the Twentieth Century*. Durham, NC: Duke University Press.

References

Stockton, K.B. (2016). The queer child now and its paradoxical global effects. *GLQ: A Journal of Lesbian and Gay Studies*, 22(4), 505–539.

Stonestreet, J. (2019, Mar. 18). Muslim parents protest LGBT indoctrination. *Christian Post*. Retrieved from www. christianpost.com/voice/muslim-parents-protest-lgbt-indoctrination.html (Accessed Nov. 13, 2019).

Stryker, S. (2009). *Transgender History*. Berkeley, CA: Seal Press.

Stychin, C.F. (2003). *Governing Sexuality: The Changing Politics of Citizenship and Law Reform*. Oxford: Hart Publishing.

Stychin, C. and Herman, D. eds. (2000). *Sexuality in the Legal Arena*. London: Athlone Press.

Sullivan, A. (1995). *Virtually Normal: An Argument about Homosexuality*. New York: Alfred A. Knopf.

Sultana, F. (2018). The false equivalence of academic freedom and free speech: defending academic integrity in the age of white supremacy, colonial nostalgia, and anti-intellectualism. *ACME: An International E-Journal for Critical Geographies*, 17(2).

Tabachnick, D.E. (2018, Sept. 26). Protecting free speech on campus: a solution in search of a problem. *The Conversation*. Retrieved from https://theconversation.com/protecting-free-speech-on-campus-a-solution-in-search-of-a-problem-103371 (Accessed Nov. 10, 2019).

Taylor, Y. (2007). *Working Class Lesbian Life: Classed Outsiders*. New York: Palgrave Macmillan.

Taylor, Y. (2016). *Making Space for Queer-Identifying Religious Youth*. Basingstoke: Palgrave Macmillan.

Taylor, Y., Hines, S. and Casey, M. eds. (2010). *Theorizing Intersectionality and Sexuality*. Basingstoke: Palgrave Macmillan.

TheWeeFlea (2019). Why Christians should support the Birmingham Muslims. *TheWeeFlea*. Retrieved from https://theweeflea.com/2019/03/27/why-christians-should-support-the-birmingham-muslims/ (Accessed Nov. 13, 2019).

Thiem, C.H. (2009). Thinking through education: the geographies of contemporary educational restructuring. *Progress in Human Geography*, 33(2), 154–173.

Thomas More Institute (2017, Dec. 31). Error has no rights. *Thomas More Institute*. Retrieved from http://thomasmore institute.org.uk/error-has-no-rights/ (Accessed Nov. 13, 2019).

Thomas More Institute (n.d.). *Thomas More Institute*. Retrieved from http://thomasmoreinstitute.org.uk/ (Accessed Nov. 13, 2019).

Todd, N.R. and Ong, K.S. (2012). Political and theological orientation as moderators for the association between religious attendance and attitudes toward gay marriage for White Christians. *Psychology of Religion and Spirituality*, 4(1), 56–70.

Transgender Trend (2019, May 22). First do no harm: the ethics of transgender healthcare, House of Lords. *Transgender Trend*. Retrieved from www.transgendertrend.com/first-do-no-harm-ethics-transgender-healthcare-house-of-lords/ (Accessed Nov. 13, 2019).

Tremblay, M., Paternotte, D. and Johnson, C. eds. (2011). *The Lesbian and Gay Movement and the State: Comparative Insights into a Transformed Relationship*. Burlington, VT: Ashgate.

Tucker, A. (2009). *Queer Visibilities: Space, Identity and Interaction in Cape Town*. Chichester: John Wiley & Sons.

Tully, A. (n.d.). No outsiders? More like no parents' rights. Society for the Protection of Unborn Children. Retrieved from https://spuc.org.uk/no-outsiders-more-like-no-parents-rights.

Tuns, P. (2018, Feb. 2). Government maintains ideological litmus test for Summer Jobs program. *The Interim*. Retrieved from www.theinterim.com/issues/society-culture/government-clarifies-ideological-litmus-test-for-summer-jobs-program/ (Accessed Nov. 11, 2019).

Turner, K. (2019, Feb. 18). Stand up for freedom. *Evangelical Alliance UK*. Retrieved from www.eauk.org/news-and-views/stand-up-for-freedom (Accessed Nov. 9, 2019).

Uhrig, S.N. (2015). Sexual orientation and poverty in the UK: a review and top-line findings from the UK household longitudinal study. *Journal of Research in Gender Studies*, 5(1), 23–72.

UK Government (2015, updated 2019). 'Prevent' Strategy. Retrieved from https://assets.publishing.service.gov.uk/government/uploads/system/uploads/attachment_data/file/445977/3799_Revised_Prevent_Duty_Guidance__England_Wales_V2-Interactive.pdf (Accessed Nov. 7, 2019).

Valentine, G. (1989). The geography of women's fear. *Area*, 21(4), 385–390.

Valentine, G. (2002). Queer bodies and the production of space. In D. Richardson and S. Seidman (eds.) *Handbook of Lesbian and Gay Studies* (pp. 145–160). London: Sage.

Valentine, G., Vanderbeck, R., Sadgrove, J. and Anderson, J. (2012). Producing moral geographies: the dynamics of homophobia within a transnational religious network. *The Geographical Journal*. http://dx.doi.org/10.1111/j.1475-4959.2012.00482.x.

Valentine, G., Vanderbeck, R.M., Sadgrove, J., Andersson, J. and Ward, K. (2013). Transnational religious networks: sexuality and the changing power geometries of the Anglican Communion. *Transactions of the Institute of British Geographers*, 38(1), 50–64.

Van Maren, J. (2018, June 18). Canada's Leftist radicals now have all the weapons they need in war against faith. *LifeSite News*. Retrieved from www.lifesitenews.com/blogs/canadas-leftist-radicals-now-have-all-the-weapons-they-need-in-war-against (Accessed Nov. 10, 2019).

Van Maren, J. (2018, June 20). Jordan Peterson: Canadian Christians must 'stand up' for religious rights after top court ruling. *LifeSite News*. Retrieved from www.lifesitenews.com/blogs/jordan-peterson-canadian-christians-must-stand-up-for-religious-rights-afte.

Van Maren, J. (2018, Nov. 19). Gay activists are coming after Christian churches next … and it's already happening. *LifeSite News*. Retrieved from www.lifesitenews.com/blogs/gay-activists-are-coming-after-christian-churches-next...and-its-already-ha (Accessed Nov. 13, 2019).

Van Maren, J. (2019, Aug. 7). Justin Trudeau's LGBT activism largely appeals to white people, who think just like him. *LifeSite News*. Retrieved from www.lifesitenews.com/blogs/justin-trudeaus-lgbt-activism-largely-appeals-to-white-people-who-think-just-like-him (Accessed Nov. 11, 2019).

VandenBeukel, J. (2016, Dec. 1). Jordan Peterson: the man who reignited Canada's culture war. *C2C Journal*. Retrieved from https://c2cjournal.ca/2016/12/jordan-peterson-the-man-who-reignited-canadas-culture-war/ (Accessed Nov. 10, 2019).

Vanderbeck, R.M. and Johnson, P. (2015). Homosexuality, religion and the contested legal framework governing sex education in England. *Journal of Social Welfare and Family Law*, 37(2), 161–179.

Vanderbeck, R.M. and Johnson, P. (2016). The promotion of British values: sexual orientation equality, religion, and England's schools. *International Journal of Law, Policy and the Family*, 30(3), 292–321.

Vanderbeck, R.M., Sadgrove, J., Valentine, G., Andersson, J. and Ward, K. (2015). The transnational debate over homosexuality in the Anglican Communion. In S.D. Brunn (ed.) *The Changing World Religion Map* (Vol. 5, pp. 3283–3301). Dordrecht: Springer.

Vanderbeck, R., Valentine, G., Ward, K., Sadgrove, J. and Andersson, J. (2010). The meanings of Communion: Anglican identities, the sexuality debates, and Christian relationality. *Sociological Research Online*, 15(2). Retrieved from www.socresonline.org.uk/15/2/3.html (Accessed Nov. 15, 2019).

Voice for Justice UK (2015). Some are more free than others …: time to say enough! *Voice For Justice UK*. Retrieved from https://vfjuk.org.uk/news-updates/some-are-more-free-than-others-time-to-say-enough/ (Accessed Nov. 10, 2019).

Voice for Justice UK (n.d.a). Free speech for all – except Christians! *Voice For Justice UK*. Retrieved from https://vfjuk.org.uk/news-updates/free-speech-for-all-except-christians/ (Accessed Nov. 11, 2019).

Voice for Justice UK (n.d.b). Liars! *Voice for Justice UK*. Retrieved from https://vfjuk.org.uk/news-updates/liars/.

Voice for Justice UK (n.d.c). Where is justice? *Voice For Justice UK*. Retrieved from https://vfjuk.org.uk/news-updates/where-is-justice/ (Accessed Mar. 18, 2020).

Wainwright, E. and Marandet, E. (2017). Education, parenting and family: the social geographies of family learning. *British Educational Research Journal*, 43(2), 213–229.

Warmington, J. (2015, Apr. 14). Rally against sex-ed curriculum about kids, not politics. *Toronto Sun*. Retrieved from https://torontosun.com/2015/04/14/massive-protest-against-sex-ed-curriculum-at-queens-park/wcm/f706a276-439a-4390-ac0f-e603e719befc (Accessed Nov. 15, 2019).

References

Warner, M. ed. (1993). *Fear of a Queer Planet: Queer Politics and Social Theory*. Minneapolis, MN: University of Minnesota Press.

Warner, M. (1999). Normal and normaller: beyond gay marriage. *GLQ: A Journal of Lesbian and Gay Studies*, (5), 119–171.

Warner, M. (2002). *Publics and Counterpublics*. Cambridge, MA: Zone Books.

Warner, T. (2002). *Never Going Back: A History of Queer Activism in Canada*. Toronto: University of Toronto Press.

Waters, J.L. (2017). Education unbound? Enlivening debates with a mobilities perspective on learning. *Progress in Human Geography*, 41(3), 279–298.

Weatherbe, S. (2015, Mar. 19). Indo-Canadian Tory MP blasts Wynne's sex ed as 'dangerous' and 'offensive'. *LifeSite News*. Retrieved from www.lifesitenews.com/news/indo-canadian-tory-mp-blasts-wynnes-sex-ed-as-dangerous-and-offensive (Accessed Apr. 19, 2018).

Weatherbe, S. (2015, Apr. 29). Ontario parents plan to pull kids out of school next week to protest Wynne's sex-ed. *LifeSite News*. Retrieved from www.lifesitenews.com/news/ontario-parents-plan-to-pull-kids-out-of-school-next-week-to-protest-wynnes (Accessed Nov.13, 2019).

Weeks, J. (2007). *The World We Have Won: The Remaking of Erotic and Intimate Life*. London: Routledge.

Weeks, J., Heaphy, B. and Donovan, C. (2001). *Same Sex Intimacies: Families of Choice and Other Life Experiments*. London: Routledge.

Weiss, M.L. and Bosia, M.J. (2013). *Global Homophobia: States, Movements, and the Politics of Oppression*. Urbana, IL: University of Illinois Press.

Wellner, F. and Marienfeld, A. (2019). Homosexuality and the AfD – that doesn't go together: the entanglement of homonationalism and heteroactivism in Germany. Conference Paper. Royal Geographical Society/Institute of British Geographers (RGS-IBG) Annual International Conference. London.

Wente, M. (2018, June 18). The TWU decision is a blow to diversity. *The Globe and Mail.*. Retrieved from www.theglobeandmail.com/opinion/article-the-twu-decision-is-a-blow-to-diversity/ (Accessed Nov. 13, 2019).

Westen, J.H. (2017, Dec. 15). Telling kids they can 'change' sex is harmful: US Catholic bishops with other faith leaders. *LifeSite News*. Retrieved from www.lifesitenews.com/news/telling-kids-they-can-change-sex-is-harmful-us-catholic-bishops-with-other (Accessed Nov. 12, 2019).

Westen, J.H. (2018). Lumen Fidei conference field notes, Dublin, Ireland.

Westlake, D. (2018). Multiculturalism, political parties, and the conflicting pressures of ethnic minorities and far-right parties. *Party Politics*, 24(4), 421–433.

White, H.R. (2015). *Reforming Sodom: Protestants and the Rise of Gay Rights*. Chapel Hill, NC: University of North Carolina Press.

Wilkinson, E. (2013). Learning to love again: 'broken families', citizenship and the state promotion of coupledom. *Geoforum*. http://dx.doi.org/10.1016/j.bbr.2011.03.031.

Williams, A. (2017, Jan. 13). Judge to examine case of Christian removed from NHS post. *Premier News*. Retrieved from www.premier.org.uk/News/UK/Judge-to-examine-case-of-Christian-removed-from-NHS-post (Accessed Nov. 14, 2019).

Williams, A. (2019, Apr. 12). One wrong word and we'll remove you from your job. *Christian Concern*. Retrieved from https://christianconcern.com/comment/one-wrong-word-and-well-remove-you-from-your-job/ (Accessed Nov. 11, 2019).

Wilson, E. (1992). *The Sphinx in the City: Urban Life, the Control of Disorder, and Women*. Berkeley, CA: University of California Press.

Woolley, F. (2018, Aug. 31). The critics are right: campus life is not what it used to be. *The Globe and Mail*. Retrieved from www.theglobeandmail.com/opinion/article-the-critics-are-right-campus-life-is-not-what-it-used-to-be/ (Accessed Nov. 10, 2019).

Yarbrough, M.W., Jones, A. and DeFilippis, J.N. eds. (2018). *Queer Families and Relationships after Marriage Equality*. London: Routledge.

Yip, A.K.T. (2008). Researching lesbian, gay, and bisexual Christians and Muslims: some thematic reflections. *Sociological Research Online*, 13(1), 1–14.

Yip, A.K.T. (2018). Research on sexuality and religion: some reflections on accomplishments and future directions. *Sexualities*, 21(8), 1291–1294.

Yip, A.K.T. and Nynäs, P. (2016). Re-framing the intersection between religion, gender and sexuality in everyday life. In P. Nynäs and A.K.T. Yip (eds.) *Religion, Gender and Sexuality in Everyday Life* (pp. 1–16). London: Routledge.

Young, I.M. (1990). *Justice and the Politics of Difference*. Princeton, NJ: Princeton University Press.

Yuval-Davis, N. (1997). *Gender and Nation*. London: Sage.

Zelikovsky, S. (2019). Transgender madness must be fought, even when conservatives support it. *LifeSite News*. Retrieved from www.lifesitenews.com/opinion/transgender-madness-must-be-fought-even-when-conservatives-support-it (Accessed Mar. 28, 2019).

Zivi, K. (2014). Performing the nation: contesting same-sex marriage rights in the United States. *Journal of Human Rights*, 13(3), 290–306.

Index